Catherine Booth

Catherine Booth

*Laying the Theological Foundations
of a Radical Movement*

JOHN READ

PICKWICK *Publications* · Eugene, Oregon

CATHERINE BOOTH
Laying the Theological Foundations of a Radical Movement

Copyright © 2013 John Read. All rights reserved. Except for brief quotations in critical publications or reviews, no part of this book may be reproduced in any manner without prior written permission from the publisher. Write: Permissions, Wipf and Stock Publishers, 199 W. 8th Ave., Suite 3, Eugene, OR 97401.

Pickwick Publications
An Imprint of Wipf and Stock Publishers
199 W. 8th Ave., Suite 3
Eugene, OR 97401

www.wipfandstock.com

ISBN 13: 978-1-62032-492-9

Cataloguing-in-Publication data:

Read, John.

    Catherine Booth : laying the theological foundations of a radical movement / John Read.

    viii + 237 pp. ; 23 cm. Includes bibliographical references and index.

    ISBN 13: 978-1-62032-492-9

    1. Booth, Catherine Mumford, 1829–1890. 2. Salvation Army—History. 3. Theology. I. Title.

BX9743.B6 R31 2013

Manufactured in the U.S.A.

To
Win and Betty,
Anne and Margaret,
Jo and Lucy

Contents

one	Introduction	1
two	Salvation	28
three	The Pursuit of Holiness	60
four	Doctrine of Holiness	85
five	The Church	119
six	Ministry	152
seven	The Sacraments	178
eight	Conclusion	205
	Bibliography	213
	Index	231

ONE

Introduction

At 4.00pm on Monday 13 October 1890 the turnstiles closed at Olympia. London's largest indoor arena was accustomed to great crowds, but the staff estimated 38–40,000 people had entered the hall, which seated 25,000, two hours before the 6.00pm start.[1] The event was the funeral service of Mrs. Booth, the wife of General Booth of The Salvation Army. *The Banner* commented: "We suppose that no woman, crowned or uncrowned, has ever before passed to her grave amidst such vast manifestations of sorrow and sympathy."[2] Catherine Booth's biographer, William Stead, wrote, "It seems probable that the future historian may record that no woman of the Victorian Era—except it be the monarch who gives her name to the epoch—has done more to help in the making of modern England than Catherine Booth."[3] What brought Catherine to this high point of public recognition?

THE SIGNIFICANCE OF CATHERINE BOOTH

Catherine Booth was recognized as one of the Victorian era's pre-eminent evangelists. Stead described her as "the most conspicuous and the most successful preacher of righteousness this generation has heard."[4] *The Manchester Guardian* praised her eloquence and "unstudied ease and grace," and concluded, "Mrs. Booth was a keen causist and a subtle dialectician. She had a strong apparatus of logic at her command, and led you into a corner with delightful ease."[5]

1. *Manchester Guardian*, "The Late Mrs. Booth."
2. *The Banner*, "The Funeral of Mrs. Booth."
3. Stead, *Mrs. Booth*, 232.
4. Ibid., 230.
5. *Manchester Guardian*, "Mrs. Booth."

Catherine Booth was also a powerful advocate of social reform. In alliance with Josephine Butler and W. T. Stead, Catherine was responsible for bringing to the notice of the public the "iniquity of state regulated vice,"[6] and for mobilizing the forces of The Salvation Army against sex trafficking and in support of the Criminal Law Amendment Act of 1885, which raised the age of consent for girls from 13 to 16. Within days of Catherine's death, William Booth published his book *In Darkest England and the Way Out* and the Army embarked on a massive program of innovative social action.[7] Stead claimed Catherine was "the prophetess of the new movement,"[8] and stated, "that the Salvation Army thus entered upon that new development is due more to her than to any other woman, and in its new social work we see the best and most enduring monument to the memory of the saintly woman and her devoted husband."[9]

Further, Catherine Booth was an effective campaigner for the rights of women. *The Manchester Guardian* claimed, "She has probably done more in her own person to establish the right of women to preach the Gospel than anyone else who has ever lived."[10] The *Daily News* attributed the Army's "astonishing success" to the "very effective way in which they have testified to their belief in the spiritual and intellectual equality of the sexes. [. . .] In all the long history of religion there is not such instance as the Army affords of the absolute sinking of the disqualification of sex."[11]

Finally, Catherine Booth was recognized as the co-founder, with her husband William, of The Salvation Army. Stead wrote, "Mrs. Booth's claim to rank in the forefront among the Makers of Modern England rests, of course, primarily upon her share in moulding and building up The Salvation Army."[12] Catherine was a wise counselor who guided William Booth and his inner circle of leaders in their decision making; she was an apologist for the movement to society's opinion formers and decision makers; but most of all she was the visionary thinker, the principal architect of the Army's theology, the one through whom Salvationism was first formed, and the one who gave it coherent and eloquent expression.

6. Booth, "The Iniquity of State Regulated Vice."
7. Booth, *In Darkest England and The Way Out*.
8. Stead, *Northern Echo*, "Mrs. Booth."
9. Stead, *Mrs. Booth*, 213-14.
10. *The Manchester Guardian*, "Memorial Notices."
11. *Daily News*, "Mrs. Booth's Funeral."
12. Stead, *Mrs. Booth*, 229.

Introduction

The noun "Salvationist" and its concomitant "Salvationism" were coined soon after the birth of the movement.[13] Salvationism has been taken to be descriptive not of the Army's creed or organizational structures, but rather of the pulsating "heart of the Army."[14] According to Shaw Clifton, Salvationism "is the sum total or combination of various distinctive characteristics that are peculiar to the Army. Salvationism is a word that denotes certain attitudes, a particular worldview. It signifies an amalgam of beliefs, stances, commitments, callings that when taken together cannot be found in any other body, religious or secular."[15] David Baxendale suggests that "Salvationism is a spiritual quality that binds together Salvationists of whatever nationality, race, or social status."[16]

Ian Randall has argued that "evangelicalism is essentially a strand of spirituality."[17] Similarly Salvationism is best understood as a mode of Christian spirituality. Although Kenneth Leech has suggested that "the word has come to be used in so general and vague a way that its continued usefulness needs to be questioned,"[18] it might be argued that in a broad sense spirituality "describes that aspect of humankind that reaches out toward the transcendent and divine, and the practices employed to assist in this quest."[19] In respect of Christian spirituality, according to Philip Sheldrake, spirituality describes "how, individually and collectively, we personally appropriate the traditional Christian beliefs about God, humanity, and the world, and express them in terms of our basic attitudes, life-style, and activity."[20] Because spirituality is formed at the nexus of ideas and experience, Alister McGrath suggests that "a substantial range of 'spiritualities' is to be expected, reflecting a set of differing (though clearly related) theological assumptions on the one hand, and a remarkable variety of personal and institutional circumstances [. . .] on the other."[21]

Conceived in this way, Salvationism emerged as a culturally engaged and engaging spirituality, which incorporated a rich variety of means of

---

13. The Army's first newspaper, published in 1878, was titled *The Salvationist*.
14. Read, "Salvationism," 8.
15. Clifton, *New Love*, 19.
16. Baxendale, "Salvationism," 501.
17. Randall, "Evangelical Spirituality," 96; See also Randall, *Evangelical Experiences*.
18. Leech, *The Eye of the Storm*, 3.
19. Read, "Spirituality and Spiritual Formation," 553.
20. Sheldrake, *Images of Holiness*, 2.
21. McGrath, *Christian Spirituality*, 10.

spiritual formation and expressions of the spiritual disciplines, encouraged, for example, by all nights of prayer, love feasts, and the development of new forms of retreat which reflected the Army's militant and missional emphases: Councils of War, Days with God, Spiritual Days, and expressed in the emergence of a new hymnody derived from popular cultural forms, and promoted by the publication of Orders and Regulations for soldiers and officers, which functioned in great part as guides to spiritual formation. The focus of this book is not however on the practices associated with the Army's nascent spirituality, but on the *formation* of a Salvationist spirituality, and in particular on the theological ideas which undergird it, the influences which shaped those ideas, and how they led to the emergence of this vibrant and distinctive spirituality in the life and thought of Catherine Booth.

John Rhemick has suggested that at the heart of Salvationism lies a theology of "grand ideas."[22] It was in Catherine Booth that a Salvationist spirituality was first formed; she was a conduit through whom it was formed in others; and a series of grand ideas lay at the heart of her Salvationism. It might seem surprising that Catherine Booth's writings should have been neglected by the movement she co-founded, when her ideas were so critical to its foundation, and yet Chick Yuill argues that "one of the tragedies of Salvation Army history [is] that, despite the proper respect which has been paid to the *person* of Catherine Booth, her *teaching* has been often largely neglected."[23]

The secondary literature is at least partly to blame for this neglect. The first biography, written by a senior Salvation Army officer, Commissioner Frederick Booth-Tucker, was wantonly verbose.[24] Buried within it were Catherine's own reminiscences, as well as lengthy quotations from correspondence and other writings, which lend scholarly value to Booth-Tucker's work without making it more readable. Every biography since has relied upon Booth-Tucker, including Stead's shorter, well-written memoir, which however was not intended to be a definitive work.[25] Many years later Catherine's grand-daughter, Commissioner Catherine Bramwell-Booth, wrote a personal and affectionate biography, which however added little to Booth-Tucker's memoir. More recently the American Salvationist scholar

22. Rhemick, *A New People of God*, 6.
23. Yuill, "Restoring the Image," 52.
24. Booth-Tucker, *Catherine Booth*.
25. Stead, *Mrs. Booth*.

Introduction

Roger Green produced an informed account of Catherine's life, but again this relies on the earlier works. William Booth was served rather better by his biographers, Harold Begbie and St John Ervine, professional writers who both produced readable accounts, and by the time William died in 1912 a substantial secondary literature also illuminated the Army's history.[26] The historical context can be derived from works of church history looking especially at the nineteenth century.[27] In recent years, after a long period in which The Salvation Army was the primary narrator of its own history, a series of scholarly studies have shed light upon the nascent Army and its setting in Victorian society. A first wave might be identified, led by a trio of American scholars—Roger Green, Norman Murdoch, and David Rightmire; closely followed by a second wave that includes Glen Horridge, Diane Winston, and Pamela Walker.[28] Roy Hattersley's popular biography, *Blood and Fire*, fed off these works.[29] The latest wave includes the works of Andrew Eason, Harold Hill, and, for Catherine Booth particularly, Krista Valtanen's unpublished doctoral dissertation, as well as the meticulous work of David Bennett, who edited and published William and Catherine's correspondence and Catherine's journal and reminiscences.[30]

Krista Valtanen was motivated in her research by her chance discovery of Stead's biography and her astonishment at Catherine's modern neglect. Valtanen asked rhetorically, "Has history, since Victorian times, genuinely done justice to Catherine Booth and her contribution?"[31] Similarly, Roy Hattersley noted regretfully that Catherine and William Booth "have been virtually forgotten outside of the ranks of The Salvation Army."[32] For Hattersley, Catherine and William "represented—as much as Brunel or Bright, Paxton, Arnold, Livingstone or Newman—much of what was

---

26. Begbie, *William Booth*; Ervine, *God's Soldier*.

27. Chadwick and Bebbington are important, but they give scant recognition to the Army in their comprehensive histories. Orr and Kent offer more on the Army. Chadwick, *The Victorian Church*; Bebbington, *Evangelicalism*; Orr, *The Second Evangelical Awakening*; Kent, *Holding the Fort*.

28. Green, *War on Two Fronts*; Murdoch, *Origins of The Salvation Army*; Rightmire, *Sacraments*; Horridge, *Salvation Army Origins*; Winston, *Red-hot & Righteous*; Walker, *Pulling the Devil's Kingdom Down*.

29. Hattersley, *Blood and Fire*.

30. Eason, *Women in God's Army*; Hill, *Leadership in The Salvation Army*; Valtanen, "Catherine Booth."; Booth and Booth, *Letters*; Bennett, *The General*; Booth, *Reminiscences*.

31. Valtanen, "Catherine Booth," 22.

32. Hattersley, *Blood and Fire*, 9.

5

best in nineteenth-century Britain. They deserve a place in the pantheon of Great Victorians."[33] However, Hattersley's work has little scholarly intent, focuses more on William than Catherine, and does not attempt to analyze Catherine's ideas. Valtanen's study breaks new ground in treating seriously Catherine's theological contribution, but is limited by its method which catalogues and describes the explicit content of Catherine's exhortations without identifying the core content of her theology. This partly explains why Valtanen concludes that Catherine was an *ephapax*, by which she means a unique individual with a singular and redemptive ministry.[34]

Andrew Eason concludes his own survey of the literature: "In spite of these recent works, much more remains to be gained from studies of Catherine Booth within her Victorian environment and in relation to her evangelical convictions."[35] The intention here therefore is to redress the deficit in understanding Catherine's evangelical convictions, understood as the underlying conceptual structure of her Salvationism. Her theology has been understood to be broadly Wesleyan, and influenced by American revivalism, but little more has been said. An attempt will be made to provide an outline of Catherine Booth's Salvationism, and to identify its sources. No attempt will be made to provide a new biography; however, much of Catherine's theological development was an outcome of her life story, and an outline is necessary to provide a context in which the formation of her Salvationism can be understood.

THE LIFE OF CATHERINE BOOTH

Catherine Booth was born Catherine Mumford on 17 January 1829 in Ashbourne, Derbyshire, to staunch Methodist parents, John and Sarah Mumford. Catherine was the only daughter of five children; of her brothers, only the youngest, John, survived infancy. In 1834 the family moved to Boston where her father established a coach-building business. Catherine's mother was her first teacher. Her early education was narrow but effective—by the age of five she could read; by the age of twelve she had read through the Bible eight times.[36]

---

33. Ibid.
34. Valtanen, "Catherine Booth," 270.
35. Eason, *Women in God's Army*, 189–90.
36. Booth-Tucker, *Catherine Booth*, I:14.

John Mumford was active in the temperance movement, and Catherine became secretary of the Boston Juvenile Temperance Society. She participated in parlor debates with her father's adult acquaintances and wrote articles anonymously for temperance magazines. Although John Mumford's Christian faith faltered, Sarah and Catherine remained "deeply attached to Methodism. Its literature was their meat and drink; its history was their pride; its heroes and heroines their admiration."[37] In his study *The Intellectual Life of the British Working Classes* Jonathan Rose suggests that "all Nonconformist sects encouraged the habits of close reading, interpretive analysis, and intellectual self improvement."[38]

In 1841 Sarah Mumford was persuaded to send Catherine to school; but in 1843 this brief experience was brought to a close by "a serious curvature of the spine." For months Catherine was forced to "lie on her face in a kind of hammock."[39] Catherine never returned to school, and instead she became her own teacher. Booth-Tucker claims, "It was during the next few years [. . .] she acquired the extensive knowledge of church history and theology which proved so useful in later years."[40] According to Booth-Tucker, Catherine studied the writings of John Wesley and John Fletcher, the works of the Lutheran historians Johann Lorenz Mosheim and Augustus Neander, and the American revivalist Charles Finney; she also read Joseph Butler's *Analogy of Religion* and Isaac Newton's writings on prophecy, and was familiar with John Bunyan's *The Pilgrim's Progress*.[41]

Roger Green describes these works as "a diverse and unfocused smattering but nonetheless attractive to Catherine."[42] However, though diverse, they do not form an unfocused list, but rather represent key influences on Catherine's thought. Jonathan Rose has argued that the reading of autodidacts in the nineteenth century tended, not least for reasons of economy and availability, to be in a sense canonical and not characteristically diverse and unfocused.[43] Each of the writers listed by Booth-Tucker was in some way canonical for Catherine. Bramwell-Booth concludes, "From these and similar books she gained her knowledge, and an informed appreciation of

37. Ibid., I:22.
38. Rose, *The Intellectual Life of the British Working Classes*, 34.
39. Bramwell-Booth, *Catherine Booth*, 27.
40. Booth-Tucker, *Catherine Booth*, I:28.
41. Ibid.
42. Green, *Catherine Booth*, 23.
43. Rose, *The Intellectual Life of the British Working Classes*, 7–8, 116–46.

the first centuries of Christianity with a precocious understanding of the teachings and problems of the Early Church."[44]

In 1844 the Mumford family moved to Brixton; Catherine's father, John Mumford, had "lapsed into drink [. . .] leaving his Boston business premises in the hands of his mortgagee."[45] Catherine's biographers imply that her education was complete by 1844.[46] However a page of notes précising a section of Butler's *Analogy* was written when Catherine was 16, that is, in 1845.[47] This confirms that Catherine continued to read with studious intent. The years 1844–51 were a time of significant personal development when the foundations of Catherine's intellectual and spiritual life were laid.

On the morning of 15 June 1846, Catherine joyfully told her mother she was "saved."[48] She had opened her hymn book to read the familiar words, "My God I am Thine! What a comfort Divine, What a blessing to know that my Jesus is mine!"[49] Later she recalled, "Scores of times I had read and sung these words, but now they came home to my inmost soul with a force and illumination they had never before possessed. It was as impossible for me to doubt as it had been before for me to exercise faith. [. . .] I no longer hoped that I was saved, I was certain of it. The assurances of my salvation seemed to flood and fill my soul."[50]

This experience followed on a "great controversy of soul"; although Catherine had always been devoted to God, she had no inner assurance of sins forgiven, and had not experienced that change of heart of which she had read and heard so much.[51] But now everything had changed: "For the next six months I was so happy that I felt as if I was walking on air. I used to tremble, and even long to die, lest I should backslide, or lose the consciousness of God's smile and favor."[52]

From 12 May 1847 through to 24 March 1848 Catherine kept a journal, recording her spiritual longings and her interest in the reforming movement then active in Methodism, as well as her struggles with the

44. Bramwell-Booth, *Catherine Booth*, 27.
45. Wright, *Boston—A History and Celebration*.
46. Bramwell-Booth, *Catherine Booth*, 28–29.
47. Booth-Tucker, *Catherine Booth*, I: facing page 27.
48. Bramwell-Booth, *Catherine Booth*, 37.
49. Booth-Tucker, *Catherine Booth*, I:33.
50. Ibid.
51. Ibid., I:32.
52. Ibid., I:34.

Introduction

symptoms of scoliosis, which along with the side effects of the treatment blighted her adolescence.[53] In a letter to her mother from Brighton, Catherine expressed her indignation at the treatment of the reformers by the Annual Conference.[54] This governing Conference, established after John Wesley's death but at his direction, consisted of one hundred ministers appointed for life. It resulted in widespread dissatisfaction, and in 1844 the first of a series of anonymous flysheets was published attacking the alleged abuses of Conference and advocating sweeping reforms. The Conference of 1847 decided to act against the reforming "men in masks" responsible. All ministers were required to sign a document declaring whether or not they were guilty. Seventy refused to sign, forty of whom offered an implicit denial. Those who remained under suspicion were required to appear before Conference and answer a direct "brotherly" question. In 1849, three ministers considered to be leaders of the agitation were expelled from the Methodist society, while others were reprimanded. This action caused the conflict to spread, and reformers began to set up their own chapels.[55]

Catherine became an outspoken supporter of the reform movement and ignored all counsels to moderation.[56] Consequently her quarterly Wesleyan Methodist membership ticket was not renewed. Catherine later reflected, "Nursed and cradled in Methodism I loved it with a love which has altogether gone out of fashion among Protestants for their church. Separation from it was one of the first great troubles of my life."[57]

There is an intriguing gap in the record for the years 1848–51. Catherine Bramwell-Booth writes, "At nineteen, the Catherine we have seen reflected in her journal vanished; there are no more self-revealing records until her love-letters begin."[58] St John Ervine describes Catherine through these years, "growing in physical pain and spiritual anguish,"[59] and "stretched on a sofa by spinal curvature and incipient tuberculosis."[60] However the letters provide a glimpse of intense personal development.

---

53. Booth, *Reminiscences*.

54. Booth, "2nd Letter to her Mother: from Brighton, 1847."

55. For the reform movement in Methodism see Davies, George, and Rupp, *A History of the Methodist Church in Great Britain*.

56. Booth-Tucker, *Catherine Booth*, I:45–50.

57. Bramwell-Booth, *Catherine Booth*, 49.

58. Ibid., 47.

59. Ervine, *God's Soldier*, I:28.

60. Ibid., I:45.

On 15 January 1853, William wrote to Catherine, "I have made Mr. Shadford believe that you really are a first rater by telling he and Mrs. S. that you are on the Bazaar Committee, Exeter Hall, and about that letter to the *Wesleyan Times*, and that great meeting."[61] Exeter Hall in The Strand was synonymous with pan-denominational evangelicalism.[62] William's picture of Catherine's activities belies that drawn by Ervine.

By the close of 1851 Catherine was attending a Reformers' chapel in Binfield Road, Clapham. Here she first met William Booth. Although the arguments of the Reformers passed William by, through a misunderstanding he was thought to be on their side, and his ticket of Wesleyan Methodist membership was withheld. In June 1851 the Reformers invited William to join them. Edward Harris Rabbits, a prosperous bootmaker and a force among the Reformers, took William under his wing.[63] Towards the end of 1851 William preached at Binfield Road. Rabbits asked Catherine what she thought of William's sermon. "One of the best I have heard in this chapel," she replied.[64]

William and Catherine met again early in 1852 when Rabbits invited some of the leading members of the Reform movement to his home for tea and conversation.[65] Their next meeting proved decisive. On Good Friday, 10 April 1852, his 23rd birthday, William ran into Rabbits who "carried him off to a service held by the Reformers in a school room[66] in Cowper Street, City Road."[67] Catherine was already there. Towards the end of the evening Catherine became unwell, and Rabbits asked William to escort her home. On the journey a deep mutual affection "flashed simultaneously into [their] hearts."[68] They became engaged on 15 May 1852. Again Rabbits proved to be a good friend, providing financial support that allowed William to leave his business and give himself to preaching the gospel.[69] However, it was a

---

61. The letter and meeting, though unexplained by William, evidently provide examples of Catherine's activism. Booth and Booth, *Letters*, 56.

62. Cf. Chadwick, *The Victorian Church*, I:5.

63. Booth-Tucker, *Catherine Booth*, I:56.

64. Bramwell-Booth, *Catherine Booth*, 60.

65. Booth-Tucker, *Catherine Booth*, I:57.

66. The Royal British Institution, a large hall in frequent use for such events. The hall was close to Whitefield's Tabernacle, John Campbell's church, where Charles Finney preached in 1849–50. Finney held his enquirer's meetings in this hall.

67. Booth-Tucker, *Catherine Booth*, I:63.

68. Begbie, *William Booth*, I:125.

69. Ibid., 112.

temporary arrangement, and together William and Catherine considered the future. Their relationships with the Reformers had become strained.[70] They were disturbed by what they saw as lawlessness, a lack of authority and respect, and a tendency to extremism.[71]

The attention of William and Catherine turned at this point to the Congregational ministry. Catherine later wrote, "This was my doing [. . .] to leave Methodism seemed an impossibility [to William]. His love for it at that time amounted almost to idolatry."[72] William was accepted as a ministerial student at the Congregational Cotton End College, having been assured that Congregationalism's Calvinism would not be forced upon him; but he was expected to be persuadable. He was asked to read Abraham Booth's *Reign of Grace*[73] and Payne's *Divine Sovereignty*.[74] Thirty pages in, William hurled *Reign of Grace* across the room; he would not go to Cotton End.[75] The Methodist Reform movement had formed a network of districts and circuits that mirrored those of the Wesleyan Methodist Conference, and the Spalding district needed a minister. Enquiries were made, and William was recommended.[76] An invitation was forwarded and accepted, and on 30 November 1852, William wrote from Spalding, "My own dear Kate, I have arrived safe."[77]

Catherine continued to be dissatisfied with the Reform movement, however, and preferred to attend Stockwell New Chapel, London, where she came under the influence of the Congregationalist minister David Thomas.[78] Catherine's letters to William reveal the extent of Thomas's influence, an influence which has not been adequately recognized. From 1852–55 at least, Catherine was effectively a member of Thomas's congregation.[79] Catherine frequently sent William sketches of Thomas's sermons.[80]

70. Cf. Booth and Booth, *Letters*, 48.
71. Booth-Tucker, *Catherine Booth*, I:64.
72. Begbie, *William Booth*, I:131.
73. Booth, *The Reign of Grace*.
74. Payne, *Lectures on Divine Sovereignty*.
75. Booth-Tucker, *Catherine Booth*, I:74.
76. Ibid., I:76.
77. Booth and Booth, *Letters*, 17.
78. Booth-Tucker, *Catherine Booth*, I:70.
79. Bramwell-Booth has Catherine hearing Thomas in July 1847; however Bennett shows this is a mistake. Bramwell-Booth, *Catherine Booth*, 45; Booth, *Reminiscences*, 26.
80. Booth and Booth, *Letters*, 36.

With her engagement, Catherine's intellectual development entered a new phase. In her reminiscences she described how she set herself to prepare for her responsibilities as a minister's wife: "I added to the number of my studies, enlarged the scope of my reading, wrote notes and made comments on all the sermons and lectures that appeared at all worthy of the trouble."[81] Catherine's interests encompassed the physical as well as the spiritual. She wrote to William on 3 January 1853, "I intend to make myself acquainted with those natural laws, on the observance of which God has made health and happiness so much to depend, more fully than I am at present."[82] Her letters to William are replete with references to her interest in natural remedies and alternative therapies such as homeopathy and hydrotherapy.[83]

Catherine's letters to William reveal her intense struggles with her own calling at this time. She reckoned she was "trimming between half service and perfect consecration";[84] but she resisted any public ministry, telling William, "I do want to be useful, but it must be in retirement and quietness."[85] She confessed, "Scores of times I have determinedly opposed what I cannot doubt were the direct leadings of the Spirit to some particular work and thereby brought condemnation and barrenness and hardness into my soul."[86] Catherine described the "strange feelings" that she should witness to and pray with friends and strangers.[87] She complained, "Why should I have such a singular and difficult work assigned me and one for which nature has so unfitted me?"[88] She was tempted to think it was "fanaticism, anything but the voice of God."[89] And yet she believed her soul was starving because she refused to walk in this path.[90] Another case was "pressing on [her] mind continually." This was "a poor, degraded, sinking drunkard, living in Russell Gardens." Catherine determined to speak to

---

81. Bramwell-Booth, *Catherine Booth*, 71.
82. Booth and Booth, *Letters*, 48.
83. Cf. Ibid., 373.
84. Ibid., 186.
85. Ibid., 145.
86. Ibid., 126.
87. Ibid.
88. Ibid.
89. Ibid.
90. Ibid.

him.⁹¹ A month later Catherine, exhilarated, having attended a meeting addressed by a brilliant temperance speaker John Gough (to which she took her father), wrote to William saying she was going again with three more guests, including "the poor man I told you about."⁹² Methodist women of an earlier generation, such as Mary Bosanquet Fletcher, inspired Catherine by their example: "I admire, revere her character as much as ever I did, and as ardently desire to follow her as she followed Christ."⁹³

William thrived in Spalding, but the separation was hard and they were uncertain of the future of the Reform movement; consequently Catherine and William cast around for an alternative route into the ordained ministry. In February 1854 William returned to London and joined another Methodist denomination, the Methodist New Connexion.⁹⁴ For a few months William attempted to study for the ministry under the supervision of Dr William Cooke, the New Connexion's foremost scholar.⁹⁵ William was a poor student but Cooke recognized his qualities and, to William's surprise, recommended him as a District Superintendent. When William demurred, he was appointed as assistant to an older man. This arrangement freed William to conduct revivals through 1854–55 in the Midlands and the North of England.⁹⁶ In June 1855 William was appointed to continue his revival ministry by the New Connexion's Annual Conference in Sheffield.⁹⁷

On 16 June 1855 William Booth and Catherine Mumford were married at Stockwell New Chapel by David Thomas.⁹⁸ For the next two years William was fully engaged in revival ministry, campaigning in Sheffield, Dewsbury, and Leeds. Catherine gave birth to their first son, William Bramwell, in Halifax on 8 March 1856. Begbie wrote of these days that "since Wesley no such evangelist had appeared in England."⁹⁹ However, the New Connexion Conference of 1857 brought William's itinerant revivalist

91. Ibid.
92. Ibid., 138.
93. Ibid., 66.
94. Booth-Tucker, *Catherine Booth*, I:106.
95. For a description of Cooke's "School of the Prophets" see Hulme, *Memoir of the Rev. William Cooke, D.D*, 98,100; For a recent appraisal of Cooke's life, work and influence see Larsen, *A People of One Book*, 91–100.
96. Booth-Tucker, *Catherine Booth*, I:113–14.
97. Ibid., I:139.
98. Ibid., I:133–34.
99. Begbie, *William Booth*, I:281.

career to an end, appointing him to the Brighouse circuit. Catherine called Brighouse "a low smoky town," and she said, "We are situated in the worst part of it."[100] The Booths' second son Ballington was born on 28 July 1857. The Brighouse people were unresponsive; it was a difficult year. At Brighouse Catherine took her first timid steps into a public ministry, leading a class meeting, teaching some of the senior girls in Sunday school, and giving a temperance lecture to the Junior Band of Hope.[101] In May 1858 William was ordained as a minister at the New Connexion's Annual Conference and appointed to Gateshead.[102] On 18 September 1858 the Booths' first daughter, Catherine, was born. After the 1859 Conference, which refused his request to be returned to evangelistic work, William was made Superintendent Minister.

One Sunday evening, as Catherine walked through the squalid, teeming streets, "it was suggested to her mind with great power" that instead of going on to the chapel she should speak to the women in the houses she was passing and invite them to the service.[103] Emboldened by a friendly response, she spoke to a woman carrying a jug of beer to her husband who was drunk and incapable of leaving the house. Catherine followed the woman indoors, listened to the couple's story, and read them the parable of the Prodigal Son; they wept freely, and after praying with them Catherine left.[104] This was the beginning of an evangelistic ministry of visitation, prayer, and practical help.[105]

In autumn 1859 the American holiness revivalists Walter and Phoebe Palmer conducted services in the region. Catherine was unable to attend their meetings, but she wrote to her parents on 16 September 1859: "The celebrated Mrs. Palmer of America, authoress of *The Way of Holiness, Entire Consecration* and *The Blessing of Salvation* [. . .] is now in Newcastle speaking every night in the Wesleyan Chapel and getting 30 and 40 of a night up to the communion rail."[106] Phoebe Palmer's preaching aroused opposition. Arthur Rees, minister of the Bethesda Free Chapel, Sunderland, issued a

---

100. Ibid., I:282.
101. Booth-Tucker, *Catherine Booth*, I:210–16.
102. Ibid., I:222.
103. Ibid., I:236.
104. Ibid., I:236–37.
105. Ibid., I:238–39.
106. Booth, "Letter to her Parents: 16 September 1859."

pamphlet excoriating the revivalism of the Palmers and attacking women's right to preach.[107]

Catherine, who had never spoken publicly but believed firmly in her right to do so, was sufficiently incensed to consider "going to Sunderland and delivering an address in answer to him."[108] In the event, she responded by publishing a pamphlet defending the principle of female ministry.[109] She wrote to her mother, "I am determined that fellow shall not go unthrashed."[110] This pamphlet is the only work in which Catherine writes with anything like scholarly intent, but it indicates the level of scholarship that underpins all her writing. Catherine constructed her argument from a range of Old and New Testament texts, and engaged in detailed exegesis of those New Testament passages that supposedly prohibited female ministry. Catherine quoted Adam Clarke; referenced Richard Watson, Philip Doddridge, Daniel Whitby, and Ingram Cobbin; argued against Alfred Barnes; discussed the nuances of the Greek text, with reference to the lexicons of Johann Friedrich Schleusner, Edward Robinson, John Parkhurst and Henry George Liddell, and Robert Scott; cited John Locke; revealed her knowledge of Phoebe Palmer's writings on female ministry; and quoted Henry Dodwell in his dissertations on Irenaeus, Justin Martyr, and Eusebius.

Despite her views Catherine remained silent in church services. On 8 January 1860 William and Catherine's fourth child, Emma Moss, was born. After the birth Catherine was unwell, but during her convalescence she became convinced she was called to a public ministry.[111] Then on Whit Sunday, 27 May 1860, towards the close of the morning service, Catherine felt the Spirit urging her to get to her feet and speak, but resisted, until "the Devil said, 'You will look like a fool.'"[112] Ready to be a fool for Christ, Catherine stepped to the front of the chapel, and said to William, "I want to say a word."[113] William, astonished, announced his wife and sat down.

---

107. Rees, *Reasons*; Pamela Walker traced a surviving copy of Rees' pamphlet to the Ryland's Library and was first to analyze both Rees' and Catherine Booth's arguments from the earliest extant primary sources. Cf. Walker, *Pulling the Devil's Kingdom Down*, 254–55.

108. Booth-Tucker, *Catherine Booth*, I:243.

109. Booth, *Female Teaching*.

110. Booth, "Letter to her Parents: 25 December 1859"; Pamela Walker was first to note this extraordinarily robust remark: Walker, *Pulling the Devil's Kingdom Down*, 26.

111. Booth-Tucker, *Catherine Booth*, I:253.

112. Booth, *Aggressive Christianity*, 138.

113. Ibid.

Catherine confessed her stubborn resistance to God's calling, and promised to be obedient in the future. To Catherine's consternation William announced her as the preacher for the evening service. That night she preached on the subject "Be Filled with the Spirit." From that day, Catherine later declared, God "has never allowed me to open my mouth without giving me signs of His presence and blessing."[114]

Catherine's pamphlet and her preaching brought her notoriety but also established her as a celebrity, and she received more invitations than she could accept.[115] She wrote to her mother, "My name is getting trumpeted around the world I suppose. Mr. Crow says it is getting into the foreign papers now, and that in one of them I am represented as having my husband's clothes on! They would require to be considerably shortened before such a phenomenon could occur would they not?"[116]

The Palmers inaugurated a revival among the churches of the North East that continued into 1861. The Booths' Bethesda Chapel was called "the Converting Shop."[117] Robert Young, minister of the Brunswick Chapel in Newcastle, reported in autumn 1859, "The Revival with which this town is favoured is advancing with increasing power and glory."[118] In the midst of this revival Catherine found her voice. Brunswick Chapel was one of many churches where she preached.

In September 1860 William's health broke, and he travelled to Matlock Spa in search of a cure. Catherine agreed to undertake William's preaching responsibilities and supervise the general management of circuit affairs.[119] William was absent for nine weeks; the congregation prospered, and Catherine preached to packed chapels in Gateshead and elsewhere. Catherine Bramwell-Booth suggests the immense strain on Catherine at this time exacerbated her sense of spiritual dissatisfaction and intensified her longing for holiness.[120]

Catherine's journal and letters reveal her long quest for holiness; but the experience had eluded her, she believed, because of her disobedience in not speaking publicly. Catherine had also resisted William's desire to take

---

114. Ibid., 141.
115. Booth-Tucker, *Catherine Booth*, I:259.
116. Booth, "Letter to her Parents: 24 September 1860."
117. Booth-Tucker, *Catherine Booth*, I:225.
118. Orr, *The Second Evangelical Awakening*, 63.
119. Booth-Tucker, *Catherine Booth*, I:258–59.
120. Bramwell-Booth, *Catherine Booth*, 200.

up a peripatetic revival ministry; this too, she believed, had compromised her absolute consecration to God. Early in February 1861 Catherine wrote to her parents describing how she had finally surrendered fully to God. On 11 February she wrote again describing more completely how, on the evening of Friday 1 February, she had entered into an experience of holiness.[121]

As a consequence of Catherine's surrender, William's hopes of evangelistic work revived. On 5 March 1861 William and Catherine wrote to the President of the New Connexion Conference, James Stacey, appealing for William's release as a revivalist.[122] They attended the Conference in Liverpool with high hopes, but once again the opposition prevailed. As a compromise, William was appointed to the Newcastle circuit with the expectation he might come to some arrangement locally that freed him for evangelistic work.[123] However, the terms were ambiguous, and after an unsatisfactory conversation with the President of Conference on 18 July 1861, Catherine recalled, "after a day's deep anxiety [. . .] we decided to send in our resignation."[124]

According to Begbie, in July 1861 William and Catherine entered what he calls the "wilderness."[125] This is somewhat misleading, since in fact they were caught up in what James Edwin Orr has called the Second Evangelical Awakening, along with evangelists such as Walter and Phoebe Palmer, Charles Finney, James Caughey, Reginald Radcliffe, Richard Weaver, and Hay Aitken.[126] According to Orr "the most effective work" in the Cornish Revivals of 1861–62 was that undertaken by William and Catherine Booth, with 4,247 new members added to the Wesleyan churches in Cornwall.[127] Their reward was hardly commensurate with their success. In June 1862 the Methodist New Connexion accepted William's resignation, regretting his revivalism; the Primitive Methodist Conference passed a resolution urging its ministers to "avoid the employing of Revivalists so called"; and in July the Wesleyan Methodist Conference, meeting in Camborne, directed its superintendents not to allow outsiders to conduct continuous services

---

121. Booth, "Letter to her Parents: 11 February 1861."
122. Booth-Tucker, *Catherine Booth*, I:277.
123. Ibid., I:294.
124. Ibid., I:304.
125. Begbie, *William Booth*, I:292–307.
126. Orr, *The Second Evangelical Awakening*, 62–75.
127. Ibid., 71, 72.

in their chapels.[128] The Booths left Cornwall in February 1863 with "the jeers of the Wesleyan President about 'the perambulations of the male and female' ringing in their ears."[129] The Booths' fifth child, Herbert Henry Howard, had been born in Penzance on 26 August 1862.

From Cornwall William and Catherine travelled to Wales, where the shipping merchants and colliery owners John and Richard Cory became patrons of their work. The Cory brothers named one of their ships *William Booth* and allocated a portion of its profits to support William's ministry.[130] During 1863 the Booths followed Walter and Phoebe Palmer to Cardiff, Walsall, and Birmingham. Leaving Birmingham, they were followed there by James Caughey. In Walsall William organized open-air services which attracted large crowds, and for the first time worked with the Hallelujah Bands.[131] In 1864 they campaigned in Leeds, Halifax, Hyde, Bury, Stalybridge, Sheffield, and Gateshead. On 4 May 1864 their sixth child, a daughter, Marion, was born in Leeds.

Increasingly William and Catherine were each valued in their own right, and from June 1864 Catherine began to accept invitations on her own. An invitation to Catherine brought her to London, alone, at the end of February 1865 to lead a campaign at the United Methodist Free Church, Rotherhithe.[132] William joined Catherine in London, and Catherine's campaign continued through to May, in Rotherhithe, Bermondsey, and finally Deptford. During this time Catherine held two meetings in connection with the Midnight Movement for prostitutes. The *Wesleyan Times* reported the occasion, "[Mrs. Booth's address] was inimitable, pointed, evangelical, impressive and sympathetic, and delivered in a most earnest and affectionate manner, drawing tears from many of those present and securing the closest attention from all. She identified herself with them as a fellow-sinner, showing that if they supposed her better than themselves it was a mistake; [. . .] Then the Saviour was exhibited as waiting to save them all, urging them by a variety of reasons to decision at once."[133]

128. Booth-Tucker, *Catherine Booth*, I:345–46.

129. Orr, *The Second Evangelical Awakening*, 72.

130. Booth-Tucker, *Catherine Booth*, I:361.

131. Ibid., I:371; "Hallelujah Bands" emerged in the early 1860s in the Midlands; formed by men who had been rough, often notorious, characters before their conversion, they held lively, unconventional meetings. Cf. Booth, *The Christian Mission Magazine*, "Hallelujah Bands."

132. Booth, *Reminiscences*, 83.

133. *The Wesleyan Times*, "Mrs. Booth amongst Lodging-House Females."

Introduction

After the meeting Catherine joined in conversation with these young women. The report continued: "Mrs. Booth, to whom they freely opened their minds, soon discovered how futile was the task of attempting to benefit them spiritually without the means of temporal deliverance."[134] Sympathetic as she was, Catherine regretted the movement's lack of practical assistance for the women and her own inability to help. The report concluded that Catherine's "adaptiveness for this work, as well as preaching the Gospel, is very plain, and in her great mission, we wish her God-speed."[135] In its report of the Bermondsey campaign the *Gospel Guide* described the preacher:

> In dress nothing could be neater. A plain black straw bonnet, slightly relieved with a pair of dark violet strings; a black velvet loose-fitting jacket, with light sleeves, which appeared exceedingly suitable to her while preaching, and a black silk dress, constituted the plain dress of this female preacher. A rather prepossessing countenance, with, at first, an exceedingly quiet manner, enlists the sympathies and rivets the attention of the audience. Mrs. Booth is a woman of no ordinary mind, and her powers of argument are of a superior character. Her delivery is calm, precise, and clear without the least approach to formality or becoming tedious.[136]

However, the following week the same writer took Catherine to task. After praising again "her quiet but confident manner, her powers of mind, her depth of thought, her clear and lucid style of argument" the writer decried the "strong influences [. . .] brought to work on the minds of the people," the energy and enthusiasm of the prayers, and the excitement of the "extraordinary measures" such as "special hymns to exciting tunes." He concluded, "There are many [. . .] who with us admire Mrs. Booth's preaching talents; but they are as much surprised as we are that a lady of such extensive mind and large Biblical information should [. . .] conduct such services."[137] A week later, a letter signed "B. S." made a strong repost: "The writer evidently is in a fog; he forgets the Spirit acts on the spirit of man, the spirit of man on the mind, and the mind on the body. The writer

---

134. Ibid.
135. Ibid.
136. *The Wesleyan Times*, "Mrs. Booth's Revival Services in London."
137. *The Wesleyan Times*, "Mrs Booth's Revival Services in London: Concluding Notice."

thinks the closet, and solitude, is best for the seeker of salvation; if so the times are altered since the day of Pentecost."[138]

On 2 July 1865, at the invitation of the East London Special Services Committee, William began to conduct services in a tent erected on a disused Quaker burial ground in Whitechapel.[139] On 17 August William reported in *The Revival*, "We have no very definite plans, we shall be guided by the Holy Spirit."[140] In the same letter William proposed the establishment of a Christian Revival Association. Catherine remembered when their future was settled.

> [William] came home one night from one of the meetings, worn out, between 11 and 12 o'clock. Throwing himself into an easy chair, he said to me, "Oh, Katie, as I passed the flaming gin palaces and the doors of the public houses tonight I seemed to hear a voice sounding in my soul, "Where can you go where there are such heathen as these and where is there so great a need for your labours?" And I felt as if I ought to stop and preach to these East End multitudes.[141]

Despite her disquiet, Catherine replied, "Well, if you feel you ought to stay, stay. We have trusted the Lord once and we can trust him again."[142] In her reminiscences she reflected, "He had no idea himself of what he was going to do and no plan of how he was going to work," and, she continued, in a line crossed out by an unknown hand as not for publication, "much less had he any notion of what was going to follow."[143] At the same time Catherine was speaking in the Assembly Rooms, Kensington, "in the very midst of the rank and fashion of the West End, so we were just about at the opposite poles [of] society," she reflected, in another crossed out line.[144] At first Catherine did not share William's vision, as is apparent from another crossed out sentence: "William's work was a tangled affair, I could not see my way through it. Of course, I was away from his battlefield, and to me it was entirely a new departure. I saw where he had gone in, but I could not

---

138. B.E, *The Wesleyan Times*, "Revival Services."
139. Sandall, Wiggins, and Coutts, *History*, I:254.
140. Booth-Tucker, *Catherine Booth*, I:392.
141. Booth, *Reminiscences*, 89.
142. Ibid.
143. Ibid.
144. Ibid., 90.

see where he was going to come out."[145] Catherine gradually became deeply involved in the life of the mission, but the separation of their spheres of work continued.

At first William had no definite plan for the future and was opposed to forming a new organization.[146] However, converts needed to be nurtured and mobilized. They would not go when sent to other churches, and if they did, they felt unwanted.[147] In February 1867 the Evangelisation Society began to support the mission's work financially.[148] The mission occupied more halls and opened new stations. On 6 April 1867 *The East London Observer* reported that "enormous audiences" had been drawn to listen to William's "exordiums" at the Effingham Theatre. In June the Eastern Star, once a public house, became the mission's first headquarters, and in September a new name appeared—the East London Christian Mission.[149] On Christmas Day 1865 a seventh child was born to William and Catherine, Evelyn Cory, known to the family as Eva, and eventually to the Army as Evangeline; and on 28 April 1867 their eighth, Lucy Milward, was born.

Catherine continued to lead her own campaigns, speaking to large congregations in London's West End and in the suburbs. The wealthy Nonconformist philanthropist Samuel Morley supported William financially, but Catherine's income was essential.[150] Catherine's campaigns publicized the work of the mission and led to the opening of new mission stations. Through the summers of 1867–73 Catherine campaigned on the south coast, in Ramsgate, Margate, Brighton, Folkestone, Hastings, Portsmouth, and Southsea, filling some of the largest theatres and music halls. The mission stations were generally small; by going outside Catherine "obtained large buildings, numerous audiences, and exerted a powerful influence upon whole neighbourhoods."[151] These were extended campaigns. Catherine was in Southsea for seventeen weeks; she rented a music hall, which was packed every night.[152] She preached on eleven successive Sundays from

---

145. Ibid., 95.
146. Sandall, Wiggins, and Coutts, *History*, I:66.
147. Ibid.
148. Booth-Tucker, *Catherine Booth*, I:431.
149. Ibid.
150. Ibid., I:400.
151. Booth, *Reminiscences*, 136.
152. Ibid., 139.

the text "Go work [today] in my vineyard."¹⁵³ After the Margate campaign a deputation of gentlemen offered to build Catherine "a church similar to Mr. Spurgeon's Tabernacle."¹⁵⁴

In October 1868 the first edition of the *East London Evangelist* was published. Booth-Tucker wrote, "The publication of the magazine afforded Mrs. Booth the fulfilment of the wish [. . .] of being able to edit a paper which should advocate more advanced views in regard to the privileges of Christians and their duty of working for God."¹⁵⁵ In 1870 the movement became The Christian Mission. Article XII of the Mission's constitution, which provided for every role to be open to godly women as well as men, testified to Catherine's influence.

William was ill for three months in the spring of 1870 from typhoid fever, which left him in a weakened state, and in March 1872 he suffered a complete breakdown.¹⁵⁶ Catherine was compelled to "take his place and do his work in the superintendence of the Mission."¹⁵⁷ At this point in the Christian Mission's history all would have been lost if Catherine had not taken charge. Norman Murdoch alleges that "Catherine never assumed a position of authority over men," but she surely did.¹⁵⁸ William's search for a cure took him to Matlock, Nottingham, Limpley Stoke, near Bath, Tunbridge Wells, Hastings, and finally Folkestone where he met Catherine who was leading a campaign. They returned to London in October, though William was still far from well and unable to resume his duties completely. During this time, Catherine "preached wherever I had an opportunity, met the evangelists/officers, cheered the sorrowful, directed the perplexed, appealed for funds, and kept everybody at work as far as I had the ability."¹⁵⁹ While William was at Tunbridge Wells, "his heart was drawn out in desire to do something for it, so he begged [Catherine] to come down and hold a few meetings."¹⁶⁰ Catherine hired the largest hall in the town and preached for two or three nights each week and four Sundays in a row. As a result a

---

153. Ibid.

154. Booth-Tucker, *Catherine Booth*, I:417.

155. Ibid., I:446.

156. Bramwell-Booth, *Catherine Booth*, 252; Begbie, *William Booth*, I:326; Booth-Tucker, *Catherine Booth*, II:17,42.

157. Booth, *Reminiscences*, 129.

158. Murdoch, "Female Ministry," 354.

159. Booth, *Reminiscences*, 130.

160. Ibid.

branch of the Mission was established. Through the 1870s, despite setbacks and retrenchments, the Mission grew steadily if unspectacularly until by the end of 1877 there were thirty-one stations in operation.[161]

The Mission's transformation into an Army was a gradual process. The conceptualization of mission as warfare and the introduction of military terminology reflected the spirit of the age. The Christian Mission became The Salvation Army at the "War Congress" held in August 1878, when the identity of the movement shifted decisively, and those assembled reported a pentecostal outpouring equipping them for the "Salvation War."[162] From fifty corps and 127 officers in 1878 the Army grew to 1,445 corps and 4,314 officers in Great Britain and 1,269 corps and 3,698 officers overseas in 1889.[163] These figures explain Stead's opinion that The Salvation Army was "a miracle of our time."[164] Norman Murdoch claims that "by 1888, overseas expansion made The Salvation Army the world's fastest growing Christian sect in an age of missions."[165] Writing in 1905 George Bernard Shaw captured a sense of the Army's impact upon national life:

> Yet in the poorest corner of this soul-destroying Christendom vitality suddenly begins to germinate again. Joyousness [. . .] rises like a flood miraculously out of the fetid dust and mud of the slums; rousing marches and impetuous dithyrambs rise to the heavens from people among whom the depressing noise called "sacred music" is a standing joke; a flag with Blood and Fire on it is unfurled, not in murderous rancour, but because fire is beautiful and blood a vital and splendid red; Fear, which we flatter by calling Self, vanishes; and transfigured men and women carry their gospel through a transfigured world, calling their leader General, themselves captains and brigadiers, and their whole body an Army.[166]

The Army aroused opposition from clergymen, magistrates, politicians, and publicans. A "Skeleton Army" was raised with serious and violent intent. Salvationists were jailed for proclaiming their faith in public. There were riots and questions in parliament. The Army featured in daily newspapers and weekly journals, and was the butt of satirical humor in

---

161. Horridge, *Salvation Army Origins*, 20.
162. *The Christian Mission Magazine*, "The War Congress."
163. Woodall, *What Price the Poor?*, 148–49.
164. Stead, *Mrs. Booth*, 199.
165. Murdoch, *Origins of The Salvation Army*, 136.
166. Shaw, *Major Barbara*, 27.

Punch. Catherine became the prime apologist for the movement, addressing crowds of opinion formers in the City and the West End of London. Collections of her addresses were published.[167] With many others the scholarly Bishop Joseph Lightfoot read her works and approved.[168] Catherine's daughter Evangeline wrote, "My mother never lost the habit of meditation. She was a diligent reader, particularly of books with which she sharply disagreed. [. . .] She met scepticism, sophistication, and aggression on their own ground. She was an intellectual among intellectuals."[169]

On Tuesday 21 February 1888 Catherine kept an appointment with her doctor, Sir James Paget, who told her that she was suffering from breast cancer and advised an immediate operation. Catherine, who was opposed to surgery, partly because of the high risks involved, but also because of her commitment to natural remedies, asked him how long she had to live. Paget told her between eighteen months and two years. In the cab on the way home Catherine prayed. William was watching for her and helped her inside the house. Smiling through her tears, Catherine told him she was dying.[170]

Catherine preached her last sermon on 21 June 1888 at the City Temple in Holborn.[171] In August she moved from the family home in Hadley Wood to the Army's home of rest for staff officers, Oceanville, in Clacton on Sea, where she remained until she died. Here the final drafts of *Darkest England* were prepared, Catherine's reminiscences were recorded, and a constant stream of visitors came on pilgrimage. According to Booth-Tucker, "her sick bed became an altar; round which there gathered daily in spirit, the great and growing Army of Salvationists scattered throughout the world."[172]

Catherine died on Saturday 4 October 1890. Her body was taken to the Army's Clapton Congress Hall, and an estimated 50,000 people came to her lying in state. The funeral service was held on Monday 13 October in Olympia's vast arena. The next day Catherine's body was processed from the Army's International Headquarters in Queen Victoria Street to Abney Park Cemetery. Three thousand officers marched in the procession; crowds

---

167. Booth, *Practical Religion*; Booth, *Aggressive Christianity*; Booth, *Godliness*; Booth, *Life & Death*; Booth, *Church & State*; Booth, *Popular Christianity*.

168. Booth, *On the Banks of the River*, 143.

169. Booth, *The Officers' Review*, "My Mother."

170. Booth, *On the Banks of the River*, 16–17.; Ervine, *God's Soldier*, 671.

171. Booth-Tucker, *Catherine Booth*, I:418.

172. Ibid., II:442.

thronged the four-mile route. Admission to the cemetery was limited to 10,000.[173]

In its obituary the *Methodist Times* described Catherine as the Army's "inspiring soul" and "restraining genius."[174] According to her son Bramwell, "In the early days of the Salvation Army movement her hand was upon many matters to an extent unknown to anyone outside the inner circle."[175] Conferences on anxious or difficult matters were held at times and in places that enabled Catherine's participation.[176] Catherine had the capacity to "at once discern and fasten on the potentialities of a situation and carry us all to the future outcome of the thing proposed":[177]

> While the Founder had the creative genius, she had the analytical mind. He [William] made things, she improved them. He inspired the Army, raised its colours (though literally the Army flag was her idea, and the design finally resolved upon was hers), pointed its weapons, and ever urged it forward to new fields of labour. She thought out the why and wherefore of it all, and in her more cultured sphere justified the Army's methods to circles which, accustomed to conventional religious expression, were shocked by ours. And further, she enhanced the reasonableness and beauty and value of the work we were doing in our own eyes. She discerned, and helped us to discern, the philosophy behind the roughness and awkwardness and seeming contradictions of the struggle, and strengthened the Founder's hands in a hundred ways.[178]

Bramwell reflected sadly, "Her voice is silent now, and her chair in the inner counsels is empty. It is a terrible and irreparable loss."[179]

THE PURPOSE OF THIS BOOK

Catherine Booth was the principal architect of The Salvation Army's theology; her Salvationism gave birth to a movement within the church marked by extraordinarily effective cross-cultural mission, an apparently complete acceptance of the place of women in ministry, and an astonishing optimism

---

173. Ibid., I:463–90.
174. Booth, *On the Banks of the River*, 146.
175. Booth, *These Fifty Years*, 22.
176. Ibid.
177. Ibid.
178. Ibid., 22–23.
179. Booth, *On the Banks of the River*, 16.

regarding the potential of human lives transformed by grace. In William and Catherine's life together it was she who provided the intellectual and theological foundation and framework for their shared mission. In so far as the radical moves and departures of the movement sprang from the theological convictions of its founders, the source lay with Catherine.

Krista Valtanen's doctoral study of Catherine identifies and analyses the explicit topics of Catherine's exhortations. However, Valtanen concludes, "Beside Booth's expressed theology, there is a strong implied theology that this study has not been able to capture in its entirety. In reality, it seems that Booth's expressed theology is driven by her implied theology."[180] The "implied"—or rather implicit and embedded—theology to which Valtanen refers is the hidden skeletal structure which gives coherence and consistency to her exhortations. Catherine's Salvationism finds fullest expression in the addresses delivered between 1879 and 1887, which were mostly prepared in brief outline and presented with great freedom. There are no scholarly references and footnotes. They were not addressed to the academy but in the most part to educated and enquiring audiences who were familiar with the religious controversies of the time, but who in Catherine's view also desperately needed to hear the gospel. In these addresses Catherine gave final expression to the ideas she had developed and refined over her lifetime.

A close reading of these addresses reveals that Catherine did, in fact, give sufficiently precise expression to her theological ideas for the underlying structure of her thought to be reconstructed and its formative influences analyzed. Although many of her exhortations in these addresses were topical and contextual, there was a strong doctrinal core which was expressed consistently—certainly in the published versions of her exhortations. The underlying theology can be discerned, not so much by reading between the lines (a method which might rightly be questioned), but by reading out of those sections, sometimes noting sentences or even phrases, where Catherine sets her ideas in their doctrinal context. The recent publication of Catherine and William's correspondence and the rediscovery and publication of Catherine's journal and reminiscences has provided another rich source for Catherine's thinking on theological matters.[181] The purpose

---

180. Valtanen, "Catherine Booth," 271.

181. Although Catherine and William's correspondence has previously been accessible through the collections in the British Library and The Salvation Army's heritage centre, Catherine's handwriting, legible only by means of a close and necessarily slow scrutiny, has in practice proved to be a stumbling block to the analysis of her ideas.

Introduction

of this book is, therefore, by means of a close reading of these primary sources, to discover and then to lay bare the underlying structure of Catherine Booth's Salvationism, to examine its characteristic features, to identify its sources, and to consider the extent of its abiding influence.

Catherine was co-founder of a *Salvation Army*. Consequently this exploration has two parts. The first three chapters examine Catherine's doctrine of salvation, which embraced the doctrines of justification and sanctification. Her soteriology had ecclesiological implications and resulted in the birth of an Army. The following three chapters examine Catherine's doctrines of church, ministry, and sacraments as they sprang from her doctrine of salvation.

TWO

Salvation

In an article "Our New Name" published in *The Salvationist* on 1 January 1879 William Booth wrote, "We are a Salvation people—this is our speciality—getting saved and keeping saved, and then getting somebody else saved, and then getting saved ourselves more and more, until full salvation on earth makes the heaven within, which is finally perfected by the full salvation without, on the other side of the River."[1]

The Christian Mission's new name expressed the beating heart of William and Catherine Booth's spirituality. Catherine Booth was indeed a Salvationist. Her doctrine of salvation lay at the very centre of her theology. By far the majority of her published addresses were devoted to this theme. The purpose of this chapter is to outline and describe her soteriology and identify its formative sources. Special attention will be given to her views of the atonement and the *ordo salutis*.

Catherine's startling expressions of dislike for certain aspects of the "substitutionary" theory of the atonement are one of the first indications that her soteriology might have a distinctive character. Given that it is thought by many commentators that John Wesley's own understanding of the atonement is best described in this way, and that it has been a *sine qua non* for many evangelicals, Catherine's trenchant criticisms raise the suspicion that she might not have grasped the importance of both objective and subjective elements to an atonement theory, or that a common sense post-enlightenment rationality blinded her to certain aspects of biblical truth, or that her insight into her avowedly Wesleyan heritage was shallow and partial.

1. Booth, *The Salvationist*, "Our New Name."

THE ATONEMENT

Catherine's view of the doctrine of the atonement has never been explicated, even though she presented it consistently. Catherine credited the religious indifference of many intelligent people of her time to a general misunderstanding of this doctrine; the presentation of "false and contradictory theories" have, she argued, "shocked and insulted their reason" and "repelled them from the subject altogether."[2]

A Governmental Scheme of Redemption

A clue that Catherine might have a distinctive view of the atonement is found in her fierce attack on the "Christs of the Nineteenth Century" in her book *Popular Christianity*.[3] Catherine argues that the "modern representation" of Christ as a "substitutionary Saviour" is a counterfeit portrayal of Christ:[4] "This Christ is held up as embodying in Himself the sum and substance of the sinner's salvation, needing only to be believed in, that is accepted by the mind as the atoning Sacrifice, and trusted in as securing for the sinner all the benefits involved in his death, without respect to any inwrought change in the sinner himself."[5]

Catherine finds a grave error in this view which encourages antinomianism: "Men are taught that Christ obeyed the law for them, not only as necessary to the efficacy of His atonement for their justification, but that He has placed His obedience in the stead of, or as a substitution for, the sinner's own obedience or sanctification, which in effect is like saying, Though you may be untrue, Christ is your truth; though you may be unclean, Christ is your chastity; though you may be dishonest, Christ is your honesty; though you may be insincere, Christ is your sincerity."[6] In contrast, the true Christ of God, for Catherine, is a Savior and Redeemer who delivers people from their sins.

> He never undertook to be true instead of me, but to make me true to the very core of my soul. He never undertook to make me pass for pure, either to God or man, but to enable me to *be* pure. He never undertook to make me pass for honest or sincere, but to

---

2. Booth, *Life & Death*, 129.
3. Booth, *Popular Christianity*.
4. Ibid., 10.
5. Ibid., 11.
6. Ibid.

renew me in the spirit of my mind so that I could not help but be both, as the result of the operation of His Spirit within me. He never undertook to love God instead of my doing so with "all my heart and mind and soul and strength," but He came on purpose to empower and inspire me to do this.[7]

Catherine declines to "go into the various theories respecting the atonement; it is enough for us to know that Christ made such a sacrifice as rendered it possible for God to be just, and yet to pardon the sinner."[8] Catherine's insight into these "various theories" may have been informed by a long-running series "The Great Propitiation" in David Thomas's journal *The Homilist*, which closely analyzed the language and themes of "some Popular Theories of the Atonement of Christ."[9] The writer, "Galileo," recognized the penal substitution theory as the most popular among evangelical Christians, but dismissed it as absurd, and it would seem to be some expressions of this originally "Calvinistic" theory that are the target of Catherine's attack.[10] Against those theories which present the atonement too narrowly as a propitiation of the wrath of God, Catherine argues that the atonement must be understood as an expression of the justice and the love of God, Father and Son:

> [Christ's] sacrifice is never represented in the Bible as having purchased or begotten the love of the Father, but only as having opened a channel through which that love could flow out to his rebellious and prodigal children. The doctrine of the New Testament on this point is not that "God so hated the world that His own Son was compelled to die in order to appease his vengeance," as we fear has been too often represented, but that "God so loved the world, that He *gave* His only begotten Son."[11]

In Catherine's view the union of the Father and the Son was perfect and entire and "equally complete with respect to the sufficiency and vicarious character of His death"; Christ was one with the Father in "the maintenance of the dignity of the law and equally inspired with boundless and quenchless love for its transgressors."[12]

7. Ibid., 11–12.
8. Ibid., 22.
9. Galileo, *The Homilist*, "The Great Propitiation."
10. Ibid., XX:294, 96.
11. Booth, *Popular Christianity*, 22.
12. Ibid.

Catherine provides a fuller explanation of her view in her address *The Need of Atonement*. A "scheme of redemption" is required that is adapted to people's need as fallen, free moral agents.[13] This scheme must "do just what we need; namely to PUT US RIGHT AGAIN."[14] That is, it must "restore us to harmony with ourselves, harmony with the moral law, and harmony with God."[15] The scheme must therefore uphold "the one great moral law which [God] has written on the tables of our hearts, written in His book and in His Gospel, operates in Heaven, and everywhere else where He reigns."[16] This law has been broken, and yet out of love God wants to save the transgressors. Justice must be done or else the universe is without law. Therefore the Son "voluntarily gave Himself a sacrifice for us, that He might redeem us from the curse of the law."[17] In *Popular Christianity* Catherine presented in summary the exact same scheme:

> The Christ of God offered Himself as a sacrifice for the sin of man. The Divine law had been broken; the interests of the universe demanded that its righteousness should be maintained, therefore its penalty must be endured by the transgressor or, in lieu of this, such compensation must be rendered as would satisfy the claims of justice, and render it expedient for God to pardon the guilty [. . .] Christ made such a sacrifice as rendered it possible for God to be just, and yet to pardon the sinner.[18]

Although Catherine does not subscribe to any particular atonement theory, her consistent portrayal of God as a lawgiver, who, in the interests of universal justice must maintain the moral law, by means of some compensation "in lieu" of the penalty being endured by the transgressor, associates her with a line of interpretation which originated in the student of Arminius, Hugo Grotius, and had become known as the "governmental" theory.

According to J. Kenneth Grider the governmental theory is eclectic and embraces many aspects of other atonement theories, including the notion that Christ's sacrifice is substitutionary.[19] The two concepts it cannot embrace are, first, that Christ was punished instead of sinful humanity;

---

13. Booth, *Life & Death*, 130.
14. Ibid.
15. Ibid., 131.
16. Ibid., 133.
17. Ibid., 135.
18. Booth, *Popular Christianity*, 21–22.
19. Grider, "The Governmental Theory".

and second, that Christ paid the debt for humanity's sin, for punishment precludes forgiveness, as does the full payment of a debt. For Grider, the governmental theory thus excludes key elements of the penal substitution and satisfaction theories. Grider follows John Miley in this analysis.[20]

In her address *The Need of Atonement* Catherine Booth is circumspect in speaking of the atonement in penal terms and as the payment of a debt. However, it cannot be said that she never speaks of Christ bearing the punishment for humanity's sin; nevertheless, it can be argued that she emphasizes rather more Christ's willing embrace of suffering in order that humanity might not suffer the punishment due for sin. Miley finds other proponents of the Grotian theory to be inconsistent because of their use of penal language, including Grotius himself.[21] However, Grotius's use of penal language appears to be less than accidental when he claims that "to bear sins by suffering, and in such a way as to liberate others thereby, can only mean to receive another's punishment."[22] In a similar fashion, Catherine affirms, "The very idea of law implies some penal consequences if it be broken," and she does not avoid claiming that Christ bore "our" punishment in his body.[23] According to Frank Foster, the history of the Grotian theory took a new turn when it was "embosomed" within the "Calvinistic orthodoxy" of New England and taken up by Jonathan Edwards and his successors.[24] Miley's prescriptive claims for the governmental view, echoed by Grider, possibly reflect the form of its rather more systematic North American development, as well as Miley's apparent opinion that the atonement is best understood by means of tightly bounded theories, as opposed, for example, to less self-contained models. Catherine's deprecatory reference to "false and contradictory theories" and presentation instead of a broadly drawn "scheme of redemption" might imply she does not share this view.[25]

Formative Influences

Catherine left no account of the extent of her familiarity with the works of John Wesley. That she quoted from the seven-volume edition of Wesley's

20. Cf. Miley, *The Atonement in Christ*.
21. Ibid., 200–201.
22. Grotius, *The Satisfaction of Christ*, 20.
23. Booth, *Life & Death*, 133,145.
24. Foster, "History of the Grotian Theory," liii–lv.
25. Booth, *Life & Death*, 129.

Salvation

works in *Female Teaching*, referencing letters from Wesley to Elizabeth Briggs and Sarah Mallett, suggests some depth to her knowledge.[26] It is probable that she was at least as well acquainted with the volumes which included Wesley's sermons and journal. According to Henry Rack, "Wesley never borrowed without change, omission, and development."[27] Much the same can be said in regard to Catherine Booth. Her reverence for Wesley, Fletcher, and her other formative influences never compromised her ability to form her own view of matters.

While John Wesley never subscribed to any particular theory of the atonement, and it would be anachronistic to suggest he did so even implicitly, many Wesley scholars believe his understanding of the atonement is best expressed in terms of "penal substitution." In support of this view, Kenneth J. Collins quotes from Wesley's *The Doctrine of Original Sin*:

> Our sins were the procuring cause of all his sufferings. His sufferings were the *penal effects* of our sins. "The chastisement of our peace," the punishment necessary to procure it, "was" laid "on him," freely submitting thereto: "And by his stripes" (a part of his sufferings again put for the whole) "we are healed"; pardon, sanctification, and final salvation, are all purchased and bestowed upon us. Every chastisement is for some fault. That laid on Christ was not for his own, but ours; and was needful to reconcile an offended Lawgiver, and offending guilty creatures, to each other. So "the Lord laid on him the iniquity of us all"; that is, the punishment due to our iniquity.[28]

Collins mounts a strong defense of Wesley's theology of the atonement against the views of scholars such as H. Ray Dunning, who argued that Wesley's use of the language of "punishment" instead of "suffering" was unbiblical and regrettable.[29]

In so far as Catherine followed in that interpretative tradition which sprang from Grotius, and included Richard Watson, Charles Finney, and Albert Barnes, it might be argued that Catherine's understanding of the atonement was rather different from Wesley's. Catherine Booth had at least

---

26. Booth, *Female Teaching*, 29.
27. Rack, *Reasonable Enthusiast*, xx.
28. Collins, *Holy Love*, 102.
29. Ibid., 103.

some knowledge of Grotius.[30] Hugo Grotius (1583–1646) set out his understanding of the atonement in response to Socinian views which were in themselves a response to the developed Calvinism of Theodore Beza.[31] Faustus Socinus objected to the idea that God's offended justice made the infliction of punishment a necessity, and that if man was to be spared then God's wrath had to fall on another, the substitute being Christ. Socinus argued that if God is indeed the offended party then he has the right to forgive sin without requiring any satisfaction whatsoever. God should not be conceived of as a judge administering the law of another from which he is not permitted to depart, but as a sovereign Lord and Prince whose will alone is the law of all things. If a private man forgives in response to true repentance without penalty he is praised for doing so. If a man can forgive a debt without payment then so can God.

In response Grotius argued that God does not act in this matter as an offended party; instead he acts as a sovereign ruler who must defend and maintain the moral law.[32] If the law is to be maintained then a penalty must be exacted. Christ's suffering and death served as a substitute for the punishment that men might have received. This allows God to extend forgiveness and at the same time maintain divine order. The atonement is thus a demonstration of both God's love and mercy.

Catherine Booth was certainly an avid reader of American revivalist Charles Finney (1792–1875) from her early teenage years. The moral law was a foundational principle within Finney's theology, and he promoted a form of the governmental theory of the atonement. Surprisingly, Keith Hardman claims that Charles Finney espoused the moral influence theory. He quotes Finney, "In the atonement God has given us the influence of his own example, has exhibited his own love, his own compassion, his own self-denial, his own patience, his own long-suffering, under abuse from enemies [. . .] this is the highest possible moral influence."[33]

Hardman continues, "In line with Finney's stress on God's moral government, he called this the governmental theory, but it is merely a variation on Abelard."[34] However, according to David Weddle, Finney also believes "it is not adequate to interpret the atonement as calling for a mere sub-

---

30. Booth, *Female Teaching*, 18.
31. Cf. Foster, "History of the Grotian Theory," xii–lvii.
32. Grotius, *The Satisfaction of Christ*.
33. Hardman, *Finney*, 385–86.
34. Ibid., 386.

Salvation

jective change in the sinner; the atonement must also fulfil an objective condition."[35] Finney's application of the principle of public justice to the atonement requires that something must be done, in the provision of some equivalent substitute in place of the execution of a penalty, before an offender can be shown mercy.[36] According to Finney the atonement is necessary not to satisfy the otherwise implacable wrath of God, but to maintain the integrity of God's moral government, thereby securing the greatest good for all creation.

Albert Barnes (1798–1870) was well known for his *Notes on the New Testament*, published from 1832. Catherine referenced the *Notes* in her pamphlet on *Female Teaching* though only to disagree with them profoundly.[37] Barnes was an exponent of the New School Presbyterianism that developed out of the New Haven theology of Nathaniel Taylor which had in turn grown out of the Calvinism of Jonathan Edwards.[38] The origins of Barnes's theory of the atonement can be traced to Edwards himself.[39] Barnes published his popular book on the atonement in 1860.[40] Barnes denies that God inflicts the punishment upon his Son that should rightly be imposed upon sinful mankind. Forgiveness cannot be freely given once punishment has been imposed. Instead the atonement is a demonstration of the justice and love of God rather than a satisfaction of the wrath of God. The atonement allows a just God who longs to forgive to do so freely. Unlike Catherine, Barnes is scrupulous in avoiding penal language, and his presentation is in line with Miley's understanding of the doctrine. This difference, along with the fact that by 1860 Catherine's views were somewhat settled, makes it unlikely that Barnes was a major influence upon her thought. Furthermore, she had already by then been exposed to variations of the governmental theory by her reading of Finney and also Richard Watson.

Richard Watson (1781–1833) was a key figure in early nineteenth-century Methodism. From 1823 he began to publish his *Theological Institutes* which systematized John Wesley's theology and established a basis for sound Methodist doctrine.[41] Catherine used Watson in the preparation

---

35. Weddle, *The Law as Gospel*, 198.
36. Ibid.
37. Booth, *Female Teaching*, 8.
38. Cf. Sutton, "Benevolent Calvinism and the Moral Government of God."
39. Foster, "History of the Grotian Theory," li–lvii.
40. Barnes, *The Atonement*.
41. Watson, *Institutes*.

of her pamphlet on *Female Teaching*.[42] Robert Chiles offers an account of Richard Watson's views on the atonement: "Richard Watson's views on the nature of the atonement are commented on by John Miley, who observes, 'We cannot accord to him any clear view.' What then distresses Miley is Watson's failure to provide a clear and steady assertion of the [. . .] moral government theory of the atonement, and his frequent lapses into variants of the satisfaction theory. Miley's bias prevents him from seeing that the satisfaction, not the governmental theory, has priority in Watson."[43]

In fact the two schemes that Watson discusses are both, to him, "views of satisfaction."[44] From Watson's description, these two views, "most prevalent among [. . .] divines," are evidently the penal substitution theory, and the governmental theory.[45] Both opinions have had "great names" as their advocates; however, the manner in which they have been expressed has been such that neither provides a satisfactory explanation of the atonement. The first opinion is "defective in not explaining what is meant by the terms 'a full equivalent' and 'an adequate compensation.'"[46] If these terms can be satisfactorily explained, however, this opinion is "greatly to be preferred."[47] The second opinion is "objectionable," because it makes the atonement an unnecessary expedient and does not prove the necessary connection between the death of Christ and the satisfaction of the law of God which would allow remission of punishment to the offenders.[48]

This appears to support Chiles's view that the governmental theory does not have priority in Watson. However, Watson's clarification of the terms in question makes this conclusion less certain. Watson explains that God provides the atonement as Judge and Lawgiver. It is as a just lawgiver that he is satisfied with the atonement offered by the vicarious death of his Son. It is not the satisfaction of an angry vengeful offended party, but rather, "The satisfaction of the mind of a just or righteous governor, disposed from the goodness of his nature to show mercy to the guilty, and who can now do it consistently with the rectitude of his character, and the authority of his laws, which it is the office of punitive justice to proclaim, and to uphold."[49]

---

42. Booth, *Female Teaching*, 19.
43. Chiles, *Theological Transition*, 158.
44. Watson, *Institutes*, II:176.
45. Ibid.
46. Ibid., II.177.
47. Ibid.
48. Ibid.
49. Ibid., II:178.

In this way the atonement upholds the honor and authority of God's law, as well as the character and the administration of the lawgiver, God. The atonement is not merely the best of all possible expedients; rather the vicarious death of an infinitely dignified and glorious being was the only way to safeguard the righteous character and administration of God. The death of Christ was a "full equivalent" and "adequate compensation" in its "judicial value," because it is, at least, "an equally powerful demonstration of the righteousness of God, who only in consideration of that atonement forgives the sins of offending men."[50]

Watson next denies that the first option, properly understood, supports antinomianism: "The Antinomians connect the satisfaction of Christ with the doctrine of the imputation of his active righteousness to believers. [. . .] They consider our Lord as a proxy for men; so that his perfect obedience to the law should be esteemed by God, as done by them; as theirs in legal construction, and that his perfect righteousness being imputed to them, renders them legally righteous and sinless."[51]

Watson denies this on four grounds. First, this doctrine is not found in Scripture. Second, this doctrine makes Christ's sufferings superfluous, "for if he has done all that the law required of us, and if this is legally accounted our doing, then are we under no penalty of suffering, and his suffering in our stead was more than the law and the case required."[52] Third, this opposes a *fiction* to the true requirements of moral government. It transfers the obligation of obedience from an individual to Christ, and leaves "man without law, and GOD without dominion, which is obviously contrary to the Scriptures, and favourable to license of every kind."[53] Fourth, "This is not *satisfaction* in any good sense; it is merely the performance of all that the law requires by one person substituted for another."[54]

Watson argues further that Antinomians are wrong to understand the terms *full satisfaction* and *full equivalent* in the sense of the payment of a debt. This confuses the cancellation of a debt of judicial obligation with the payment of a debt of money which by its payment on our behalf cancels out all future obligation. Watson concludes, "With such explanations of the terms of the first of the two opinions on the satisfaction of Christ, above

---

50. Ibid., II:181.
51. Ibid.
52. Ibid.
53. Ibid., II:182.
54. Ibid.

given, it may be taken as fully accordant with the doctrine of the New Testament on this important subject."[55]

However, it would appear that given such explanations, the first of the opinions now looks very much like the second, and even more so were the objectionable aspects of the second also changed, that is, by upholding the authority of God, as well as his honor, and by allowing that the death of Christ is a necessary as well as a wise and fit expedient of government. Indeed, according to Watson, when interpreted in this way the two opinions do indeed "come substantially to an agreement."[56] Watson has in fact adapted the penal substitution theory to a governmental context, removing its objectionable substitutionary and antinomian aspects, creating an explanation of the atonement which is very much like the scheme of redemption later to be expressed by Catherine Booth, and confirms Frank Foster's view that "in his theory of the atonement [Watson] rests directly and confessedly upon Grotius."[57]

Crucially, Catherine affirms with Watson that the atonement fully and uniquely satisfies the requirements of justice—in contrast to Finney, for whom the atonement "honors" the law, and Barnes, for whom the atonement is a "demonstration" of God's justice. Richard Watson is rather more likely, therefore, to be the source and provider of scholarly support for Catherine's views than Finney or Barnes.

Collins, who represents Wesley as holding to a penal substitution view of the atonement, suggests that "the logic of this interpretation necessarily demands either universalism, on the one hand, or unconditional election, on the other hand."[58] Accordingly, Collins affirms that universalism, properly understood as the offer of salvation to all, is a part of Wesley's view. However, for Wesley, according to Collins, "the atoning work of Christ is not the *formal* cause of justification but the *meritorious* cause; that is, the atonement is the basis upon which the offer of forgiveness is made to *all*."[59] But this construction undermines the sense in which Christ's death is completely substitutionary; and this is also one of the reasons why Catherine Booth objected to some representations of the substitutionary view. Collins later notes another adjustment that Wesley made to the substitutionary

---

55. Ibid., II:186.
56. Ibid., II:180.
57. Foster, "History of the Grotian Theory," xl.
58. Collins, *Holy Love*, 107.
59. Ibid.

scheme. For Wesley, though initially sanctifying grace is freely given in conjunction with justification and forgiveness, the active obedience of Christ in fulfilling the law is *not* imputed to the believer.[60] Once again, this was one of Catherine Booth's objections to some popular substitutionary theories.

So greatly did Wesley wish to emphasize that Christ's obedience to the law is *not* substitutionary of a believer's own personal obedience, that in quoting from Thomas Cranmer's *Homily on Salvation* he omitted all reference to this thought. Collins concludes, "Wesley disassociated the fulfillment of the law from atonement and justification, and in the words of Lindstrom, 'attached it instead to sanctification.'"[61] It is evident that John Wesley was as alert to the antinomian dangers of a substitutionary view of the atonement as Catherine Booth.

To conclude, although Catherine's espousal of at least some aspects of a governmental theory of the atonement might suggest that in this core element of her soteriology she was influenced by Finney and American revivalism, in fact it was thoroughly Wesleyan concerns that brought her to this view, including, expressed negatively, her antipathy towards antinomianism, and more positively, her conviction that salvation embraces both justification and sanctification. Catherine's insistence that the purpose of the atonement is not only to justify, but also to "restore us to harmony with ourselves, harmony with the moral law, and harmony with God," suggests that ultimately a concept of restorative, as opposed to retributive justice, lies behind her scheme.[62]

LAW AND CONSCIENCE, LOVE AND GRACE

The harmony between the justice and the love of God are critical in Catherine Booth's soteriology. This harmony springs from the interplay of four closely associated root concepts: law and conscience, and love and grace. This short section will explore these concepts.

Law and Conscience

Catherine's emphasis on law and conscience reflects the influence of Bishop Joseph Butler and her early reading of the *Analogy of Religion*.[63] Catherine

---

60. Ibid., 112.
61. Ibid., 113.
62. Booth, *Life & Death*, 131.
63. Butler, *The Analogy of Religion*.

derived her epistemology from Butler. Ernest Mossner summarized one element of Butler's apologetic in the Analogy: "As most evidence has not the value of absolute demonstration, man necessarily acts in his daily existence frequently without certain knowledge. Indeed 'probability is the very guide of life.' This rule of probability applies to all functions of human life, not only to matters of practice, but also to matters of speculation."[64]

To William Booth, troubled by doubt while he was at Spalding, Catherine wrote, "All is mystery around me, above me, below me, within me, before me, but yet I believe, act, plan, live according to what I can understand [. . .] All men do this. As to the natural world, they acknowledge their ignorance, but yet believe in it and act upon it, as though they perfectly understand every law, and operation, and tendency."[65]

According to Albert Barnes, Butler "pointed the unbeliever to a grand system of things [. . .] deeply mysterious, yet developing great principles, and bearing proof that it was under the government of God."[66] For Terence Penelhum the *Analogy* demonstrates "that for anyone who *does* accept Christian revelation, it is inconsistent not to view the natural world and our life within it as a source of moral teaching."[67] Catherine delighted in the universal moral law by which God governs creation, as she delighted in the gospel: "The great glory of the Gospel of Christ is that it brings us back to love His Law, and as the angels delight in it, and as all holy intelligences delight in it, so we delight in it, and the righteousness of the Law—high, deep and broad, and long as it is—shall be fulfilled in us, 'who walk not after the flesh, but after the Spirit.'"[68]

Butler's moral philosophy was rooted in the natural supremacy of conscience.[69] Conscience as "that faculty of the soul which pronounces on the character of our actions" is critical to Catherine's scheme.[70] She describes conscience as a "constituent part of our nature [. . .] common to man everywhere and at all times."[71] It is "an independent witness standing as it were between God and man; it is *in* man, but *for* God, and it cannot

---

64. Mossner, *Bishop Butler*, 82.
65. Booth and Booth, *Letters*, 136.
66. Barnes, "Introductory Essay," 2.
67. Penelhum, *Butler*, 107.
68. Booth, *Aggressive Christianity*, 108–09.
69. Cf. Sturgeon, "Nature and Conscience in Butler's Ethics."
70. Booth, *Practical Religion*, 180.
71. Ibid.

Salvation

be bribed or silenced. Some one has called it 'God's Spirit in man's soul.' Another, 'God's vice-regent in the soul of man.'[72] [. . .] All other of our faculties can be subdued by our will; but this cannot."[73] The gospel, for Catherine, does not deliver people from the rule of conscience, set as it is to the moral law; instead the gospel enlightens the conscience and gives the believer power to obey its voice.[74]

Love and Grace

John Wesley and Joseph Butler famously did not get on when they met. Butler told Wesley, "Sir, the pretending to extraordinary revelations and gifts of the Holy Ghost is a horrid thing, a very horrid thing!," and "You have no business here. You are not commissioned to preach in this diocese. Therefore I advise you to go hence."[75] This did not stop Wesley calling the *Analogy* "that fine book," though it was probably "too hard for most of those for whom it is chiefly intended."[76] Law and conscience were important to Wesley, but it is Catherine's emphasis on the themes of love and grace that most clearly reveal her debt to Wesley. In 1852, when the opportunity arose for William to train as a Congregationalist minister, the plan foundered on the rock of Calvinism: "We knew that the basis of the Congregational theology was Calvinism. We were both saturated, as it were, with the broadest, deepest and highest opinions as to the extent of the love of God and the benefit flowing from the sacrifice of Jesus Christ. We were verily extremists on this question."[77]

In her Arminianism Catherine was thoroughly Wesleyan. In boundless love God reaches out to all humankind without exception in prevenient grace. For Catherine Booth, as for John Wesley, the possibility of salvation begins with the prevenient grace of God. In consequence of original sin people are incapable of seeing their own fault, ending their rebellion, and returning to God. The partial restoration of their faculties by the Spirit is what makes salvation possible: "God has taken compassion on us, and sent His Spirit into the world for this purpose—'To convince the world of sin,

---

72. A phrase used by Jonathan Edwards in a sermon entitled *True Grace distinguished from the Experience of Devils*.

73. Booth, *Practical Religion*, 180–81.

74. Ibid., 182, 83.

75. Wesley, *The Works of John Wesley*, XIII:500.

76. Wesley, *Journals and Diaries*, 18–24, XXII:134.

77. Begbie, *William Booth*, I:133.

of righteousness, and of judgement.' Thus he opens our eyes, and shows us our lost estate."[78]

In Catherine's thought the supreme realities of law and conscience, love and grace are apparent in the workings of providence. Catherine believed in a retributive as well as a benevolent providence. Not only in the age to come will people reap what they sow: "How often does the conscience writhe for years under a sense of retributive providence, and how is every personal, domestic and commercial affliction embittered by the perhaps silent, but stinging acknowledgement, 'As I have done to others, so hath God requited me' (Judges 1:7)."[79]

The workings of providence are no less real for sometimes being unseen; but they are visible and to be celebrated in the success of The Salvation Army: "We believe that there are laws in the spiritual kingdom as unerring in their operation, and as certain in their results, as any physical laws; and that if we conform ourselves to those laws, and act upon them, we may be as certain of a good harvest morally as the husbandman can be naturally. In other words, we believe *we shall reap according as we sow*; and we contend that the history and success of the Salvation Army prove it."[80]

God's boundless love reaching out to fallen humanity, by the workings of providence governed and regulated by the moral law, creates the conditions under which the possibility of salvation begins.[81]

THE *ORDO SALUTIS*

While affirming Catherine Booth's sense of connection with her Methodist roots, Roger Green has questioned just how well she understood her Wesleyan heritage, claiming "that for all her reading and native intelligence, Catherine did not have Wesley's comprehensive depth or theological vision." He continues, "Neither did she deal with many of the finer details of Wesley's theology," including Wesley's concept of the *ordo salutis*; the relationship of prevenient grace to justifying and accompanying grace; his

---

78. Booth, *Aggressive Christianity*, 25.
79. Booth and Booth, *Letters*, 92.
80. Booth, *Church & State*, 47.

81. The interplay of these themes also explains Catherine's, and William's, positive attitude towards nature and modernity evidenced, on the one hand, by their enthusiasm for 'natural' cures such as homeopathy and hydrotherapy, and on the other by their ready adoption of the communications and transport technologies of the industrial age – a significant factor in the dynamic worldwide growth of the Army.

Salvation

use of the analogy of faith; and his constant use of the quadrilateral. Green concludes, "Neither in her writing nor her preaching did Catherine demonstrate a command of these and other detailed and precise theological issues and she could not have been expected to do so."[82]

Perhaps few among his followers can be compared to Wesley to their personal advantage, but Green has underestimated the extent of Catherine's insight into the concept of the *ordo salutis* at least. Catherine never used the term in her writings. However, she was in her own way as much a preacher of the *ordo salutis* as Wesley, and an exploration of her understanding of the *ordo salutis* is essential to comprehending her soteriology. Catherine saw her task in preaching as first, to ascertain for herself and then assist the members of her congregation to identify where precisely on the *via salutis* they stood and then to take the next step. In her address *Dealing with Anxious Souls,* Catherine discussed the sequential steps to salvation of conviction, repentance, and faith. It is the highest privilege, she declared, to point a seeker to "the Lamb of God, and to show him the way of faith more perfectly [. . .] Let us mind the ORDER OF GOD in our dealing with souls."[83] In her addresses Catherine presents a full-orbed scheme of salvation in which conviction, repentance, faith, justification, regeneration, obedience, consecration, entire sanctification, and final glorification all find their place.

The twin themes of justification and sanctification provide the structure in Catherine Booth's *ordo salutis*. According to Krista Valtanen, "These two themes are related, and it is only together that they form Booth's complete *ordo salutis*, which was to bring about the change she desired in her listeners."[84] Catherine's personal experience undergirds her teaching of these two themes; however, as significant as justification and sanctification are for Catherine, they do not form her complete *ordo salutis*. Although Catherine never expounds this in a single address, the interconnected stages of what she clearly thought of as a process or an order of salvation can be discovered. Within her *ordo salutis*, prompted by the prevenient grace of God, conviction arises followed by repentance, and faith, while justification is accompanied by regeneration, and confirmed by assurance. Sanctification is the natural outcome of the life of the Spirit conferred in the saving action of God in Christ and by the Spirit; although its reception requires a

---

82. Green, *Catherine Booth*, 101–2.
83. Booth, *Practical Religion*, 108.
84. Valtanen, "Catherine Booth," 170.

further step of repentance, or consecration, and faith. The consequence of a life of obedient faith is continuance in a state of full salvation and final glorification. In its essential form Catherine Booth's *ordo salutis* is thoroughly Wesleyan. According to Kenneth J Collins:

> The Wesleyan *ordo salutis* can perhaps best be portrayed by the image of a large modern suspension bridge whose purpose is to carry traffic in one direction only. [. . .] Continuing this analogy, the two main columns which support this expanse and which mark off significant points on the journey can be referred to as justification and entire sanctification, and although the second column represents a closer approach to the ultimate goal than does the first, the chief structural relation between them is one of parallelism.[85]

Collins's model is as descriptive of Catherine Booth's *ordo salutis* as it is of Wesley's. Collins criticizes H. Ray Dunning's conceptualization of the connection of the two major structures within Wesley's *ordo salutis* as being like the relation between two foci of an ellipse, on the basis that "elliptical orbits are characterized by a process of alternating progression and regression around two fixed points," and therefore Dunning's "choice of imagery is inappropriate for displaying the structural interrelation between justification and sanctification,"[86] which is, in contrast, "linear, chronological, and teleological."[87] The figure of an ellipse as a metaphor for the Wesleyan *ordo salutis* can, however, survive Collins' criticism, if the fall in Adam and then the restoration in Christ are each considered as a journey through the two opposite half circumferences of an ellipse. The starting point of the fall and the end point of salvation stand at the same apse: humankind formed in the image and likeness of God; and the starting point of salvation and the end point of the fall stand together at the opposing apse: the total depravity of humankind. The journey from glory to depravity and on from depravity to glory forms one single elliptical orbit. Unlike the metaphor of a suspension bridge, the metaphor of the orbital progression through an ellipse preserves the notion of salvation as the restoration of the image of God in fallen humankind—an idea which is at the very heart of Catherine Booth's soteriology, and which, Albert Outler has argued, is "the axial theme of [John] Wesley's soteriology."[88]

85. Collins, "Wesleyan Ordo Salutis," 26.
86. Ibid., 25.
87. Ibid.
88. Outler in Wesley, *Sermons*, 1–4, II:185.n70

Salvation Begins

Catherine describes as "*the most important question* that can possibly occupy the mind of man," "how much like God we can be [. . .] preparatory to our being perfectly like Him, and living as it were, in His very heart for ever and ever in Heaven."[89] For Catherine the end point of salvation is to be fully restored to the image and likeness of God and to a full and complete relationship with him. Consequently the starting point is the loss of the image in the fall and humankind's absolute estrangement from God. For Catherine this loss is absolute and is reflected in her orthodox Wesleyan doctrine of original sin. The doctrines set out in The Salvation Army's foundation deed of 1878 included in Article 5 an avowal of humankind's fallen state: "We believe that our first parents were created in a state of innocency but by their disobedience they lost their purity and happiness and that in consequence of their fall all men have become sinners totally depraved and as such are justly exposed to the wrath of God."[90]

In Catherine's words, "all hearts are depraved by nature, and therefore out of harmony with God and incapable of entering into the privileges and duties of His Kingdom."[91] All share in this inherited corruption of humankind's nature. In proof, Catherine refers first to the many assertions of this truth in the Bible, referencing Jeremiah 17:9, "that the heart of man is deceitful above all things, and desperately wicked."[92] Second she refers to human history, "written in blood and watered by tears."[93] But third, "we prefer to come to experience."[94] Instead of appealing to a first-hand familiarity with gross immorality in her hearers, Catherine suggests that, through favorable circumstances and the constraints of providence, they may be like Nicodemus—outwardly moral, respectable, even religious, and yet still guilty of a heart of indifference towards religion, hard and dishonorable thoughts towards God, unwillingness to forsake sin, and failure to "love God with all your heart, and your neighbour as yourself."[95]

Of critical importance to the overall shape of her soteriology is that in her doctrine of original sin Catherine followed John Wesley rather than

---

89. Booth, *Godliness*, 143.
90. Sandall, Wiggins, and Coutts, *History*, I: 289.
91. Booth, *Life & Death*, 22.
92. Ibid., 23.
93. Ibid.
94. Ibid.
95. Ibid., 24.

Charles Finney, who declared the orthodox doctrine a lie, and protested, "*Orthodoxy!!* There never was a more infamous libel on Jehovah! It would be hard to name another dogma which more violently outrages common sense. It is nonsense—absurd and utter NONSENSE!"[96] In Finney's scheme, "Adamic nature is potential, the plastic material of self-actualization."[97] Human nature is not sinful in itself but morally neutral. An individual's failure as a free moral agent to exercise their free will to make correct moral choices is what renders them sinful, guilty before God, and exposed to his condemnation and wrath.

Although Catherine followed Wesley and not Finney in her doctrine of sin, she did believe it was possible to overstate man's fallen condition. Man remains "a wonderful being [. . .] made originally in the image of God [. . .] although fallen, eclipsed, dwarfed, yet the outline of man's make—his faculties, capacities, possibilities—remain the same. Some theologians in their desire to exalt God, very much debase and under-estimate man; whereas the best way to glorify the Creator is to give Him full credit for the excellency of His workmanship."[98] John Wesley, too, held that the image of God in man was defaced but not wholly obliterated.[99] Undergirding this view is the doctrine of prevenient grace, whereby God graciously, with salvific intent, restores to fallen humanity some degree of his image and likeness.

Catherine's appeal to her hearers to acknowledge the reality of original sin through an examination of their own hearts is an appeal to conscience. It is the work of the Holy Spirit to awaken people to their lost condition, to arouse them to a point of conviction: "God has taken compassion on us, and sent His Spirit into the world for this purpose—'To convince the world of sin, of righteousness, and of judgement.' Thus he opens our eyes and shows us our lost estate."[100] But the Holy Spirit can and does choose to undertake this work through human agency. The work of the apostle Paul, Catherine noted, was "to open the eyes of the unconverted, and turn them from darkness to light, and from the power of Satan unto God." Paul was

---

96. Finney, *Sermons on Gospel Themes*, 80.
97. Weddle, *The Law as Gospel*, 153.
98. Booth, *Life & Death*, 115.
99. McGonigle, *John Wesley's Doctrine of Prevenient Grace*, 25.
100. Booth, *Aggressive Christianity*, 25.

Salvation

able to do this because "he had a power in him which every really renewed child of God has—the Holy Ghost—to equip him for this work."[101]

In Catherine's view the church is called, in the power of the Holy Spirit, to be an expression of the prevenient grace of God. The mission of the church is not only to call sinners to repentance, but to create conviction—hence the need for *aggressive* Christianity. Hence also the necessity of using all possible means to achieve this end. It was this heartfelt conviction that made William and Catherine, first, revivalists, and then, founders of The Salvation Army. The new measures which aimed at the conviction and persuasion of the sinner intellectually and emotionally, and which acknowledged human beings as physical, social beings, were for the Booths an expression of the power of the Holy Spirit at work in and through the church. Law and conscience are the great allies of mission: "The eyes of the soul must be opened to such a realization of sin, and such an apprehension of the consequences of sin, as shall lead to an earnest desire to be *saved from sin*. God's great means of doing this is the law, as the schoolmaster, to drive sinners to receive Christ as their salvation."[102] The Army's social mission must also be understood in this light. For this aspect of mission is also an expression of prevenient grace. The invitation to eat and drink, the provision of hospitality, the alleviation of poverty, the healing of the sick are a free expression of God's love for humankind.

Repentance is the necessary human response to the conviction of the Holy Spirit. Catherine often emphasizes the human capacity to choose, to will to be saved. This change of will is a consequence of conviction, a result of the Holy Spirit's illumination. But in Catherine's view it appears to be the exercise of a natural human capacity to make a moral choice. Catherine denies that this is self-salvation. She sees the change exemplified in Romans 7 where those who are willing to keep the law, willing to obey God, are yet unable to do so: "Though they are brought round from the voluntary choice or embrace of evil, and the voluntary service of the Devil, round to the voluntary choice and embrace of righteousness and the service of God, they are not yet *able* to do it."[103]

According to Catherine, there is all the difference in the world between "being willing to let Jesus Christ save me from my sins, and saving

---

101. Ibid., 28–29.
102. Booth, *Godliness*, 5.
103. Booth, *Aggressive Christianity*, 30.

myself from them."[104] God demands this change in the attitude of the will as a "CONDITION OF THE EXERCISE OF HIS POWER." Catherine illustrates by the story of Jesus healing a man with a withered hand. Jesus asked the man to stretch out his hand. The man could have argued that this was an unreasonable request. Jesus' intention was that the man should respond with his will and say, "Yes, Lord." In the stretching, in the responsive action, Jesus healed him; instantaneously and contemporaneously with his willing came the healing. In an address provocatively titled *Save Thyself* Catherine illustrates the therapeutic nature of salvation as well as the necessity of human action by another story from the Gospels: "Will you pass through the crowd and come now and touch the hem of his garment ? If so, you shall be healed of whatsoever plague you have, and songs of praise and thanksgiving shall well up from your satisfied soul continually. But you must press through; you must wrestle and struggle, not with Him, but with yourself and your sins, to get at Him. Will you strive to enter in?"[105]

Catherine denies that there is any merit in such actions, as if they might be part of a process of self-salvation. Rather, it is a "*condition* of His receiving us that we leave all of ours, to receive of His."[106] Catherine is aware of the controversy surrounding her views.[107] She acknowledges those New Testament texts which are thought to suggest no human action or effort is required to be saved, but, "As many texts, quite as relevant, quite as important and just as much inspired [. . .] represent it as an exceedingly *difficult* thing to be saved; requiring as much of human effort and sacrifice as though Salvation all depended on ourselves."[108] Included are those uncompromising verses which represent Jesus saying, "Cut off that right hand, and pluck out that right eye."[109]

The synergism of divine initiative and human response working together in the process of redemption has been characterized as co-operant grace and is often thought to be a Wesleyan distinctive. Catherine appears to be aligning herself with this position in her stress on the importance of an active human response to the offer of salvation. However, Kenneth Collins has argued that Wesley's statements concerning free will have been

104. Ibid.
105. Booth, *Life & Death*, 169.
106. Ibid., 170.
107. Ibid., 155–71; Booth, *Aggressive Christianity*, 21–38.
108. Booth, *Life & Death*, 157.
109. Booth, *Aggressive Christianity*, 27.

misunderstood if they are interpreted in this way.[110] To do justice to Wesley, Collins argues, "a synergistic paradigm, which contains both divine and human acting, must itself be caught up in an *even larger conjunction* in which the Protestant emphasis on the sole activity of God, apart from all human working, is *equally* factored in."[111] Collins quotes Outler, who, comparing Wesley to Arminius, writes, "Arminius held that man hath a will to turn to God *before* grace prevents him, whereas, for Wesley, it is the Spirit's prevenient motion by which we ever are moved and inspired to *any* good thing."[112] However, Catherine clearly expresses Wesley's position over and against Arminius's in the following statement: "Having, by the Holy Ghost made us realise our desperate condition, then comes the Gospel to meet us just where we are, on condition that we abandon our evil ways, and do the works meet for repentance, which we are *able to do* by the power of the Holy Spirit."[113]

Without prevenient grace, humanity is entirely hopeless. Crucially in *Saving Faith* Catherine, speaking of seekers in her congregation who she believes are longing for deliverance and striving against sin, argues that this is a sign of prevenient grace working in them: "People do not see what a great deal they owe to the convincing and preventing power of the Holy Spirit helping their infirmity, even now, to cut off and pluck out the right hand and the right eye and bringing them to a waiting attitude before God."[114]

Wesley and Fletcher stood together in asserting the necessity of prevenient grace to human freedom of the will: "We [Wesley and Fletcher] both steadily assert that the will of man is by nature free only to evil. Yet we both believe that every man has a measure of free-will restored to him by grace."[115] This assertion allows Wesley to uphold a doctrine of original sin which includes the notion of total depravity, for if Wesley were to assert that man could exercise free will irrespective of prevenient grace, that would imply a necessary limitation to the extent of man's depravity. Furthermore, it also "logically follows that 'irresistible grace' has to operate at least at

---

110. Collins, *Holy Love*, 79.

111. Ibid., 12–13.

112. Albert Outler in Wesley, *Sermons*, 1–4, II:157, n.3; cited in Collins, *Holy Love*, 79.

113. Booth, *Aggressive Christianity*, 27.

114. Booth, *Godliness*, 12–13.

115. John Wesley, "Some Remarks on Mr. Hill's 'Review of all the Doctrines Taught by Mr. John Wesley,'" Wesley, *The Works of John Wesley*, X:392.

Catherine Booth

some point in the Wesleyan order of salvation."[116] For if men and women in the natural state are unable to accept or reject grace, then the gift to be able to do so, that is to exercise free will, must be irresistibly restored. That Catherine believed this is evident from many of her statements. She states, "Man is fallen, and cannot of himself obey even his own enlightened intelligence. There must be an extraneous power brought into the soul."[117] The alternative is to uphold humanity's natural capacity to exercise free will, by redrafting the doctrine of the fall. This alternative was available to Catherine in that Charles Finney and the theologians associated with Harvard's New Divinity made this move. The consequence for Finney was a suspicion that in his doctrine of free will, sin and the fall, he was heterodox and semi-Pelagian, at best. However, Catherine remained resolutely Wesleyan.

In Catherine Booth's *ordo salutis* true repentance is an essential concomitant of saving faith. Because of her distrust of antinomianism, Catherine frequently contrasts true, saving faith with false, dead faith. Saving faith is not a mere intellectual perception, or even conviction of the truth.[118] Neither is it sympathetic feelings or emotions, no matter how intense or strong.[119] Saving faith is trust, which implies and includes an act of voluntary commitment, as a bride might trust her husband, "she trusts him *with herself,*" or as someone sick might trust a physician: "You believe in his skill and obey his orders."[120] Faith is: "Risking my all, for this life and for the next, on the truthfulness and goodness of God, and daring to live and act contrary to everyone around me, as if all that God HAS SAID WERE TRUE!"[121]

John Wesley claimed, "It is the work of God alone to justify, to sanctify, and to glorify; which three comprehend the whole of salvation."[122] This is equally true of Catherine Booth's view. Repentance and faith are grace-given possibilities; from first to last redemption is the work of God; and God alone.

---

116. Collins, *Holy Love*, 80.
117. Booth, *Church & State*, 11.
118. Booth, *Life & Death*, 72–73.
119. Ibid., 74.
120. Booth, *Godliness*, 17.
121. Booth, *Life & Death*, 76.
122. John Wesley, "Predestination Calmly Considered" in Wesley, *The Works of John Wesley*, §48, X:230.

Salvation's First Focus

Catherine held to an orthodox Protestant view of justification by faith.[123] God's pardoning grace is given freely, not on the basis of human merit or action, but on the merits of Christ and his atonement. The "real faith" required is simple trust in Christ's power to save:[124] "Believe that God does now accept you wholly for the sake of the sacrifice of His blessed Son; that He justifies you freely from all things from which you could not be justified by the law. You stand a condemned, guilty, Hell-bound criminal, and nothing but His free, sovereign mercy can save you. Throw yourself upon this, and the moment you do so in real faith you will be saved."[125]

Catherine seldom preached justification as a discrete topic, possibly because her congregations consisted largely of professing Christians who were perhaps more inclined to hold concerns regarding the doctrines of election and assurance. Catherine also believed that to preach justification alone was to run the risk of preaching an antinomian gospel. Catherine believed that through the atonement God justifies unrighteous people, but at the same time he makes them new creatures with the potential to become saints.[126] She lamented, "How people separate what God does for us outwardly through the sacrifice of His Son from what He does inwardly by the operation of His Spirit!"[127]

Not only does Jesus Christ pardon people for past sin; he also gives them power to withstand temptation. The regeneration of the Holy Spirit is the *"renewing* of the *spirit* of [the] mind"; it is to be "created anew in Christ Jesus."[128] "What God does for us through Jesus Christ outside of us is one thing, and what He does in us by Jesus Christ is another thing, but the two are simultaneous, or one so immediately succeeds the other, that we hardly discern the interval."[129]

Regeneration is not the creation of a new soul, or the introduction of "a new something apart from ourselves" living "alongside the old, unrenewed,

---

123. Notwithstanding that she denied the doctrine of the *active* imputation of Christ's righteousness.
124. Booth, *Aggressive Christianity*, 37.
125. Ibid.
126. Booth, *Life & Death*, 131.
127. Ibid.
128. Booth, *Aggressive Christianity*, 85.
129. Ibid.

wicked heart till death," but a restoration of the old soul.[130] This theme of restoration comes to full fruition in Catherine's doctrine of holiness. The Holy Spirit is the one who makes people holy, by restoring in them the *imago Dei*, conceived of as the image and likeness of Christ.

Catherine describes regeneration, to be born again of the Spirit, as union with Christ.[131] The means by which Christ makes us new creatures, is that "*He unites me to Himself.*" This mystical union, which Catherine admits she cannot explain, is not separate from regeneration, but is another facet of it; it is the "Union of My Soul with Him."[132] This union is spoken of in the Old and New Testaments as knowing God, and abiding in Christ. The possibility of this vital union with Christ is the very heart of the gospel. Catherine compares it to marriage: "He 'marries' me to Himself. He unites me 'to another' husband, and then I attain power to bring forth fruit unto God. A beautiful—a wonderful figure!"[133] She continues, "The mystery is too great to be explained, but [. . .] united to Christ I have power to conquer, to subdue, to trample under foot those things which heretofore have been my master, and by virtue of Him I retain the power, and no other way."[134] To compare a person's spiritual union with Christ with marriage is to conceive of their relationship with God in Christ as a binding covenanted relationship of love which forms one from two and yet leaves both free and intact as persons. For Catherine personally, this union set her under Christ in an obligation and loyalty born in the freedom of love; it brought her into a new milieu of influence and authority, and into a new world of transformed relationships. Catherine first compared this spiritual union with Christ in the Spirit to marriage in a letter to William dated 16 January 1853.[135] This union, a deep participation in Christ, is the objective beginning of sanctification.

Justification and regeneration, though received by simple faith, are accompanied by the witness of the Spirit, the assurance of forgiveness, of acceptance, and new life in Christ: "By assurance, I mean the personal realisation of my acceptance in Christ; my acceptance by the Father; my present

---

130. Catherine is denying the idea that Christians have 'two natures'. Booth, *Life & Death*, 21.

131. Booth, *Aggressive Christianity*, 85.

132. Ibid., 86.

133. Ibid., 85–86.

134. Ibid., 86.

135. Booth and Booth, *Letters*, 57.

acceptance—I mean the inward assurance, which men and women find for themselves, or have revealed in themselves, which they know as a matter of consciousness. Not that which their minister tells them; not that which they learn from books; not even that which the Bible only tells them."[136]

Catherine's personal experience lent the power of conviction to her preaching on the subject of assurance and the witness of the Spirit. Catherine Bramwell-Booth suggests Catherine's experience was important not only to herself but also to the future Salvation Army: "Her preaching exercised a vital influence on its formative years. The majority of early converts in The Salvation Army were saved from flagrant sin [. . .] but for Catherine Booth's own experience that assurance might all too readily have come to be associated with salvation from gross sinning alone. How clearly she taught that everyone, child or grown-up, stood in equal need of the inner witness of sonship, the secret token of acceptance with God."[137]

She also understood from her own experience, as well as from Wesley and Fletcher, that although this first focal point of salvation, an experience of justification and regeneration confirmed by the witness of the Spirit, held latent within itself the potential of a holy life, an experience of holiness was neither immediate nor assured. In Catherine's experience the distance between the focal points of justification and entire sanctification along the axis line of salvation was to be measured in years.

Salvation Continues

Expressions of longing for the blessing of holiness are scattered throughout Catherine's reminiscences and correspondence. She confided to her diary on 1 June 1847, "Oh, when shall I be a Christian indeed without any inbred [sin]." Catherine's letters to William are full of life, enthusiasm, and passionate conviction. They do also, however, tell of spiritual frustration and disappointment. Writing to William in January 1853, Catherine lamented her loss of joy since the first days of her conversion: "My soul is now like the temple, deserted, bereft of the abiding manifestation of God's presence, receiving only now and then a transitory ray, a short and flickering illumination. But I am tired of living thus; my soul pants, yea, even fainteth again to behold the brightness of his glory, to abide in the sunshine of his smile."[138]

---

136. Booth, *Aggressive Christianity*, 68.
137. Bramwell-Booth, *Catherine Booth*, 36–37.
138. Booth and Booth, *Letters*, 57.

It is possible Catherine was aware of Phoebe Palmer's "shorter way" to holiness by June 1847 and yet it hardly proved to be a shorter way for her.[139] The struggles of these years confirmed her conviction that the conditions of entire sanctification were full consecration and simple faith.

In Catherine Booth's theology, the two great focal points of salvation, justification and sanctification, are symmetrical as regards the conditions that apply, humanly speaking, to their attainment. Repentance and faith follow on from conviction prior to justification; and similarly consecration, conceived of as a deeper work of repentance and of faith (that simple trust in God's work and provision), follow on from the work of the Holy Spirit in convincing the justified sinner of the continuing reality of inbred sin. Catherine wrote, "Further, there are *two indispensible conditions of attaining this blessing—entire consecration and faith in His promises*."[140] In so far as justification and sanctification were the symmetrical focal points of her soteriology, Catherine followed John Wesley who wrote: "A gradual work of grace constantly precedes the instantaneous work both of justification and sanctification. But the work itself (of sanctification as well as justification) is undoubtedly instantaneous. As after a gradual conviction of the guilt and power of sin you was [sic] justified in a moment, so after a gradually increasing conviction of inbred sin you will be sanctified in a moment. And who knows how soon. Why not now?"[141]

The symmetry might be derived from Wesley but the experience for Catherine was highly personal.[142] Catherine believed that the inner conflict she experienced over these years sprang from her failure to be obedient to God's calling to speak in public. Through her fear and timidity she lost a sense of the divine presence and the power and happiness she had once enjoyed. It was when she came to a point of resignation and repentance in this matter that her sanctification became possible.[143] The remaining step was that of simple faith, and it was in taking this step that Catherine and William's reading of Phoebe Palmer proved helpful.

139. Catherine prays in her diary, 'Lord, bless my dearest mother tonight [. . .] help her at all times to offer me, her unworthy child, upon the altar that sanctifies the gift.' Booth, *Reminiscences*, 14.

140. Booth, *Holiness*, 14.

141. John Wesley, Letter to Arthur Keene (21 June 1784), Wesley, *The Letters of the Rev John Wesley*, VII:222.

142. The difference between Wesley's notion of repentance prior to sanctification and Catherine's notion of full consecration will be discussed in a following chapter.

143. Booth, *Aggressive Christianity*, 137–39.

Salvation's Second Focus

On Thursday 21 June 1888, Catherine gave her last public address to an audience consisting "for the most part of business gentlemen and outside friends" at the City Temple in London. For the last time she proclaimed her message of justification and sanctification.

> Perhaps on no point has the Salvation Army suffered persecution more than on this one point of its teaching—that it teaches a Saviour not only willing to pardon but who does pardon absolutely, and who communicates a sense of that pardon by His Holy Spirit to the hearts of those who truly repent and sincerely believe, with a living faith, in Him, and not only washes their past sins away but has the power to keep them from their sins, and will, if they trust in Him, enable them to live in righteousness and holiness all their lives, walking in obedience to His commands, keeping that inner law of which we have just heard—the law of Christ—which is the most perfect law and fulfils all others—loving the Lord thy God with all thy heart, mind, soul and strength, and thy neighbour as thyself.[144]

Catherine chose not to "contend [over the] names or terms by which this experience is expressed"; although she preferred simple terms such as "Holiness" or "Godliness" to potentially contentious terms such as "Christian perfection."[145] Catherine very occasionally recognized that she was contending for "inner" or "entire" sanctification, and she was consequently not denying the sense in which sanctification is given, or begins, with justification.[146] However, in her addresses "holiness" and "sanctification" refer invariably to "entire sanctification" and Catherine's usage is followed in this study. Catherine's indifference to terminology does not mean that there is not a strong governing concept at the heart of her doctrine. Holiness is, for Catherine, the restoration of the *imago Dei* by means of the recreation and reformation of the believer in the likeness of Christ.[147]

Catherine believed that the Holy Spirit could and would confirm the work of sanctification in the heart of the believer. This knowledge that God has acted as he has promised does not come from learning, or the assurances of a minister, or even from taking the promises of Scripture at face

---

144. Booth, *The War Cry*, "Mrs. Booth's Last Public Address."
145. Booth, *Holiness*, 7.
146. Ibid.
147. Booth and Booth, *Letters*, 130.

value; it is a "conviction wrought in the heart" by the Holy Spirit.[148] Catherine believed in the perceptible inspiration of the Holy Spirit: "Wait, and there will come a voice from the excellent glory. There will come light as from the Shekinah, which will reveal it in your spiritual consciousness, and you will thus know that thing for ever."[149]

For Catherine receiving, being filled, and being baptized with the Spirit were synonymous. In her address *Filled with the Spirit* Catherine equates "higher-life religion" with the "Pentecost [. . .] offered to all believers."[150] In the same address Catherine offers a brief description of the Spirit's work: "Oh! it is the most precious gift He has to give in earth or in Heaven—to be filled with the Spirit, filled with Himself [. . .] taken possession of by God; moved, inspired, energised, empowered by God, by the great indwelling Spirit moving through all our faculties, and energising our whole being for Him."[151]

Catherine was using pentecostal language to describe entire sanctification by 1853 at the latest; that is, before she read William Arthur's pentecostal book *The Tongue of Fire*, and before Phoebe Palmer began to include pentecostal language in her own writings.[152] As Catherine closely studied John Fletcher's *Checks to Antinomianism*, Fletcher can be named as the authoritative source of Catherine's pentecostalism.[153] However, as Laurence Wood has shown, Catherine's usage was not untypical of mid-century Methodism.[154]

Salvation's End

The end of salvation, teleologically, for Catherine Booth, is glorification.[155] The Salvation Army's well known phrase "promoted to Glory" is not a comforting euphemism for the unavoidable reality of death, but a statement of faith in humankind's eternal destiny; "Glory" in this instance is not a synonym for Heaven, but for the status achieved upon the perfect restoration of the image and likeness of God in Christ. Catherine was in accord with

148. Booth, *Aggressive Christianity*, 73.
149. Ibid., 190.
150. Ibid., 148,49.
151. Ibid., 154.
152. Booth and Booth, *Letters*, 130,333; White, *The Beauty of Holiness*, 128.
153. Bramwell-Booth, *Catherine Booth*, 28; Wood, *Pentecost in early Methodism*, xiii.
154. Wood, *Pentecost in early Methodism*, xiv.
155. Booth, *Life & Death*, 52.

Wesley who said of justification, sanctification, and glorification, that these "three comprehend the whole of salvation."[156]

However, Catherine's eschatological hope burned bright for this world as well as the next. William memorably expressed their shared hope of the coming millennium in his article *Salvation for Both Worlds*: "Christ is the deliverer for time as truly as for eternity. He is the Joshua who leads men in our own day out of the wilderness into the Promised Land, as His forerunner did the Children of Israel thousands of years ago. He is the Messiah who rings glad tidings! He is come to open the prison doors. He is come to set men free from their bonds. He is indeed the Saviour of the world!"[157] Andrew Miller dates William Booth's embrace of millennialism to the 1880s and considers it to be the result of the transatlantic influence of the American Holiness Movement.[158] However, the Booths' millennialism was central to their theology from the first, not a late addition, and not unusual for mid-century Methodists.[159] Catherine was speculating as to how and when the millennium might come by 1853 at the latest.[160]

The taproot of Catherine Booth's millennialism is to be found in John Fletcher's *Checks to Antinomianism* and in his doctrine of dispensations. Catherine followed John Fletcher in believing that the present dispensation, the dispensation of the gospel, or the Spirit, would end in a global Pentecost that would usher in the millennium.[161] According to Laurence Wood, John Wesley shared this belief with Fletcher.[162] According to Catherine, "God's ultimate idea for the world [. . .] is the true millennium which is to come, towards which all real progress tends."[163] She complained to those who did not share her hope of the assured success of the Christian mission, "Don't

---

156. John Wesley, "Predestination Calmly Considered" in Wesley, *The Works of John Wesley*, §48, X:230.

157. Booth, *All the World*, "Salvation for Both Worlds."

158. Miller, "Eschatological Ethics," 42.

159. David Bebbington has identified a surge in Methodist post-millennialism in the mid to late 1840s. "Another dimension of Methodist piety was a sublime confidence in the future. It was not just that members felt assured of going to heaven, for they also believed that the cause of Christ was destined, according to the promises of Scripture, to triumph all over the earth." Bebbington in Cooper and Gregory, *Revival and Resurgence*, 235; See also Reasoner, *The Hope of the Gospel*.

160. Booth, *Reminiscences*, 98.

161. Wood, *Pentecost in early Methodism*, 146.

162. Ibid., 170.

163. Booth, *Church & State*, 15.

tell me that the dispensation of the Spirit is going to end in this ignominious fashion. I don't believe it."[164]

The Booths' eschatology is reflected in the Darkest England scheme and explains, first, why they ever contemplated such a grand and ambitious scheme of social reform, and second, to what extent it was indeed their scheme, and not that of a second generation of Army leaders who were possibly rather more socialistic and less evangelistic than William and Catherine.[165] The final drafts of the *Darkest England* manuscript were prepared at Clacton where Catherine lay dying. W. T. Stead acted as a voluntary secretary and amanuensis in getting the manuscript into shape. Stead described his final conversation with Catherine: "I told of her of the confidence with which the General's scheme inspired me, and the new radiance that glowed before me into the future [. . .] 'And I,' said Mrs. Booth, 'and I most of all [. . .] yes, thank God, we may rejoice that something on an adequate scale is to be done at last; through all these years I have laboured and prayed that this matter might be done..'"[166]

CONCLUSION

Failing to uncover the foundational ground of Catherine Booth's theology, Krista Valtanen describes Catherine as an *ephapax*, "In the end [Catherine] is not the product of a sect or party in theology, but rather an *ephapax*—an individual with a strong message of revival, who stood at the meeting point between Victorian English society, nineteenth-century transatlantic revivalism and the nascent Salvation Army."[167]

However, an exploration of Catherine Booth's soteriology reveals that she was indeed—though neither sectarian nor partisan—a product of a particular strand of theology. Her doctrine of the atonement reflected her thoroughly Wesleyan theological concerns. Her *ordo salutis* was profoundly indebted to John Wesley and his successors. Catherine Booth's impact on history was not a consequence of theological innovation, but of her faithfulness to the tradition she received, accompanied by a determination to carry through the emerging implications of that theology fearlessly, and above all practically. Catherine was influenced by Charles Finney, not in

---

164. Ibid., 78.
165. For an expression of this view cf. Murdoch, "Frank Smith: Salvationist Socialist," 1.
166. Stead, *Mrs. Booth*, 213.
167. Valtanen, "Catherine Booth," 2.

her core theology, but in its practical expression, towards a Salvationism worked out in evangelism, revivalism, and social reform. Catherine was influenced by John Wesley and John Fletcher towards a Salvationism that proclaimed the grace-created potential in human beings, of being restored in the image and likeness of their Creator, to live a holy life in the power of the Holy Spirit.

THREE

The Pursuit of Holiness

Four words sum up the significance of the doctrine of holiness for Catherine Booth: central, decisive, integral, and catalytic. Holiness was central to Catherine's conception of the gospel; decisive for her Wesleyan identity; integral to The Salvation Army's reformist and revivalist mission; and catalytic within her own life and ministry. Catherine declared, if holiness "be not the central idea of Christianity, I do not understand it."[1] Salvation, rightly understood, is a full salvation which includes forgiveness and justification but *also* regeneration and sanctification. For Catherine the decisive test for her faithfulness to her spiritual progenitors in Methodism was her faithfulness to the holiness teaching of Wesley and Fletcher. She did not aspire to be a theological innovator but rather a faithful teacher of Methodism's *grand depositum*.[2] Catherine believed that The Salvation Army was called to embody holiness, and so integral was this to the Army's mission that only in so far as it fulfilled this calling could its existence be justified.[3] On Pentecost Sunday 1860 Catherine Booth found her voice, broke her silence, and testified and preached in public for the first time. In February 1861 she entered into a deeper experience of sanctifying grace. Her discovery was a catalyst for personal transformation. Before, despite the strength of her faith, personality, and opinions, Catherine was characteristically troubled, uncertain, and fearful; after her experience she became characteristically assured and confident. In these two events Catherine

---

1. Booth, *Godliness*, 149.

2. "This doctrine [entire sanctification] is the grand depositum which God has lodged with the people called Methodists; and for the sake of propagating this chiefly He appears to have raised us up." Wesley, Letter to Robert Carr Brackenbury (15 September 1790), Wesley, *The Letters of the Rev John Wesley*, VIII:238.

3. Booth, *Godliness*, 167.

Booth discovered her destiny as a preacher of holiness and with it a holy boldness.[4]

In her lifetime Catherine won a reputation as a preacher of holiness in the tradition of John Wesley and John Fletcher. In his history of the Second Evangelical Awakening J. Edwin Orr recovered Catherine Booth's role in the revival and holiness movements of the nineteenth century, and John Kent's work *Holding the Fort* acknowledged the significance of William and Catherine and placed their work and theology within an historical context.[5] Kent was also the first to recognize how great an influence the American Phoebe Palmer had upon William and Catherine, particularly in Catherine's account of how she entered into the blessing of entire sanctification. However, Kent bound Catherine too strongly to Phoebe Palmer. As one of the few scholarly works to consider the Army's founders, Kent's conclusions have become the presumptions of writers as diverse as Roy Hattersley and David Bebbington.[6] Significantly for the Army's own self-understanding, scholarly historians of the movement such as Roger Green, Norman Murdoch, and David Rightmire have also followed Kent.[7] Yet Kent does not seem to have based his conclusions on a wide reading of Catherine's work, but to have extrapolated from one, admittedly significant, letter. Chick Yuill alone has questioned Kent's conclusions and examined Catherine's writings in an attempt to identify other possible sources and influences. In an essay on Catherine's doctrine of holiness, Yuill identified the additional influence of William Boardman, and reset Catherine's teaching in a Wesleyan context.[8] However, the scope and purpose of his work limited the extent and the depth of Yuill's research.

The questions therefore remain: to what extent did Holiness Movement figures such as Phoebe Palmer and William Boardman help to shape the development and presentation of Catherine Booth's doctrine of holiness? Were there any other contemporary influences? To what extent was Catherine's doctrine innovative or unique?

---

4. Cf. Stanley, *Holy Boldness.*
5. Orr, *The Second Evangelical Awakening*; Kent, *Holding the Fort.*
6. Hattersley, *Blood and Fire*; Bebbington, *Evangelicalism.*
7. Green, *Catherine Booth*; Murdoch, *Origins of The Salvation Army*; Rightmire, *Sacraments*; Rightmire, *Sanctified Sanity.*
8. Yuill, "Restoring the Image."

SEEKING HOLINESS

Catherine's quest for holiness can be traced to the early summer of 1847 when at the age of 18 she spent some weeks in Brighton convalescing. Possibly inspired by her reading of Mrs. Rowe's *Devout Exercises of the Heart* she began to keep a journal.[9] An entry dated 14 May records her heart-felt prayer:

> I entered into a fresh covenant this morning with my Lord, to be more fully given up to him. Oh, to be a Christian indeed; to love thee with all my heart is all my desire. I do love thee, but I want to love thee more. I want to enjoy thee more. [. . .] Oh, for more of thy love! Just now reveal thyself to my longing soul and let me be satisfied with beholding thy beauty. [. . .] Give me a full salvation from sin. Let me glorify thee with my every breath.[10]

Numerous entries record her longings after holiness, perfect love, perfect peace, a clean heart, a constant abiding in Christ, freedom from inbred sin, and the quickening of the Spirit.[11] On the first anniversary of the day she became "a child of God, an heir of heaven," Catherine prayed, "Take me for another year, let me bear abundantly more fruit, let the Sun of Righteousness shine in full lustre on my soul, and make me spotless and pure."[12] Catherine's longings expressed in the inherited language of Methodism reveal how deeply she had internalized the spirituality of Wesley and Fletcher.

On 8 July 1847, Catherine wrote, "I have received a letter from Mr. Wells today, who took so kind an interest in my welfare while at Brighton. He writes very kindly and urges me to press after a full salvation. Oh, that I could believe for it. I feel convinced it is unbelief that keeps me out of the possession of this glorious blessing."[13] From August through to October Catherine read the life of Mary Bosanquet Fletcher and found encouragement there.[14] On 28 November 1847 she recorded her reaction to reading the life of William Carvosso:

---

9. Rowe, *Devout Exercises of the Heart*. Catherine misspelled 'Rowe' as Roe, which may indicate familiarity with the journal of Miss Roe, who was better known by her married name, Hester Ann Rogers.

10. Booth, *Reminiscences*, 2.

11. Ibid., 4, 5, 6, 7, 10, 11.

12. Ibid., 9,19.

13. Ibid., 24.

14. Ibid., 29, 31.

O, what a man of faith and prayer was he. My expectations were raised when I began the Book. [. . .] This day I have sometimes seemed on the verge of the good land. O, for mighty faith! I believe the Lord is willing and able to save me to the uttermost. I believe the blood of Jesus cleans [sic] from all sin, and yet there seems something in the way to prevent me fully entering in. [. . .] My chief desire is holiness of heart.[15]

On 3 June 1852, a few weeks after she became engaged to William, Catherine wrote, "Conscious through the day of increased desires to live altogether for God. Have been reading Mahan on Perfection, the best work on the subject I ever read. My previous views confirmed and some points cleared up. Oh, to enjoy this glorious salvation."[16] Yet still the experience eluded her. On 28 August 1860 she wrote to William from Gateshead: "Oh, why could I not believe for the blessing of holiness? I tried but I have not learnt to take the naked word as a sufficient warrant for my faith. I am looking for 'signs.' Oh, pray for me. I have solemnly pledged myself to the Lord to seek till [sic] I do find this pearl of great price. Will you not join me in seeking it too?"[17]

The reference to the "naked word" is evidence of Catherine's familiarity with the ideas of Phoebe Palmer. On 21 January 1861 Catherine wrote to her parents, telling of a step forward in her quest for holiness, and affirming, "I shall be eternally grateful that I have read Mrs. Palmer's books. They have done me more good than anything met with. I do most earnestly urge you to get one of them at once, entitled *Faith and its Effects*. [. . .] Get it, and read it both of you, and may the Lord bless it to your hearts as he has done to me."[18]

However, Phoebe Palmer was not Catherine's only companion on her spiritual journey at this time. In September 1860 she read William Arthur's *Tongue of Fire*.[19] In February 1861 Catherine also read William Boardman's *The Higher Christian Life*.[20] Soon after, inspired by her reading of Palmer and Boardman, Catherine testified that she entered into an experience of entire sanctification.

---

15. Ibid., 32.
16. Ibid., 41.
17. Booth and Booth, *Letters*, 324.
18. Booth, "Letter to her Parents: 21 January 1861."
19. Arthur, *Tongue of Fire*.
20. Boardman, *Higher Life*.

Catherine was seventeen when she came into the assurance that she was indeed a child of God. Despite her inherited Wesleyan belief in the blessing of holiness, and her personal commitment to seeking it, Catherine was 32 years old by the time she came into the assurance that she was indeed sanctified as well as justified. Why did her quest take so long?

Catherine was not alone in having an expectation of holiness that was not matched by her personal experience. This disjunction was common among Methodists. The tension it created provided the energy that made the long memoirs of a Methodist saint like Mary Bosanquet Fletcher not only readable but gripping.[21] Through the challenges and struggles of the unfolding years, Mary continued to seek the deeper blessing of which she believed she had enjoyed a foretaste. It was perhaps more common for Methodists to live with the unrealized expectation than to live in the experience; more common to preach holiness in faith, than to live it by faith. This was something Catherine did herself, preaching holiness faithfully before she experienced it. According to David Bebbington, "By the 1860s the idea that there is a decisive second stage in Christian sanctification was at a low ebb among the generality of Wesleyans."[22]

For earnest seekers such as Catherine Booth, William Boardman appeared to simplify a message that had become shrouded in arcane and confusing language. Boardman attempted to keep faith with the integrity of the holiness traditions he represented in his work; he was a sympathetic and ecumenically minded interpreter.[23] Phoebe Palmer shortened the long journey into holiness by providing a helpful way of conceptualizing and then taking the necessary step of faith. Together Boardman and Palmer solved the pressing problem of the doctrine of entire sanctification for Catherine—how do you appropriate it, how do you experience it? That they did so for many others explains the popularity of their writings.

EXPERIENCING HOLINESS

On 11 February 1861 Catherine wrote to her parents describing how she had come into an experience of the blessing of holiness. Catherine begins her account with a reference to William Boardman's book: "In reading that

---

21. Moore, *The Life of Mrs. Mary Fletcher*; for an examination of the dramatic power of these narratives, see Erickson, "Perfect Love," 79–81.

22. Bebbington, *Evangelicalism*, 153.

23. Boardman, *Higher Life*, 40.

precious book, *The Higher Life*, I perceived that I had been in some degree of error with reference to the nature, or rather the manner, of sanctification, regarding it rather as a great and mighty work to be wrought in me through Christ, than the simple reception of Christ as an all-sufficient Saviour, dwelling in my heart, and thus cleansing it every moment from all sin."[24]

Catherine describes her earnest seeking through the week, how she gave all of Thursday and Friday to the subject, reading and praying, and trying to believe. She continues: "On Friday morning God gave me two precious passages. First, 'Come unto me, *all* ye that *labour* and are *heavy laden* and I *will* give you rest.' Oh how sweet it sounded to my poor, weary, sin-stricken soul. [. . .] The second passage was those thrice-blessed words, 'Of him are ye in Christ Jesus *who* is made unto us wisdom, righteousness, *sanctification* and redemption.'"[25]

Even so, Catherine struggled to believe in God's promises, until "a little after six in the evening when William joined me in prayer":[26] "We had a blessed season. While he was saying, 'Lord, we open our hearts to receive thee,' that word was spoken to my heart, 'Behold, I stand at the door, and knock. If any man hear my voice, and open unto me, I *will* come in and sup with him.' I felt sure he had long been knocking, and oh, how I longed to receive him as perfect Saviour!"[27] Still Catherine was unable to take the step of faith. After they had prayed, Catherine lay back on the sofa, exhausted. Then came the breakthrough, inspired by Phoebe Palmer's teaching.

> William said, "Don't you lay all on the altar?" I said "I am sure I do." Then he said, "And isn't the altar holy?" I replied in the language of the Holy Ghost, "The altar is *most* holy, and whatsoever toucheth it is holy." "Then," said he, "are you not holy?" I replied with my heart full of emotion and [?] faith, "Oh, I think I am." Immediately the word was given me to confirm my faith, "*Now* are ye clean through the word which I have spoken unto you." And I took hold, with a trembling hand, and not unmolested by the tempter, but I held fast the *beginning* of my confidence, and it grew stronger, and from that moment I have dared to reckon myself dead indeed unto sin, and alive unto God through Jesus Christ my Lord.[28]

---

24. Booth, "Letter to her Parents: 11 February 1861."
25. Ibid.
26. Ibid.
27. Ibid.
28. Ibid.

Catherine's description of her feelings after the event also suggests Phoebe Palmer's influence: "I did not feel much rapturous joy, but perfect peace, the sweet rest which Jesus promised to the heavy-laden."[29]

FORMATIVE INFLUENCES

Phoebe Palmer

Phoebe Palmer's influence is particularly evident in William's inspired catechism which carried Catherine across the threshold and into an experience of entire sanctification.[30]

William: Don't you lay all on the altar?
Catherine: I am sure I do.
William: And isn't the altar holy?
Catherine: The altar is *most* holy, and whatsoever toucheth it is holy.
William: Then, are you not holy?
Catherine: Oh, I think I am!

John Kent, who was first to recognize this influence, rightly claims that "the three questions which William Booth asked his wife summarized exactly Phoebe's characteristic thesis, that one is obliged to believe that one is sanctified once one has laid one's all upon the holy altar."[31] Kent's argument has proved influential and most writers since have accepted his conclusions, apparently without question. Roger Green follows Kent in emphasizing Palmer's influence although he confusingly associates the first section of Catherine's testimony with Palmer.[32] Hattersley bases his account entirely on Kent.[33] Unfortunately David Bebbington also follows Kent in an all too rare reference to The Salvation Army in his magisterial work, concluding, "Sanctification understood in Mrs. Palmer's fashion was duly embodied in the Army's doctrinal standards."[34] However unquestionable the fact of Phoebe Palmer's influence may be on Catherine's initial testimony to sanctification, Bebbington's conclusion, as will be seen, is not correct.

29. Ibid.
30. Ibid.
31. Kent, *Holding the Fort*, 327.
32. Green, *Catherine Booth*, 106.
33. Hattersley, *Blood and Fire*, 115–16.
34. Bebbington, *Evangelicalism*, 165.

According to Chick Yuill, Phoebe Palmer speaks "more than anyone else of her time to the sincere seeker, such as Catherine Booth, who longs to claim the desired blessing but does not know how to do it."[35] For Charles White, "Phoebe Palmer uncoupled [the] tension between gradual and instantaneous sanctification in Wesley's thought, placing all her emphasis on the instantaneous."[36] White summarizes, "The thesis of her first book is that there is a shorter way to holiness; 'long waiting and struggling with the powers of darkness is not necessary' because 'There is a shorter way!' In fact, the shorter way is the only way."[37]

The shorter way involves three consecutive steps: first, entire consecration; second, faith; and third, testimony.[38] While these steps have been commonly understood to provide an instantaneous entry into sanctification, Elaine Heath has argued that the shorter way for Phoebe Palmer was understood to be both an event and a process.[39] Palmer's "altar theology" rests on two concepts: first, that the altar sanctifies the gift, and second, that Christ himself is the altar. Four New Testament texts provide support. In Matthew 23:19 Jesus answers his critics by arguing from Exodus 29:37 that an offering to God is not holy in and of itself; rather it is the altar that sanctifies the gift. The idea that Christ himself is the altar is taken from Hebrews 13:10: "We have an altar from which those who minister at the tabernacle have no right to eat." Palmer follows Adam Clarke by interpreting the altar as Christ, an interpretation that Heath argues is consistent with tradition and supported by contemporary scholarship.[40] Romans 12:1 is the essential third text: "Therefore, I urge you, brothers, in view of God's mercy, to offer your bodies as living sacrifices, holy and pleasing to God—this is your spiritual act of worship." A fourth text (1 John 1:7b) confirms that once we have placed our lives on the altar "the blood of Jesus, his Son, purifies us from all sin." In Palmer's own words: "This [act of commitment], I was given to see, was in verity [the] placing all upon the altar that sanctifieth the gift, and I felt that, so long as my heart assured me that I did thus offer all, that it was a solemn duty as well as a high and holy privilege, to believe that

---

35. Yuill, "Restoring the Image," 62.
36. White, *The Beauty of Holiness*, 129–30.
37. Ibid., 130.
38. Heath, *Naked Faith*, 22.
39. Ibid.
40. Cf. Ibid., 24.

the blood of Jesus cleanseth at the present and each succeeding moment, so long as the offering is continued."[41]

Palmer's testimony points to a potential weakness in her argument. Phoebe's heart assurance is that she has placed her all on the altar; it is not the inner assurance of the Holy Spirit that she has indeed been sanctified. Indeed in Phoebe's own experience this witness was denied. Phoebe wrote that no "wonderful manifestation [. . .] at once [followed] as a reward of my faith." All she had was "faith—*naked faith in a naked promise.*"[42]

Catherine's letter to her parents can itself be considered a product of Palmer's influence, for in Palmer's scheme the obligation to testify to the blessing was binding, often precedes the emotional assurance of sanctification, and was essential to retaining the blessing.[43] John Kent would therefore appear to be justified in claiming that, "Once one grasps the kind of shorthand that was being used, Mrs. Booth's letter ceases to be a simple account of a subjective experience, the story of how the Booths discovered holiness for themselves, and becomes instead a description of an exercise in Phoebe Palmer's spiritual discipline."[44]

However this does not necessarily justify Kent's additional claim that "what the Booths adopted in 1861 was the revivalist doctrine which Mrs. Palmer brought with her from the United States";[45] and he is not justified in his claim that the letters make it "quite clear" that the Booths "had completely accepted Phoebe Palmer's doctrine of holiness."[46] Kent ignores two salient questions. First, is it only Phoebe Palmer's influence that can be discerned in Catherine's letter: and second, to what extent did Phoebe Palmer's doctrine influence Catherine Booth's actual teaching of the doctrine of holiness?

William Boardman

In quoting Catherine's letter Booth-Tucker omits the reference to William Boardman's book *The Higher Christian Life*, which may explain why Boardman's influence was only finally noted by Chick Yuill in his essay

---

41. Phoebe Palmer, Guide to Holiness I (1839–40), 210, cited in White, *The Beauty of Holiness*, 23.
42. Wheatley, *The Life and Letters of Mrs. Phoebe Palmer*, 42.
43. White, *The Beauty of Holiness*, 139.
44. Kent, *Holding the Fort*, 327.
45. Ibid.
46. Ibid., 326.

on Catherine's doctrine of holiness. John Kent seems not to have been aware of it. In fact, in the same way that the final section of Catherine's letter paraphrases Palmer, so the first section paraphrases Boardman.

William Boardman was a member of Phoebe Palmer's circle in New York and attended the Tuesday Meetings for the Promotion of Holiness. Boardman's book was immensely popular and influential on both sides of the Atlantic.[47] It was written in an informal style using what Boardman called the "historical and inductive" method; that is, the book relied on stories of sanctification from Christian history and the present day for its persuasive power rather than a reasoned explanation of the theology of holiness.[48] It also had an ecumenical intent, describing three broad views of sanctification—Lutheran, Wesleyan, and Oberlinian—and attempting to reveal the greater though simple truth that lay behind all three: the possibility of a higher Christian life.

This simple truth was in effect an argument from analogy, that just as salvation in the sense of justification comes by faith, so *full salvation* comes through *full trust* in Jesus.[49] The experience of a state of sanctification in itself is not the thing at issue. "Whoever can say," according to Boardman, "Jesus is mine and I am His, that He is complete and I am complete in Him," and say the truth, "has the experience, whether he has an experience to relate or not [. . .] Christ, without any marked experience whatever, is all-sufficient."[50] What is attained in this experience of the higher Christian life, what is objectively and subjectively received and trusted in, is Christ, Christ in all his fullness, Christ as all in all. "That is all," Boardman says, "and that is enough."[51] As for some rewarding sense of holiness of heart, according to Boardman, there is nothing "but a sense of self-emptiness, and vileness, and helplessness" accompanied by "a sense of absolute dependence upon Christ for holiness of heart and life."[52] What follows is the work of faith as Christ the potter takes hold of the clay placed in his hands, and a new starting point has been gained, a new and higher level reached.[53]

---

47. Bebbington, *Evangelicalism*, 164.
48. Boardman, *Higher Life*, xlv.
49. Ibid., 93, 31.
50. Ibid., 38–39.
51. Ibid., 43.
52. Ibid., 43–44.
53. Ibid., 44–45.

Boardman's influence upon Catherine is evident in her reference to "the simple reception of Christ as an all-sufficient Saviour," and in her speaking of holding fast to the *beginning* of her confidence. She concludes, "I have no words to set forth the sense I have of my own vileness. [. . .] But then I have said, the Lord has not made my salvation to depend in any measure on my own worthiness or unworthiness, but on the worthiness of my Saviour."[54] There is strength in Chick Yuill's claim that Boardman provided Catherine with "a platform on which to build her theology of holiness, a theology which stood on the simple logic that Christ, who had made a perfect atonement, could do a perfect work in the life of the believer."[55]

Although Christ is central to Boardman's scheme, he was at pains to express his doctrine in Trinitarian terms:

> Strictly and literally, Jesus is our justification, and sanctification, and glorification; and the Holy Spirit is our justifier, sanctifier, and glorifier. When, therefore, we trust wholly in Jesus for all, we do not rob the Holy Spirit of the honour justly His due, but we honour Him by complying with His teachings and shewing *[sic]* His work. [. . .] So, likewise, by trusting wholly in Jesus, we honour also the Father. And this for two reasons. [. . .] First, Jesus is the express image of the Father—the Father's representative to us, the fullness of the Father made manifest in flesh. [. . .] And then, again, the Father is the author and planner of salvation through faith in His Son.[56]

This is an important point, for the relationship of Christology to pneumatology in the doctrine of sanctification was to become a pressing question in the development of the Holiness Movement through Catherine Booth's lifetime, not least through a hitherto largely unrecognized influence on Catherine Booth, the writings of the Methodist scholar William Arthur.

William Arthur

There is no obvious or certain evidence in the letter that Catherine was helped in her quest by reading William Arthur's popular and influential exposition of Pentecost, *The Tongue of Fire*. However Arthur's book helped to create the context of heightened evangelical expectation into which Boardman's book was launched and his teaching took root. According to Melvin

---

54. Booth, "Letter to her Parents: 11 February 1861."
55. Yuill, "Restoring the Image," 70.
56. Boardman, *Higher Life*, 80.

Dieter, "It fanned the expectations for a new 'Age of the Spirit' which would restore the power of primitive Christian spirituality to the Church, re-energise its evangelism, and hasten the establishment of the Kingdom of God on earth."[57] William Arthur was in some ways a surprising prophet, an establishment figure who was on the opposing side to William and Catherine in the internecine struggles within the Methodist Connexion in the 1850s.[58] Arthur was no rash revivalist; although he had gained a reputation for the power and eloquence of his preaching he was rather more of a bureaucrat than an evangelist. Arthur was a personal friend of Jabez Bunting and actively took his side against the Reformers and against James Caughey. He was a member of the Legal Hundred, rose to become President of the Conference, and was described as Methodism's "first man."[59] His writings may have come out of the mid-century Methodist mainstream establishment, but they fanned Catherine's expectations at this critical time. However, it is also possible that Catherine may have been encouraged in what she came to regard as her misconception that sanctification was "a great and mighty work to be wrought in [her] through Christ" by reading *The Tongue of Fire*.[60] Arthur described the moment when the Holy Ghost manifests the divine favor:

> This manifestation may be gentle, or it may be rapturous; but in any case it is comforting. [. . .] The thirst of the soul has no deeper seat than is now reached. Wisdom has no remonstrance, expectation no disappointment, fear no warning. It may be in a profound calm, it may be in an unspeakable joy; but it is with core-deep consciousness that the soul feels it has now touched, yea, tasted, its supreme good, and that, for time or for eternity, it need no more than to abide in this blessedness, and improve this fellowship.[61]

This is a markedly different view from that of Phoebe Palmer, with her altar theology, and "naked faith in the naked word." Although Palmer's shorter way may have helped Catherine, arguably in her mature teaching of holiness Catherine came closer to Arthur than to Palmer.

---

57. Dieter, *The Holiness Revival*, 250.
58. Cf. Taggart, *William Arthur*.
59. Ibid., 1.
60. Booth, "Letter to her Parents: 11 February 1861."
61. Arthur, *Tongue of Fire*, 53.

HOLINESS AND REVIVAL

More than twenty years separate Catherine's letter to her parents and her published addresses on holiness. These were not uneventful or inconsequential years. It is by no means a logical necessity that Catherine's eventual understanding of the doctrine of holiness is to be found intact and entire in her testimony of 1861.[62]

For some later Salvationist historians, the years 1861 through to 1865 were the Booths' "wilderness" years. They were undoubtedly difficult years, but they were also fruitful years during which the Booths built a reputation as revivalists. They plunged into that growing and developing network of relationships which identifiably became the Holiness Movement, and which would provide invaluable support in every conceivable manner to their own ministry and that of the nascent Salvation Army. According to James Edwin Orr, "the most significant and the most fascinating home development of the 1859 Awakening was the birth of The Salvation Army."[63] He continues, "The Salvation Army arose as a permanent expression of the 1859 Revival in its double ministry of evangelism and social uplift."[64] It was in these years that William discovered the necessary connection between holy living and successful evangelism, for, writes Orr, "he preached one to achieve the other."[65]

Orr's conclusions make it surprising therefore that Kent should speak of the Booths "following the trend of evangelical fashion" and turning back to "the idea of holiness in the early 1870s."[66] Kent also claimed that when they did so, "it was to Mrs. Palmer's writings that they clearly referred."[67] It is not necessary to turn to an independent source to test these conflicting views, for Kent's opinion is challenged by his own text. Kent admits that Palmer "was not mentioned by name as a source."[68] He might have also added that neither did Catherine Booth use such Palmerian terms as "shorter way," "altar theology" or "naked faith," and rarely if ever used such emblematic Palmerian texts as "the altar sanctifies the gift."

---

62. And therefore, in some significant part, the Army's.
63. Orr, *The Second Evangelical Awakening*, 104.
64. Ibid.
65. Ibid., 103.
66. Kent, *Holding the Fort*, 327.
67. Ibid.
68. Ibid.

Kent has turned a positive into a negative; the positive fact presented in his text being that by 1870 the Christian Mission was holding special weekly meetings for the promotion of holiness.[69] There is a tendentious subtext in Kent's description that this initiative "amounted to the third occasion on which William Booth had tried to capture attention by using the holiness theme."[70] Kent cannot deny the growth of the Holiness Movement or William and Catherine Booth's participation in that growth, but he does attribute their "comparative breakthrough" to the excitement that the Americans, Robert and Hannah Pearsall Smith, stirred up around holiness teaching.[71] With the event of the Brighton Congress in 1875, according to Kent, Pearsall Smith gave "the Salvation Army a much needed stimulant for growth."[72]

It is unfortunate that Kent provides an authoritative source for David Bebbington, who concludes that after the Brighton Convention of 1875 the message of holiness was "taken up by many other bodies, including The Salvation Army, but the Keswick idiom became dominant."[73] He states that "in the early phase following its emergence in the 1870s, the Salvation Army was a vigorous holiness organization, concerned to carry 'the fire of the Holy Ghost' into all its work. Its message reflected the American influence on Britain."[74] It is safer in this area to follow Orr's conclusion, which is, that in contrast to the Keswick movement, The Salvation Army adopted a much more Wesleyan view of holiness.[75] Melvin Dieter agrees with Orr: "The historic relationship between William and Catherine Booth and the early holiness movement revivalists in England compared with the Booths' own roots in the Wesleyan evangelical tradition established Wesley's doctrine of Christian holiness as a central emphasis in the Army's teaching and practice. It became the dynamic of its evangelism and social movements."[76]

---

69. Catherine recalls, "The Christians who gathered around [William, in 1865] deserted him almost to a man before a fortnight had passed away. They did not agree with his holiness teaching; he laid too much stress upon the necessity of good works." Booth, *Reminiscences*, 90.

70. Kent, *Holding the Fort*, 329.

71. Ibid.

72. Kent's partial explanation for the Army's "apparent success." Ibid., 335.

73. Bebbington, *Evangelicalism*, 151.

74. Ibid., 165.

75. Orr, *The Second Evangelical Awakening*, 127.

76. Dieter, *The Holiness Revival*, 257.

PHOEBE PALMER'S QUESTIONABLE INFLUENCE

John Kent's assertion, that the Booths adopted Phoebe Palmer's revivalist doctrine in 1861 and that from then on they completely accepted her doctrine of holiness, has been noted. Palmer's influence upon William and Catherine in the 1860s is beyond doubt, and it has been seen that her altar theology was critical in assisting Catherine to embrace the doctrine of holiness as a personal experience. Phoebe Palmer presented a contemporary model of female ministry that Catherine first defended and then embraced for herself, and together the Palmers provided a model of shared ministry that the Booths emulated and which became a model for ministry in The Salvation Army. The Salvation Army has truly launched a host of "perambulating males and females" upon the world.[77] Nevertheless, John Kent's only evidence for his claim that the Booths adopted Phoebe Palmer's theology as their own is Catherine's letter to her mother describing her experiences in early 1861. It remains an open question whether, or to what extent, Phoebe Palmer influenced Catherine Booth's particular presentation of the doctrine of holiness.

According to Charles White, "Phoebe Palmer simplified and popularized John Wesley's doctrine of entire sanctification, modifying it in six different ways."[78] Only in the last two of these ways does White consider Palmer an innovator. In the first she follows John Fletcher; in the second, third, and fourth ways White finds Palmer following Adam Clarke. First, Phoebe Palmer identified entire sanctification with the baptism of the Holy Spirit; second, she linked holiness with power; third, she emphasized the instantaneous aspect of sanctification to the exclusion of the gradual; fourth, she taught that entire sanctification is not so much the goal of the Christian life as its beginning; fifth, through her "altar theology" she reduced the attainment of sanctification to three simple steps of entire consecration, faith, and testimony; and finally, she held that the words of the Bible were sufficient evidence of sanctification and no external subjective manifestation, or sense of assurance, was necessary.[79]

Elaine Heath holds that at least some of these innovations were the work of Palmer's followers and interpreters rather than of Palmer herself. However, as a summary of the ways in which Phoebe Palmer may be held

---

77. Orr, *The Second Evangelical Awakening*, 72.
78. White, *The Beauty of Holiness*, 198.
79. Ibid.

The Pursuit of Holiness

to have been an innovator in her doctrine of holiness, White's list provides a useful point of comparison with Catherine Booth's holiness teaching.

Two things can immediately be said: first, that Catherine does not follow Palmer in the two ways in which White finds Palmer to be uniquely innovative; but second, that there are continuities, if not similarities, between Palmer and Catherine in the other four ways in which, according to White, Palmer modifies John Wesley's doctrine of sanctification.

White identifies Palmer's altar theology as her own innovation, with its three simple steps of entire consecration, faith, and testimony. Catherine commonly taught the first two steps of entire consecration and faith as the essential conditions of sanctification: "Further, there are *two indispensible conditions of attaining this blessing—entire consecration and faith in His promises.*"[80] However in her teaching of consecration Catherine never argued from Palmer's distinctive verse Matthew 23:19 that the altar sanctifies the gift. For Catherine, consecration is a simple though potentially difficult and painful act of obedience to the revealed will of God. "Will you say, 'I accept thy plan for myself, my time, my influence, my money, my children, my home, and my future; I accept it?'"[81] That acceptance and obedience was the crucial aspect of consecration which Catherine constantly emphasised. In Catherine's personal experience it was her unwillingness to accept the call of God to preach the gospel that rendered her own obedience incomplete and consecration imperfect. When she accepted and acted on this calling there was no longer a barrier to her entering into the experience of holiness. Consecration is therefore an act of renunciation and submission to God in all things which is for Catherine synonymous with repentance. The failure to repent and consecrate in this sense of obedience is the most common obstacle to a person being sanctified and it must not be dealt with lightly.[82] Saving faith is not for Catherine "naked faith in the naked word." Its focus is not primarily the word of God, but Christ himself. Faith is an act of trust in and commitment to Jesus Christ, comparable to the trust in and commitment to a physician by someone who is sick, who believes in his skill, places their life in his hands, and obeys his orders.[83] Finally Catherine does not insist on testimony as a necessary third step. She does not seem to have ever repeated the testimony found in her letter to her

---

80. Booth, *Holiness*, 14.
81. Booth, *Life & Death*, 199.
82. Booth, *Godliness*, 174.
83. Ibid., 17.

parents. The only further condition Catherine lays down in her pamphlet on holiness is "walking by faith in humble submissive obedience to the light [God] gives you."[84]

White also identifies Palmer as an innovator in holding that the word of Scripture was the only witness required for someone to be sure they had been sanctified. This was Palmer's most controversial departure from Wesley's doctrine of sanctification. Nathan Bangs, the eminent Methodist historian, theologian, and preacher, though a close friend of the Palmers, took issue with Phoebe on this point, supporting the Wesleyan doctrine of the assurance of the Spirit as the necessary confirmation of God's sanctifying work and denying Palmer's theological syllogism with its inherent potential for self-deception as to the attainment of entire sanctification.[85] In this crucial aspect Catherine did not teach that "naked faith in the naked word" was sufficient, and that the only required word of assurance was the word of Scripture; rather she consistently taught, following Wesley, the necessity of the graciously given witness of the Holy Spirit, which is an "inward assurance, which men and women find for themselves, or have revealed in themselves, which they know as a matter of consciousness"; this assurance cannot be given by a minister, it cannot be learned from books, it is "not even that which the Bible only tells them."[86] This is the "assurance of faith, a conviction wrought in the heart by the Holy Ghost."[87]

According to Al Truesdale, "Palmer did not simply correct popular Wesleyanism. In important respects she replaced it by setting aside its reification of experience and inserting a predictable theological formula that minimized (if not negated) experience, and could not fail to deliver certainty. In the replacement, there were no experiential patterns to approximate and no hurdles to overcome."[88] Truesdale describes reification as the fallacy of attributing "objective substantiality to an idea or abstraction."[89] The term was coined by the philosopher Alfred North Whitehead who described it as "the Fallacy of Misplaced Concreteness."[90] According to Truesdale reification occurs in holiness teaching when the experience of

84. Booth, *Holiness*, 16.
85. Dieter, *The Holiness Revival*, 24.
86. Booth, *Aggressive Christianity*, 68.
87. Ibid., 73.
88. Truesdale, "Reification," 116–17.
89. Ibid., 102.
90. Whitehead, *Science and the Modern World*, 51.

one person is presented as normative for all, thereby falsely objectifying sanctification. Truesdale argues that Palmer's reinterpretation of the witness of the Spirit as the witness of the Word removes this danger, reclaiming freedom for the seeker to claim the blessing without the imposition of an experience objectified without regard to their own personality, culture, and religious tradition. However, although Catherine affirms the witness of the Spirit she does not specify the nature of the witness without regard to these factors. When faith follows on consecration and "the Master comes to His Temple" the reality of his presence will be known, but "the manifestation will be according to your nature. One will fall down and weep in quietness, and the other will get up and shout and jump."[91] This is remarkably similar to William Arthur's description, that the "manifestation may be gentle, or it may be rapturous; but in any case it is comforting [. . .] It may be in a profound calm, it may be in an unspeakable joy."[92] Whether or not such a responsive flexibility in her expectations excuses Catherine from the charge of reification, Truesdale's insight helps to establish a critical distance between Catherine's doctrine and Phoebe Palmer's.

It is clear therefore that Catherine Booth did not adopt Phoebe Palmer's doctrine of holiness in at least these two major distinctive characteristics. The question remains whether in some of the more general aspects of her doctrine Catherine was indebted to Palmer. White identifies John Fletcher, Adam Clarke, and William Arthur as the formative influences upon Palmer in regard to the remaining four categories, and it must be noted first that Catherine was familiar with the work of these writers and came to them either before she came to Palmer or else independently of her reading of Palmer. There can therefore be no prior expectation that in these aspects of her doctrine Catherine was influenced by Palmer rather than directly by Fletcher, Clarke, and Arthur.

The first of the four ways identified by White is Palmer's frequent identification of entire sanctification with the baptism of the Holy Spirit. White attributes this to the influence of first, John Fletcher, and second, William Arthur. Krista Valtanen avers that Catherine never makes this association.[93] However, in her address *Filled with the Spirit* Catherine equates "higher-life religion" with the "Pentecost [. . .] offered to all believers."[94] In

---

91. Booth, *Aggressive Christianity*, 98.
92. Arthur, *Tongue of Fire*, 53.
93. Valtanen, "Catherine Booth," 194.
94. Booth, *Aggressive Christianity*, 148–49.

the same address Catherine offers a brief description of the Spirit's work: "Oh! it is the most precious gift He has to give in earth or in Heaven—to be filled with the Spirit, filled with Himself [. . .] taken possession of by God; moved, inspired, energised, empowered by God, by the great indwelling Spirit moving through all our faculties, and energising our whole being for Him."[95]

Catherine was using pentecostal language to describe entire sanctification by July 1853, when she wrote to William, "I am looking up to Jesus for a further baptism of his loving, meek, self sacrificing spirit."[96] And at this stage, before she had come into the assurance that she was herself entirely sanctified, Catherine's notion of holiness was precisely what it would be in the 1880s—that is, the restoration of the image and likeness of God to humankind by means of the transforming power of the Holy Spirit.

> That is it; to be like Jesus, and oh, what can our ambition aim at higher? To be like him is to be eminent on earth for goodness, beloved of all; to be precious to heaven; to be envied and dreaded of hell; to be loved of God, aye, precious as the apple of his eye. [. . .] We both may really be like him if we only will. Let us think about the glory of being like him, till our wills are brought to desire it above all things else, and then the transforming power will descend and the glorious work will be done.[97]

A few days later Catherine wrote again, presaging the future scene in their Gateshead home, "I wish you were here so that we could [. . .] kneel together at this sofa and plead and wait for a fresh baptism of the Holy Spirit for a renewal of our souls in true holiness."[98]

Chick Yuill has argued, "Although Catherine Booth herself sometimes referred to holiness as the "baptism in the Spirit," for her the phrase represented a powerful metaphor rather than a rigid doctrinal statement."[99] Certainly Catherine does not seem to use the phrase consistently to describe a discrete stage on the *via salutis*. However, the baptism of the Holy Spirit is more than a metaphor for her. Catherine uses pentecostal terminology consistently. First, Pentecost was that singular and unrepeatable historical event when the Holy Spirit was poured out upon the disciples of Jesus in

---

95. Ibid., 154.
96. Booth and Booth, *Letters*, 130.
97. Ibid.
98. Ibid., 131.
99. Yuill, "Restoring the Image," 85.

The Pursuit of Holiness

fulfillment of the prophecy of Joel. Second, because the current dispensation is the age of the Spirit, it is the privilege of every believer to be filled with the Holy Spirit. This pentecostal infilling is the means by which the believer is enabled to live a holy life.[100] But a third Pentecost is possible, equally dependent on the first. Catherine narrates a story of an all night of prayer attended by around one thousand people. Around six in the morning the Holy Spirit descended upon the gathered assembly, laying strong men prostrate under the power of God.[101] Such an event could also be described as a Pentecost. The War Congress of August 1878 was announced by the single word, "Pentecost."[102]

According to Charles White, pentecostal language does not appear in Palmer's writing until after 1856. In December that year Palmer realized "that the baptism of the Spirit given at Pentecost empowered and impelled its recipients to speak for Christ."[103] At the same time she realized that the same empowerment and therefore calling was given to women as well as men. White believes this may reflect the influence of *The Tongue of Fire*, which was first published in 1856. Although Arthur may also have influenced the development of Catherine's thought, he quite evidently did not initiate it. Catherine's very first sermon delivered on Whit Sunday 1860 was on the subject "Be Filled with the Spirit," and on 17 September 1860 Catherine wrote to William saying she planned to preach again on the same theme, but she could only find one chapter in Finney on the subject and wanted a "good definition" of what it meant; consequently William's thoughts would be welcomed.[104] Catherine did not turn to Palmer's work for help, nor did she find much help in Finney. Two days later Catherine wrote again to William, "I have been reading Arthur's *Tongue of Fire* [. . .] it is some time since I enjoyed a book so much."[105] William Arthur's surprisingly visionary exposition of Pentecost was a consequence of working out the implications of Wesley and Fletcher's view that the present dispensation was the age of the gospel, the age of the Holy Spirit. It is an extended response to the question, what does Pentecost mean for the church, for the kingdom of God, for the world? It was in fact not so much a vision as

---

100. Booth, *Aggressive Christianity*, 149.
101. Ibid., 159.
102. Sandall, Wiggins, and Coutts, *History*, I:231.
103. White, *The Beauty of Holiness*, 128.
104. Booth and Booth, *Letters*, 331.
105. Ibid., 333.

an extended, imaginative interpretation of Wesley and Fletcher's dispensationalism. Patrick Streiff has claimed: "Throughout his life, Fletcher's view of the future was marked by the expectation of a new, more comprehensive operation of God's grace, but for the later Fletcher, with his pneumatological preoccupations, apocalyptic gave way more and more to the expectation of a new Pentecost and a Church of the Spirit."[106]

It can be seen therefore that whatever similarities or continuities there might be, Catherine's doctrine of holiness is neither derived from nor dependent on Palmer on this particular point of doctrine.

According to White, in regard to items two, three, and four on his list, Palmer was influenced by Adam Clarke, and it has been noted that Catherine was already familiar with Clarke's writings. In respect of White's second point, in a manner similar to Phoebe Palmer, Catherine does associate holiness with power. To be baptized with the Spirit is to be baptized with power. The great work of the power of God is "to subdue the naturally evil, wicked, and rebellious heart of man."[107] To receive the Holy Spirit is to be endued with power, "the direct, pungent, enlightening, convicting, transforming power of the Holy Ghost."[108] A child filled with the Holy Spirit has greater power to help, bless, and benefit the soul than any adult, however intelligent, educated, eloquent, or influential they might be.[109] In respect of White's third point, that Phoebe Palmer emphasized the instantaneous aspects of sanctification to the detriment of the gradual, it is less certain that Catherine can reasonably be accused of this. Catherine never taught Phoebe Palmer's shorter way. She certainly never suggested there was an easy way to attain holiness. Nevertheless Catherine did believe that it was the privilege of every believer to be entirely sanctified; however young or weak in spirit or temperament, if they met the required conditions they could enter into the experience. Yet although she would usually close a holiness address with a call for an immediate response, she did not normally press the matter, but instead concentrated on meeting objections and assisting her hearers to understand and apply the conditions regardless of the time that might take.

> The Lord will search you and when he has revealed the extent of the disease—when you have gone down low enough in self-despair,

---

106. Streiff, *Reluctant saint?*, 46.
107. Booth, *Aggressive Christianity*, 193.
108. Ibid., 189.
109. Ibid.

The Pursuit of Holiness

when you come down right to the depths and cry "Unclean, unclean; I can do nothing to cure myself, heal me"—He will make a perfect cure and put a song of thanksgiving in your mouth, and give you the sunlight of His smile continually. Many people are not allowed to wait long enough for these probings of the Spirit. They are hurried too quickly into a profession of the blessing, then when they fall away they say it was not what they believed it to be, but this does not make the faith of God of none effect.[110]

In the grand picture of things the emergence of The Salvation Army as a community of the justified and sanctified—a salvation people—is the strongest evidence that William and Catherine Booth believed not only that salvation was not, in the end, about these instantaneous moments on which a revival ministry necessarily focused, but on the processes before and after, the fostering of which was essential if a people were to be formed in holiness. In regard to White's fourth point, in the same way as Phoebe Palmer, Catherine did teach that sanctification was the beginning of the Christian life. This did not preclude growth in holiness or Christ-likeness; rather it was the condition for it.

> Neither is sanctification *final growth*. It does not imply final attainment. You must discriminate between purity and maturity. You may have the most perfect baby but he is not a man yet. He has to grow and develop and increase; but people really and truly do not begin to grow in grace until they are sanctified. It is more frequently a falling down and a getting up again than an even onward progress in grace and salvation. Hence if you really want to grow in grace, if you want to rise to the possibilities of your nature in the salvation of God, you must be delivered from sin, for sin undoes you, knocks you down into the mud, as it were, and you have to be, as the apostle says, "always laying the foundation for repentance from dead works." How can such people grow? Instead of growing on, and on, and on, until they attain the stature of the perfect man in Christ Jesus, they stop short in perpetual boyhood.[111]

There are therefore some similarities and continuities between Phoebe Palmer's doctrine of holiness and Catherine's. However, their views are by no means in perfect alignment, and it could be argued that it is where Palmer is most in debt to her Wesleyan heritage that the congruence with Catherine's doctrine is most apparent. Indeed White has argued that in her

---

110. Booth, *Holiness*, 14.
111. Ibid., 8.

doctrine of holiness Palmer was not so much innovating as "carrying Wesleyan doctrines to their natural conclusion."[112]

> She was working out their inner logic. If it is true that all Christians will eventually be sanctified, and if it is true that it is better to be sanctified than merely justified, and if it is true that God can sanctify the believer now just as easily as a thousand years from now, and if it is true that God gives sanctification in response to the believer's faith, then every Christian should be sanctified now. Wesley preached each of the protases, and he admitted the truth of the apodoses.[113]

However accurate White's conclusion may be, in virtually every point detailed above it can be said that Catherine stands closer to John Wesley than to Phoebe Palmer. Furthermore the distinctive theological locus of sanctification for Catherine is the theme of the restoration of the *imago Dei* after the image and likeness of Christ, whereas the distinctive theological locus for Phoebe lies in her altar theology.[114] The judgment must be made—over and against the conclusions of John Kent and the assumptions of those that followed him—that it was not Phoebe Palmer's doctrine of holiness that Catherine Booth adopted and "duly embodied in the Army's doctrinal standards," but instead a doctrine that relied rather more on her own Wesleyan antecedents and what she in turn made of them.[115]

In the area of eschatology, according to Woodrow Whidden, Phoebe Palmer's views, though infrequently expressed, were rather closer to premillennialism than that of her circle.[116] Whidden describes Palmer's expectation of the Lord's second coming as "personal, visible, cataclysmic, and imminent."[117] He argues that Palmer expected an imminent "literal, visible, cataclysmic second coming of Jesus Christ," that would herald the end of the world.[118]

Here then, is a further difference between Phoebe Palmer and Catherine Booth, for Catherine was a postmillennialist. According to Robert Clouse, "The distinctions [between premillennialism and postmillennialism]

112. White, *The Beauty of Holiness*, 204.
113. Ibid.
114. Cf. Palmer, *Entire Devotion to God*, 3–8.
115. Bebbington, *Evangelicalism*, 165.
116. Whidden, "Eschatology, Soteriology and Social Activism," 95.
117. Ibid., 96.
118. Ibid., 94.

involve a great deal more than the time of Christ's return. The kingdom expected by the premillennialist is quite different from the kingdom anticipated by the postmillennialist, not only with respect to the time and manner in which it will be established but also in regard to its nature and the way Christ will exercise control over it."[119]

Premillennialism supposes a radical disjunction between the present age or dispensation, in effect the end of history, while postmillennialism supposes an equally radical and historical continuity. Mildred Bangs Wynkoop identifies the emergence of premillennialism as a symptom of the break up, in certain sectors of the Holiness Movement, of what she calls the "Wesleyan synthesis" and the disruption of Wesleyan patterns of theology by the intrusion of alternative theological and philosophical root-systems.[120] The eschatological choice lies between an essentially apocalyptic or historical idea of existence: "The historical interpretation emphasized the continuity of events to provide the meaning of the present. The apocalyptic stressed the discontinuity of events, the breaking in on history of new, unrelated forces and events. The historical has to do with the ongoing, day-by-day, moral, responsible linking of human choosing into character. Apocalyptic is the intrusion of crises that force a change of direction which is not linked to any human choice. The historical is morally related. The apocalyptic is amoral."[121]

Notwithstanding these differences the Palmers and the Booths were friends and allies in their revival ministries. When Phoebe Palmer died, the obituary in *The Christian Mission Magazine* was fulsome in its praise: "Her visit to this country some thirteen years ago was made a blessing to thousands, and by her labours and writings she has done more to advance the cause of holiness than any man or woman this century."[122]

CONCLUSION

In looking at Catherine's spiritual experience, this chapter has taken the view that Phoebe Palmer was a catalytic influence upon Catherine Booth, stirring her to engage in public debate for the cause of women's ministry, modeling a powerful preaching and teaching ministry, assisting her

---

119. Clouse, *The Meaning of the Millennium*, 7; cited in Underwood, "Millenarianism," 82–83.

120. Wynkoop, "Theological Roots," 79.

121. Ibid., 83.

122. *The Christian Mission Magazine*, "Mrs. Phoebe Palmer."

move into an experience of holiness and affirming the Holy Spirit's role in sanctification. But the argument put forward has been that the pattern of Catherine's holiness teaching was not the same as Phoebe Palmer's and not derived primarily from her. Undoubtedly there are similarities in the teaching of these two mid-century Methodist women preachers, but there are also significant differences, not least that Catherine never explicitly taught Phoebe Palmer's formulaic shorter way, whatever its advantages and benefits, or its pitfalls and shortcomings might have been.

It is acknowledged that Phoebe Palmer did have an impact on the formation of Catherine Booth's doctrine of holiness, but it has been argued here that her influence has been greatly overstated by John Kent and those who have followed him. Yet Catherine did not regard innovation or independence of thought as virtues in regard to the formation of doctrine and she was not at all afraid to express her appreciation for some other teacher or preacher of holiness. Who were, therefore, the major influences on the development and presentation of Catherine Booth's holiness teaching?

FOUR

Doctrine of Holiness

Phoebe Palmer claimed that the foundation of her doctrine of holiness was not "Wesley, not Fletcher, not Finney, not Mahan, not Upham, but the Bible."[1] In contrast, writing to Richard Cope Morgan in 1865, defending her doctrine of holiness against an accusation of perfectionism, Catherine Booth claimed her views were "substantially one with Upham, Wesley, Fletcher, Finney, and the holiness people of America."[2] Catherine owned the Bible as her first authority to no less a degree than did Phoebe Palmer.[3] At the same time there is no reason her list of those with whom she identified herself should be treated lightly or ignored. Instead, the validity of her claim for some degree of affinity with each of these authorities should be tested.

CATHERINE BOOTH'S DOCTRINE OF HOLINESS

One of the clearest expositions of Catherine's doctrine is found in her address *Holiness*. Catherine begins by describing two different stages of Christian experience she finds in Scripture.[4] The first stage applies to those "babes in Christ," who are either near the beginning of their Christian life, or who through a want of light or obedience have not moved up to a higher level of experience.[5] This stage is characterized by dispositions, motives, and feelings which "they know to be incompatible with the law and will of

---

1. Palmer, *The Promise of the Father*, 227.
2. Booth-Tucker, *Catherine Booth*, I:543.
3. For an examination of Catherine Booth's biblicism see Larsen, *A People of One Book*, 89–111.
4. Booth, *Holiness*, 3.
5. Ibid.

God, and the mind of Christ."[6] Catherine claims, however, that the scriptural passages describing "a far higher and more glorious state of experience" are "far more numerous."[7] This level of experience is the "glorious top stone which [God] has put on the temple of grace," which Catherine names as "sanctification, holiness complete, and unreserved consecration to God."[8] This doctrine is the "central truth of Christianity."[9]

Catherine continues by clarifying what, for her, this state of experience is not. First, holiness is not "freedom from infirmity."[10] It is not to be made perfect in respect of "apprehension, memory or capacity."[11] Catherine acknowledges that some theological controversy has arisen out of varying definitions of sin. "If a lapse of memory, a mistake in judgment, a surprise or aberration of feeling is a sin," she does "not contend that we are saved from these"; however, Catherine does not count these as sins.[12] Second, holiness is not deliverance from temptation.[13] As Christ was tempted and yet was without sin, so Christians are also tempted. "Saying 'yes' to temptation is sin."[14] Third, sanctification is not final growth.[15] Instead, holiness is the condition which allows the Christian to grow from spiritual childhood into maturity.[16]

Having explained what holiness is not, Catherine explains what holiness is, in her thinking. Holiness is a perfection of intention, "a purifying of the motives, purposes, desires and affections of the soul, and a thorough committal on the side of God and right at all costs."[17] Expressed negatively, it is a "a deliverance from sin," expressed positively, it is "an inward transformation into the very likeness of Christ," and what links these two descriptions is the conception of holiness as "full conformity of heart, and mind, and will, to the law and mind of God."[18] Holiness is perfect love for God and

6. Ibid.
7. Ibid., 4.
8. Ibid., 5.
9. Ibid., 6.
10. Ibid.
11. Ibid., 7.
12. Ibid.
13. Ibid.
14. Ibid.
15. Ibid., 8.
16. Ibid.
17. Ibid.
18. Ibid.

humankind, for love is the fulfilling of the law. Elsewhere Catherine writes of perfect love, "Give me a man sincere and thorough in his love, and that is all I want; that will stretch through all the ramifications of his existence; it will go to the ends of his fingers and his toes, through his eyes, and through his tongue, to his wife, and to his family, to his shop, and to his business, and to his circle in the world. That is what I mean by HOLINESS!"[19] This intimate identification of holiness as perfect love, and the fulfillment of the great commandments, through an inward transformation into the likeness of Christ, lies at the heart of Catherine's soteriology.

Catherine next presents three arguments for the attainability of this experience. First, holiness is "expressly, emphatically, and repeatedly commanded."[20] In evidence Catherine expounds three texts, quoting the King James version from memory, without references: Matthew 5:48, "Be ye therefore perfect, even as your Father which is in heaven is perfect"; Matthew 22:37-39, "Thou shalt love the Lord thy God with all thy heart, and with all thy soul, and with all thy mind. This is the first and great commandment. And the second is like unto it, Thou shalt love thy neighbour as thyself"; and Hebrews 12:14, "Without holiness no man shall see the Lord [sic]."[21] Second, Catherine argues for the attainability of holiness "from the provisions of the Gospel."[22] Christ's work as mediator had a twofold aspect; it is restorative as well as atoning, bringing "us back to complete and eternal harmony with God,"[23] and restoring "our lost integrity and purity."[24] Catherine's third argument for the attainability of holiness is that it is "repeatedly made the object of inspired prayer."[25] Here Catherine references the prayers of Christ, including, "Sanctify them through Thy truth" (John 17:17); and the prayer of Paul for the Thessalonians, "And the very God of peace sanctify you wholly; and I pray God your whole spirit and soul and body be preserved blameless unto the coming of our Lord Jesus Christ" (1 Thessalonians 5:23).[26]

---

19. Booth, *Godliness*, 93–94.
20. Booth, *Holiness*, 8.
21. Ibid., 9.
22. Ibid.
23. Ibid., 10.
24. Ibid.
25. Ibid., 11.
26. Ibid.

In the next section Catherine describes "the way by which this blessing must be obtained."[27] First, "a definite idea of the blessing" is necessary, and a person needs to be clear in seeking from God salvation and deliverance from sin.[28] This does not mean seeking a particular kind of experience, however, "for the ways by which God brings souls into this experience are quite as diversified as the ways in which he brings them into pardon and peace at first."[29] Second, the Holy Spirit must be allowed time and freedom for his work of conviction. "You must allow the Spirit to work in a godly sorrow for all sins [. . .] of the past."[30] This work of conviction must not be rushed.[31]

Finally, in this section, Catherine states, "There are two indispensable conditions of attaining this blessing—entire consecration and faith in his promises."[32] Catherine believes consecration is "generally the defective point" in a person's failure to enter into holiness, rather than faith, which causes little trouble when consecration is complete.[33] Consecration is, for Catherine, synonymous with submission and obedience. Catherine illustrates by the story of Abraham who stepped out on God's promises without hesitation or argument.[34] The second indispensable condition is faith, which is the simple trust that as we "CLAIM THE BLESSING," God "does now forgive our sins and cleanse us from all *this unrighteousness*, and that having cleansed the temple He now comes in and takes *possession*."[35]

The Holy Spirit witnesses to Christ's sanctifying presence: "He lights up the Shekinah of his presence in the believer's soul, and then is fulfilled the promise, 'I will come unto him, and make my abode with him, I will sup with him and he with me.'"[36] Having received the blessing of holiness, the believer should continue "walking by faith in humble submissive obedience to the light he gives," and in doing so the continued maintenance of

---

27. Ibid., 13.
28. Ibid.
29. Ibid.
30. Ibid.
31. Ibid., 14.
32. Ibid.
33. Ibid.
34. Ibid., 15.
35. Ibid.
36. Ibid., 16.

Doctrine of Holiness

the blessing is sure and secure.[37] Catherine's confident exposition of these themes indicates her understanding of theological tradition.

ENDURING INFLUENCES

John Wesley

To what extent was Catherine Booth indebted to John Wesley in her doctrine of holiness? Catherine's introduction reflects the popularity in holiness discourse of William Boardman's notion of "higher life" religion, but the Wesleyan influences are apparent throughout her account.

Wesley's most complete exposition of his doctrine of holiness is found in *A Plain Account of Christian Perfection*.[38] In his 1740 sermon on *Christian Perfection*, included in the *Plain Account*, Wesley identified four ways in which Christians may not be perfect.[39] They cannot be expected to be free from ignorance, infirmity or temptation, nor can they be perfect in a manner which does not admit of degrees, that is a continual increase in maturity or perfection. Catherine's description of what holiness is not is almost identical to Wesley's, and her intention is precisely the same as Wesley's: that is, to clear the ground for a description of what holiness is. Catherine's definition of holiness is identical to Wesley's. Christian perfection is for Wesley, a "purity of intention," it is "one desire and design ruling all our tempers."[40] Expressed negatively, it is deliverance from sin. Jesus saves "his people from their sins; not only from outward sins, but from the sins of their hearts."[41] At root, it is perfect love, the fulfillment of the great commandment, "loving God with all our heart, and our neighbour as ourselves."[42] Expressed positively, it is an inward transformation into the very likeness of Christ, the restoration of the divine image and likeness: "This great gift of God, the salvation of our souls, is no other than the image

---

37. Ibid., 15.
38. Wesley, "Plain Account."
39. Ibid., §12,374.
40. Mahan, *Christian Perfection*, 16–17; Mahan is citing Wesley, "Plain Account," §27,444.
41. Wesley, "Plain Account," §12,377.
42. Mahan, *Christian Perfection*, 16–17; Mahan is citing Wesley, "Plain Account," §27,444.

of God fresh stamped on our hearts. It is a 'renewal of believers in the spirit of their minds, after the likeness of Him that created them.'"[43]

In respect to the possibility of entire sanctification Catherine argued in her address from the commands of Scripture, the provision of the gospel, and also from the prayers of Jesus and Paul. The catechism included in the *Plain Account* covers the same ground. The same commands of Scripture are detailed,[44] the same promises that God can save his people from all sin are cited,[45] and the prayers of Jesus in John 17 and of Paul in 1 Thessalonians are also given as a surety for the possibility of entire sanctification.[46] Wesley is probably the original source for this section of Catherine's address.

In her emphasis on the Holy Spirit's work of conviction, Catherine is in accord with Wesley, and their language is similar. According to Wesley, through the convicting work of the Spirit, "now first do they see the ground of their heart [. . .] [and] all the hidden abominations there, the depths of pride, self will, and hell."[47] This "fiery trial" "continually heightens both the strong sense they then have of their inability to help themselves, and the inexpressible hunger they feel after a full renewal of his image, in 'righteousness and true holiness.'"[48]

In her address Catherine next describes the two indispensable conditions of attaining the blessing—entire consecration and faith. Phoebe Palmer set three conditions—consecration, faith and testimony; but for Wesley, faith is the only condition to receiving sanctification. Moreover consecration is not for Wesley a condition of sanctification but the fruit of, or even a synonym for, sanctification. Catherine was not alone in establishing these two conditions; they were commonplace in Holiness Movement teaching. But her use of this phraseology would seem to differentiate her teaching from Wesley's at this critical point.

However, two rejoinders can be made. First, in her address Catherine spoke of consecration in two different ways. Early in her address Catherine named the blessing as "sanctification, holiness complete, and unreserved consecration to God," an entirely Wesleyan usage.[49] And second,

---

43. Wesley, "Plain Account," §12,378.
44. Ibid., §17,390.
45. Ibid., §17,389.
46. Ibid., §17,390.
47. Ibid., §13,381.
48. Ibid.
49. Booth, *Holiness*, 5.

in describing what she meant by consecration, Catherine did not use the metaphors of Phoebe Palmer's "altar theology" but described submission and obedience as the required response to the convicting work of the Spirit—a response, effectively, of repentance. And while John Wesley stops short of calling repentance a condition of sanctification, he does at the same time consider "evangelical repentance" to be a necessary response to conviction. Kenneth Collins summarizes: "For Wesley, repentance and works suitable for repentance are in some sense *necessary* for entire sanctification."[50] Wesley shrank from applying any conditions other than faith, maintaining that "though it be allowed that both the repentance and its fruits are necessary to full salvation, yet they are not necessary either in the *same sense* with faith or in the *same degree*."[51] Catherine does not appear to share Wesley's acute concern to emphasize the role of free grace responding to simple faith as the only necessary means of sanctification.

Such differences might appear to support Robert Chiles's thesis that one of the negative developments in Methodist theology after the death of Wesley was a transition from an emphasis on free grace to free will.[52] John Knight took issue with Chiles's conclusions, finding evidence that after 1770, and against antinomianism, Wesley himself placed greater emphasis on human freedom and man's works. In turn, Kenneth Collins found that Knight failed to take sufficient notice of Wesley's continued emphasis on "the divine initiative in salvation as evidenced by his lucid discussion of prevenient, convincing, and sanctifying grace."[53] However, the backdrop to Catherine Booth's own *ordo salutis* is equally that of prevenient grace; and furthermore her conception of regeneration as spiritual union with Christ in the Spirit undermines the notion that she might have considered the necessary submission and obedience prior to the exercise of faith in sanctification to be possible as an entirely unaided exercise of human free will.

Simple or naked faith is for Wesley the one condition of sanctification, although with the proviso, required by the place of repentance in his scheme, that it is the only *immediate* and *proximate* condition.[54] Wesley defines the faith required as "a divine evidence and conviction, first, that

50. Collins, *Holy Love*, 284.

51. John Wesley, Sermon 43 "The Scripture Way of Salvation," in Wesley, *Sermons*, 1–4, §111, II:67.

52. Chiles, *Theological Transition*.

53. Collins, "Wesleyan Ordo Salutis," 31.

54. Collins, *Holy Love*, 286.

God hath promised it in Holy Scripture [. . .] secondly, that what God hath promised he is able to perform [. . .] [and] thirdly [. . .] that he is able and willing to do it *now*."[55]

For Wesley, as for Catherine in her interpretation of Wesleyan perspectives, there is an intimate connection between exercising faith and receiving the assurance of the Spirit, and he therefore continues, "To this confidence, that God is both able and willing to sanctify us *now*, there needs to be added one thing more, a divine evidence and conviction that *he doth it*."[56] In understanding the witness of the Spirit to be an essential concomitant of entire sanctification Catherine is in agreement with Wesley.

In broad outline, and also in much of the detail, Catherine Booth's doctrine of holiness derives from John Wesley's. The most significant difference lies in Catherine's emphasis on the need for repentance/consecration in conjunction with faith as necessary to entering into the experience of entire sanctification. In this it might be argued that Catherine did not so much add to Wesley as clarify and emphasize an aspect of Wesley's own scheme, but it is acknowledged that this is indeed a difference.

Charles Finney

That Catherine Booth was influenced by Charles Finney is a matter of record. Writing to William on 30 August 1853 she declared, "I wish I could talk an hour to Finney. I should like to see him if he ever comes to England again."[57] Booth-Tucker summarized Finney's influence on Catherine:

> Finney was to Mrs. Booth what Wesley had been to the General. Without agreeing with him on every point, she appreciated his massive intellect, enjoyed his lawyer-like logic, dived into the depths of his philosophy, and, above all, admired the zeal and Holy Ghost power which permeated the life and writings of the great revivalist. Among the few modern books which have received the hearty imprimatur of the Salvation Army have been the "Revival Lectures" and "Autobiography" of Finney [. . .] he was a theologian after Mrs. Booth's own heart, imparting life and spirituality to subjects which were usually handled in a dull, dry manner, and bringing within the reach of the ordinary mind questions which had usually been abandoned to the consideration of divines. As

---

55. John Wesley, Sermon 43 "The Scripture Way of Salvation," in Wesley, *Sermons*, 1–4, §111, II:67–68.

56. Ibid., §111, II:68.

57. Booth and Booth, *Letters*, 145.

a controversialist, Finney was inimitable, smiting the errors of Calvinism, Antinomianism, and Universalism hip and thigh, with a trenchancy and power that left little to be desired. Mrs. Booth studied his writings perhaps more than those of any other author, and continued to do so, and to recommend them to others, to the end of her life.[58]

According to Booth-Tucker, uppermost in the minds of William and Catherine when they contemplated a proposed integration of the Army into the Church of England was the security of their holiness doctrine as taught by "Finney, Wesley and Fletcher."[59] *The Wesleyan Times* describing revival services conducted by Catherine in Rotherhithe in March 1865 reported, "She has reminded many of our friends more of the manner of a Finney than of many other revivalists."[60] And yet, when their teaching is closely compared it would appear that for Booth-Tucker to say Catherine did not agree with Finney on every point is an understatement. Catherine's theology differs from Finney's not only in its detail but in its structure.

This is hardly surprising when the native soil of their theologies is compared. Finney was not raised as a Presbyterian, but that was the theological context in which he was converted and then nurtured as a young Christian. Finney's apparent Arminianism developed in reaction to that nurturing Calvinism.[61] The primary influence on Charles Finney's theology was Jonathan Edwards.[62] On 20 April 1827, Samuel Aikin wrote to Lyman Beecher describing Finney's discovery of Edwards, and Edwards's civilizing impact on Finney's harsh and rough hewn speech:

> He is greatly reformed, and I apprehend that reading those very quotations which you make from Edwards on Revivals was the means of his reformation. Until he came to my house [. . .] he had never read the book, and here it was frequently in his hands during the revival; also other volumes of that great writer; and he often spoke of them with rapture. Indeed, next to the Bible, no book was read so much [. . .] as Edwards on Revivals and on the Affections.[63]

58. Booth-Tucker, *Catherine Booth*, II:123–24.
59. Ibid., II:428.
60. *The Wesleyan Times*, "Albion Street, Rotherhithe."
61. Cf. Hardman, *Finney*, 45–47.
62. However Hardman is sceptical as to the extent of Finney's insight into Edwards' thought ibid., 120.
63. Beecher, *Autobiography*, 91.

Finney was influenced by Methodist theology and revivalism, but not as directly as he was influenced by the moderated Calvinism of New Divinity scholars such as Lyman Beecher and Nathaniel Taylor.[64] Finney's modified Calvinism shares common elements and emphases with Catherine's Wesleyan doctrine but there are also significant differences. Furthermore some of Finney's adaptations distance his theology not only from Old School Calvinism but also from some distinctive elements of Wesleyan thought. In every instance where Catherine Booth faces a choice about whether to follow Finney and depart from some distinguishing aspect of Wesleyan doctrine, she chooses Wesley over Finney. However, where Finney emphasizes some shared point of doctrine Catherine follows Finney enthusiastically. This is where Finney's influence upon Catherine is most evident, and it is because some of these points are so critical in the presentation of Catherine's doctrine that Finney's influence appears to be so great.

It has already been seen that—in contradistinction to Finney—Catherine holds to a Wesleyan doctrine of the Fall. Catherine follows Wesley in considering that God's prior action in prevenient grace restoring a sufficient measure of free will provides the only possible ground for the human response to the free offer of salvation in repentance and faith. Essential differences between Catherine and Finney are evident again in their understanding of Christian Perfection. For Catherine regeneration, conceived of as union with Christ in the Spirit, is a deep and supernatural act of transformation, the condition which renders sanctification possible.[65] And for Catherine sanctification entails a fresh purifying and new moral empowerment, which is effected by the infilling or baptism of the Holy Spirit.

Finney's quest for entire sanctification took on urgency during his early days in Oberlin. He recalled being led "into a state of great dissatisfaction with my own want of stability in faith and love [. . .] [God] did not suffer me to backslide [. . .] but I often felt myself weak in the presence of temptation."[66]

> I was led earnestly to inquire whether there was not something higher and more enduring than the Christian church was aware of; whether there were not promises, and means provided in the Gospel, for the establishment of Christians in altogether a higher form of Christian life. I had known somewhat of the view of

---

64. Hardman, *Finney*, 23, 123.
65. Booth, *Church & State*, 38.
66. Finney, *Memoirs*, 340.

sanctification entertained by our Methodist brethren. But as their idea of sanctification seemed to me to relate almost altogether to states of the sensibility, I could not receive their teaching. However, I gave myself earnestly to search the Scriptures, and to read whatever came to hand upon the subject, until my mind was satisfied that an altogether higher and more stable form of Christian life was attainable, and was the privilege of all Christians.[67]

Finney first presented his doctrine of Christian Perfection in his *Lectures to Professing Christians*. It is evident immediately that Finney's view of sanctification is grounded in the same set of heterodoxies as his doctrine of salvation. According to Keith Hardman, "all the characteristic traits of his earlier thinking are included," chief among them being the denial of a fallen nature or inherited depravity.[68] According to Finney, Christian Perfection is both attainable and a duty.[69] It is a perfect obedience to the law of God: "It is to love the Lord our God with all our heart and soul and mind and strength and to love our neighbour as ourselves."[70] Finney believes that men and women have a natural ability to obey the law of God. What they seem to lack is the moral ability, which is to say, they are unwilling to obey. But Finney believes this to be a contradiction, in that to be a moral agent, which is definitive of humankind, is to have the ability to choose. He therefore follows Edwards, or so he believes, in declaring, "Strictly speaking, there is no such thing as Moral Inability."[71]

Therefore, all that is required for a person to be entirely sanctified is for them to yield absolutely to God's will.[72] In this moment of submission, "they are filled with all the fullness of God."[73] This is not sanctification by works, according to Finney. In the same way that people are saved by faith in Christ, they are sanctified by faith in Christ.[74] The act of submission is in itself an act of faith, obedience being an indispensable aspect of saving

---

67. Ibid.
68. Hardman, *Finney*, 332.
69. Finney, *Professing Christians*, 252.
70. Ibid., 255.
71. Ibid., 256; For a discussion of Edward's influence on Finney see Guelzo, "An Heir or a Rebel? Charles Grandison Finney and the New England Theology."
72. Finney, *Professing Christians*, 257.
73. Ibid.
74. Ibid., 269.

faith. What is required is "to receive Christ in all his relations,"[75] that is, not only as a justifying but also as a sanctifying Savior:

> They need to receive him AS A KING, to take the throne in their hearts, and rule over them with absolute and perfect control, bringing every faculty and every thought into subjection. The reason why the convert thus falls under the power of temptation, is that he has not submitted his own will to Christ, as a king, in everything, as perfectly as he ought, but is, after all, exercising his own self-will in some particulars.[76]

For Finney, entire sanctification and entire consecration are synonymous. The "simple and primary meaning" of sanctification "is a state of consecration to God".[77] "To sanctify is to set apart to a holy use—to consecrate a thing to the service of God. A state of sanctification is a state of consecration, or a being set apart to the service of God."[78]

By his emphasis on consecration Finney appears to place a heterodox stress on the human rather than the divine action in sanctification. Indeed Keith Hardman accuses Finney of once again standing on Pelagian ground.[79] Hardman considers that Finney's emphasis on the reception of Christ in the power of the Spirit as essential to sanctification is misleading, because Finney believes "Christ and the Holy Spirit can work on human beings only by bringing motives for action to bear on them, or by persuading them to act for their own benefit."[80] The power of the Holy Spirit is for Finney the power of persuasion; it effects no change in a person's nature. Finney can therefore claim, "A state of entire and permanent sanctification is attainable in this life on the ground of natural ability."[81]

In his preface to the revised 1851 edition of the *Lectures on Systematic Theology*, George Redford, the editor, wrote:

> In many respects Mr. Finney's theological and moral system will be found to differ both from the Calvinistic and Arminian. In fact, it is a system of his own, if not in its separate portions, yet in its construction; and as a whole is at least unique and compact; a system

---

75. Ibid., 275.
76. Ibid., 276.
77. Finney, *Views of Sanctification*, 14.
78. Ibid., 14–15.
79. Hardman, *Finney*, 334.
80. Ibid.
81. Finney, *Views of Sanctification*, 68.

Doctrine of Holiness

which the Author has wrought out for himself, with little other aid than what he has derived from the fount itself of heavenly truth, and his own clear and strong perception of the immutable moral principles and laws by which the glorious Author of the universe governs all his intellectual creatures.[82]

Finney's system may not have been Calvinistic or Arminian. It certainly was not Wesleyan. Catherine Booth's debt to Wesley has already been explored. But her emphasis on "entire consecration" would suggest she was also indebted to Finney. In February 1861 Catherine wrote to her parents telling of her longings after holiness and lamenting, "I only want perfect consecration and Christ as my all."[83] In February 1863, Catherine wrote to her mother from Cardiff, "I had a meeting this morning in the Baptist Chapel, at which I spoke with great liberty for an hour. We had thirty or forty up for full consecration. It was a blessed season."[84] In 1879 she wrote of an impending visit to Hartlepool and stated, "This is the place where I held my first consecration services eighteen years ago. There were two hundred and seventy cases in ten days, and grand ones, too."[85] Many other examples could be given. Consecration, spoken of in seemingly Finneyan terms, was evidently part of Catherine Booth's vocabulary. For Catherine, as well as Finney, sanctification can properly be described as "this walk of full consecration and whole-hearted devotedness to God."[86]

It has already been seen, however, that Catherine placed a similar emphasis on consecration in relation to sanctification as she did on repentance in relation to justification, and that for Catherine it was synonymous with the deeper work of repentance that Wesley considered necessary in some way prior to sanctification. Moreover, Catherine did not regard either repentance or consecration as naturally possible, because "man is fallen, and cannot of himself obey even his own enlightened intelligence. There must be an extraneous power brought into the soul."[87] In her scheme, without grace and divine empowerment, repentance and consecration were impossible. Of prevenient grace before repentance, Catherine declared, "Though you are, in one sense, dead in trespasses and sins, yet the Spirit

82. Redford in Finney, *Systematic Theology*, Preface.
83. Booth-Tucker, *Catherine Booth*, I:271.
84. Ibid., I:357.
85. Ibid., II:174.
86. Booth, *Aggressive Christianity*, 149.
87. Booth, *Church & State*, 11.

of God has already breathed upon your soul, and He now waits for the response of your will in order that He may accomplish this great change in you."[88] For Catherine, grace, which effects a deep spiritual union with Christ, creates both the possibility and the duty of holiness.

In his sermon *On Perfection* John Wesley described Christian Perfection in similar if not identical terms: "We cannot show this sanctification in a more excellent way, than by complying with that exhortation of the Apostle: 'I beseech you, brethren, by the mercies of God, that ye present your bodies' (yourselves, your souls and bodies; a part put for the whole, by a common figure of speech) 'a living sacrifice unto God'; to whom ye were consecrated many years ago in baptism. When what was then devoted is actually presented to God, then is the man of God perfect."[89]

The similarities in language between Wesley and Finney disguise semantic differences and create a real possibility of confusion. Is it possible that Catherine was simply not aware of the significant differences between John Wesley's theology and Charles Finney's? Is it possible that her Salvationism was at some fundamental level compromised because it rested on two ultimately incompatible schemes? Is it possible that Catherine's doctrine of sanctification was as a consequence confused and pastorally dangerous at root, and not in the end comprehensible, coherent, or practical?

Evidence to the contrary, that Catherine Booth not only did not agree with Finney on all points but was aware of what those points might be, is found in the publication by the Army in 1926 of an abridgement of Finney's lectures on revival, edited by Booth-Tucker.[90] Booth-Tucker's omissions and editing are significant. According to Booth-Tucker's introduction, General Bramwell Booth, who was enthusiastically introduced to Finney's writings by his mother Catherine, described Finney as a "Presbyterian Salvationist."[91] Bramwell's neat description owns and distances Finney at the same time and sets the context and the bounds within which his writings are to be appreciated by a discerning Salvationist. Although the flavor of Finney's theology survives to some extent, Booth-Tucker either omits or edits ruthlessly references to Finney's particular heterodoxies. For example, the preamble to Finney's lecture on *Be Filled with the Spirit*, which in the original

88. Booth, *Life & Death*, 27.
89. John Wesley, Sermon 76, "On Perfection," §10, in Wesley, *Sermons, 1–4*, III:75–76.
90. Booth-Tucker, *The Successful Soul Winner*
91. Ibid., Introduction.

Doctrine of Holiness

affirms that a person by virtue of natural ability has all the power they need to obey God, and the Holy Spirit is not necessary to enable obedience, is omitted entirely.[92] In his lecture *Directions to Sinners*, Finney complains that sinners often mistakenly think they require a change of heart before they can believe. According to Finney, God requires sinners to love him, to believe the gospel, and to repent; to do these things is to change one's heart and "to make you a new heart, just as God requires."[93] This paragraph in the Army edition is changed to read: "Others think they must wait for God to change their hearts. That is the very thing God is waiting to do as soon as the sinner repents, submits, believes."[94] Finney's meaning has been substantially changed. By 1926, Booth-Tucker and Bramwell Booth were aware of the differences between Finney's theological emphases and their own, and it is reasonable to conclude that Catherine shared this awareness with her son, Bramwell, and son-in-law, Booth-Tucker, not least because in her own writings Catherine demonstrated that these were indeed the points at which she disagreed with Finney.

Finney most boldly expressed his thoughts on this subject in a sermon *Sinners Bound to Change their own Hearts*.[95] Catherine expressed her own different views in an address entitled *New Life*. Catherine wrote, "Your heart is wicked, and therefore it is contrary to its evil nature to love God. Before you can love Him, your wicked heart must be changed. And this is the reason why you cannot enter His Kingdom except ye be born again."[96] Reflecting on what Jesus meant by telling Nicodemus that he had to be born again, Catherine concludes, "Evidently He meant the beginning of true spiritual life to the soul. He intimates that so great a change must take place in our souls as could only be illustrated by the great change which takes place in our bodies at our natural birth."[97]

According to Finney, "Sanctification does not imply any constitutional change, either of soul or body. It consists in the consecration or devotion of the constitutional powers of body and soul to God, and not in any change wrought in the constitution itself."[98] For Finney, in precisely

---

92. Finney, *Lectures on Revivals*, 97.
93. Ibid., 845.
94. Booth-Tucker, *The Successful Soul Winner* 94.
95. Finney, *Sermons on Important Subjects*, 1–42.
96. Booth, *Life & Death*, 25.
97. Ibid., 20.
98. Finney, *Systematic Theology*.

the same way that regeneration does not imply or require a change in human nature, neither does sanctification. But this is not how Catherine understands sanctification. For Catherine, God's scheme of salvation is a scheme of restoration. God's purpose is "to heal me, and make me over again, and restore me to the pattern He intended me to be."[99] Catherine expresses her view with a passion and intensity to equal Finney's but her view could not be more different: "I challenge anybody to disprove by the Bible that he proposes to *restore* me—brain, heart, soul, spirit, body, every fibre of my nature—to restore me perfectly, to conform me wholly to the image of His Son."[100] These differences in their doctrines of regeneration and sanctification suggest that Catherine's pneumatology might be rather more complete than Finney's and play a rather more important role in her doctrine of holiness.

Catherine discovered in Charles Finney's writings a strand of truth which affirmed aspects of the gospel that she thought had too often been denied or simply forgotten. The importance of human action, the significance of the will, the place of the emotions, the duty of sanctification— Catherine found all of these emphasized in Finney, and she emphasized them too in her doctrine of sanctification, in her teaching of the necessity of entire consecration to the will of God, and in her very manner of preaching the possibility of holiness. Catherine appreciated much else that she found in Finney, not least his denial of Calvinistic doctrines such as unconditional election, a limited atonement, irresistible grace, and the perseverance of the saints. However, whenever Finney differed from John Wesley, in turn Catherine differed from Finney and agreed with Wesley. John Wesley affirmed the doctrines of total depravity and the necessity of a new birth in regeneration. John Wesley believed that only prevenient grace created the possibility of a human response in repentance towards God, as a first step in the restoration of humankind to the image and likeness of God. Catherine Booth affirmed and believed in these things too. Charles Finney undoubtedly influenced Catherine Booth's doctrine of holiness, but the effect was to amplify and strengthen aspects of the doctrine that Catherine had already found in Wesley.

---

99. Booth, *Godliness*, 165.
100. Ibid.

Asa Mahan

Asa Mahan is not included in Catherine's list of 1865; however, by her own evidence Mahan had some influence upon her understanding of Christian Perfection. On 3 June 1852, Catherine confided to her journal, "Conscious through the day of increased desires to live altogether for God. Have been reading Mahan on Perfection, the best work on the subject I ever read. My previous views confirmed and some points cleared up. Oh, to enjoy this glorious salvation."[101]

Asa Mahan's book, *Scripture Doctrine of Christian Perfection*, was first published in 1839.[102] Mahan was President of Oberlin College, where Charles Finney was on the faculty. Mahan took to Oberlin "an aching void in his heart."[103] His deep need was met when, having read Adam Clarke describe God's promises of holiness, he experienced a manifestation of the presence of Christ, which he later described as his first baptism of the Holy Spirit.[104] Mahan's experience was contemporaneous with Charles Finney's explorations. As a consequence of their preaching on the subject they were asked by a student in a public meeting, "When we look to Christ for sanctification, what degree of sanctification may we expect from him? May we look to him to be sanctified wholly, or not?"[105] The student earnestly appealed to his beloved instructors, Mahan and Finney, for "a specific answer to this question."[106] The question caused Finney and Mahan to turn to the writings of John Wesley, but Wesley evidently influenced Mahan rather more than Finney. Mahan defines Christian Perfection in Wesleyan terms:

> Christian Perfection [. . .] is the consecration of our whole being to Christ, and the perpetual employment of all our powers in his service. It is the perfect assimilation of our entire character to that of Christ, having at all times, and under all circumstances, the "same mind that was also in Christ Jesus." It is, in the language of Mr. Wesley, "In one view, purity of intention, dedicating all the life to God. It is the giving God all the heart; it is one desire and design ruling all our tempers. It is devoting not a part, but all our soul, body and substance to God. In another view, it is all the mind

---

101. Booth, *Reminiscences*, 41.
102. Mahan, *Christian Perfection*.
103. Madden and Hamilton, *Freedom and Grace*, 59.
104. Ibid., 61.
105. Mahan, *Christian Perfection*, 232.
106. Madden and Hamilton, *Freedom and Grace*, 61.

that was in Christ Jesus, enabling us to walk as he walked. It is the circumcision of the heart from all filthiness, from all inward as well as outward pollution. It is the renewal of the heart in the whole image of God, the full likeness of him that created it. In yet another, it is loving God with all our heart, and our neighbour as ourselves."[107]

At this time Mahan, a New Divinity Presbyterian, taught a modified Calvinism, which was not dissimilar to Finney's, but he was more moderate and scriptural in his claims for natural human ability than Finney and placed greater stress on the role of grace. For example, Mahan acknowledged the promise found in Ezekiel, "a new heart also will I give you, and a new spirit will I put within you,"[108] along with the requirement to "make to yourselves a new heart and a new spirit," and, he wrote, "I suppose, that all such commands are based upon the provisions of divine grace."[109] Mahan continued, "The sinner is not required to 'make himself clean,' or to 'make to himself a new heart,' in the exercise of his unaided powers; but by application to the blood of Christ, 'which cleanseth from all sin.' The grace which purifieth the heart is provided: the fountain, whose waters cleanse from sin, is set open."[110]

Central to Mahan's doctrine was the reception of Christ as a sanctifying as well as a justifying Savior. In his autobiography Mahan expressed this work in the fullest terms: "To fully qualify him for his high calling, Christ Himself, through the Spirit, enters the citadel of the soul, puts to death 'the lusts that war in the members,' 'destroys the body of sin,' sanctifies to Himself 'the whole spirit, and soul, and body,' and then, under the power of the Spirit, sends the believer into the world, as the Father sent Him into the world."[111]

Although Mahan's work was pleasing to Catherine, confirming her in her views, informing her on other questions, and reinforcing the vocabulary of holiness she would one day use herself, it did not help her to enter into an experience of holiness, nor did she place Mahan on the list of authorities she quoted to Morgan in defense of her doctrine.

107. Mahan, *Christian Perfection*, 16–17; Mahan is citing Wesley, "Plain Account," §27,444.
108. Mahan, *Christian Perfection*, 32.
109. Ibid., 113.
110. Ibid.
111. Mahan, *Autobiography*, 313.

Doctrine of Holiness

In 1870 Asa Mahan's book *The Baptism of the Holy Ghost* was published.[112] Mahan observed, "In no era of church history, since the primitive age passed away, has the mission and 'promise of the Spirit' occupied so much attention among all classes of believers as now."[113] In response to this interest, which he believed was a glorious sign of the times, Mahan presented a doctrine of sanctification in pentecostal terms, identifying the "Baptism of the Holy Ghost" with entire sanctification, and making the narrative of Acts chapter 2 normative for the reception of the blessing.

Donald Dayton believes the difference between Mahan's two most popular books illustrates a paradigm shift in the teaching of the Holiness Movement that took place through the nineteenth century.[114] According to Dayton, the adoption of "Pentecostal" and "baptism of the Holy Ghost" language by holiness teachers involved much more than a shift in terminology. In Dayton's view, when "Christian Perfection" becomes the "baptism of the Holy Ghost," there is necessarily a major theological transformation.[115]

For Dayton, this transformation includes a radical shift from Christocentrism to an emphasis on the Holy Spirit; an emphasis on the power of the Spirit over the fruit of the Spirit, which raises the leading question of the nature of the gifts of the Spirit; an intensification of expectations of the millennium; a shift from the goal and nature of the holy life towards the event in which the change takes place; and an emphasis on the baptism of the Spirit as a "conscious" event, which leads towards the questions of evidence such as speaking in tongues.

Dayton's view that the pneumatological aspects of sanctification grew in interest through the middle years of the century is supported by Mahan himself.[116] However, Madden and Hamilton argue, "There was no new direction to Mahan's thought; there was simply a new dimension added to the old one, and he continued to defend all strands, old and new, throughout his career."[117] They draw attention to Mahan's familiarity with both the phrase and its usage at the time of his earlier work.[118]

---

112. Mahan, *The Baptism of the Holy Ghost*.
113. Ibid., 15.
114. Dayton, "Mahan," 60.
115. Ibid., 64.
116. Mahan, *The Baptism of the Holy Ghost*, 15.
117. Madden and Hamilton, *Freedom and Grace*, 190.
118. Ibid.

Catherine Booth

The same shift can be observed in the writings of Catherine Booth, at least to some extent, but as with Mahan, Catherine was using pentecostal language well before the 1870s. That she was doing so in a consistent manner long before the publication of Mahan's book precludes the possibility that she was influenced directly by Mahan. After Mahan moved to England in 1873 his books and his teaching became catalytic elements in the progress and development of the Holiness Movement. Mahan participated in the Oxford Convention held from 29 August to 7 September 1874, and again in the Brighton Convention held from 29 May to 7 June 1875. The room in which he presented his teaching on the baptism of the Holy Ghost was "always crowded."[119] The Booths shared with Mahan a network of mutual friends and acquaintances including Admiral Edmund Gardiner Fishbourne, who was deeply influenced by Mahan.[120] Fishbourne, a "wealthy and eccentric" "gentleman-evangelist," was appointed as one of the referees for The Christian Mission in 1868,[121] and was also a close friend and adviser of Robert Pearsall Smith in 1875.[122] Fishbourne was a well connected friend. *The Illustrated London News* of April 1858 recorded his participation in a fund-raising dinner attended by over 150 gentlemen, including "the Duke of Beaufort, Viscount Lismore, Viscount Maldon, Lord Rokeby, Lord Grey de Wilton, Lord Cosmo Russell,"[123] and a number of MPs, Sheriffs, and other distinguished guests.[124] Mahan became an "ardent supporter" of The Salvation Army.[125] In retirement in Eastbourne he worshipped at Longstone Hall, with a holiness congregation "loosely associated" with the Army.[126] When Mahan died on 4 April 1889 Colonel Reece attended the funeral, representing General Booth.[127]

Asa Mahan influenced Catherine Booth's doctrine of holiness in that he supported and reinforced her in many of her views. However, there is no evidence that Mahan inspired any innovations or departures from her essentially Wesleyan doctrine.

119. Ibid., 200.
120. Ibid., 199.
121. Sandall, Wiggins, and Coutts, *History*, I:251.
122. Kent, *Holding the Fort*, 147; Bebbington, *Evangelicalism*, 160.
123. *Illustrated London News*, "The London Homeopathic Hospital."
124. Ibid.
125. Madden and Hamilton, *Freedom and Grace*, 199.
126. Ibid., 219.
127. Ibid., 220.

Thomas Upham

The inclusion of Thomas Cogwell Upham as the first person on Catherine's list in her letter to Morgan is intriguing and unexpected. An address of Upham's, *The Kingdom of God is within You*, was published in the July 1870 edition of *The Christian Mission Magazine* and this also suggests that Upham was genuinely valued by the Booths.[128] In his address Upham quotes from the writings of St Augustine, François Fenelon, and Madame Guyon. Upham has been described by David Bundy as "an enigmatic figure in the historiography of the nineteenth century."[129]

Born in 1799, Thomas Upham became Professor of Moral and Mental Philosophy at Bowdoin College, Maine, USA, in 1825, after serving briefly as a Congregational minister.[130] In philosophy he was strongly influenced by the Scottish Common Sense Realism of Thomas Reid.[131] In matters of faith he was deeply affected by Phoebe Palmer. In December 1839 Upham was the first man to attend one of Palmer's "Tuesday Meetings for the Promotion of Holiness."[132] Asa Mahan and William Boardman also attended Palmer's meetings. In February 1840 Upham entered into an experience of entire sanctification.[133] David Bundy claims Upham's "personal experience became paradigmatic for the expectations of religious transformation" in the Tuesday meetings.[134]

Darius Salter describes Upham as "the progenitor of the ecumenicity created by the American search for entire sanctification."[135] Upham's writings were marked by an intense spirituality which derived from his studies of seventeenth and eighteenth century European mysticism.[136] His biography of Madame Guyon "received widespread publicity and review."[137] Melvin Dieter affirms that "he permanently infused into the holiness tradition in America a deep sense of experiential kinship with such Catholic

---

128. Upham, *The Christian Mission Magazine*, "The Kingdom of God is Within You."
129. Bundy, "Thomas Upham," 23.
130. Ibid., 25.
131. Ibid., 26.
132. Ibid., 28.
133. Ibid.
134. Ibid., 32.
135. Salter, *Spirit and Intellect*, 94.
136. Ibid., 95.
137. Dieter, *The Holiness Revival*, 47.

perfectionists."[138] Upham's teaching emphasised "the importance of the inner, contemplative, devotional life of holiness."[139]

In his teaching of the possibility of "divine union," which led him to speak of "mere sanctification," in comparison with this higher more exalted state, Upham appeared to some of his friends, as well as to commentators such as Darius Salter, to have moved in a dangerously heterodox direction. Catherine would never have followed Upham in this particular move.[140] In Catherine's thought "divine union" is a synonym for regeneration.[141] Harriet Beecher Stowe, who wrote her anti-slavery novel *Uncle Tom's Cabin* while staying with Phebe and Thomas Upham, believed Upham's emphasis on spirituality restored a much needed balance to the activism of their times.[142]

To the extent that Catherine was influenced by Upham it might be said that he added philosophical, historical, ecumenical, and devotional depth to her doctrine of sanctification. In Thomas Upham's writings, Catherine Booth discovered views regarding free will, the place of the moral law, and the nature of faith which she had embraced and which she had found in other writers, from Joseph Butler through to Charles Finney.

Robert Pearsall Smith and the Keswick Movement

Catherine also claimed that her views on holiness were essentially one with those she called "the holiness people of America." William Boardman and Phoebe Palmer, whose influence upon Catherine has already been examined, might be considered to be sufficiently significant and typical exemplars. Boardman's protégés, Robert and Hannah Pearsall Smith, would not have been known to Catherine in 1865, but John Kent ascribed William and Catherine Booth's "comparative breakthrough" to the excitement which Robert Pearsall Smith stirred up around holiness teaching.[143] With the event of the Brighton Convention in 1875, according to Kent, Robert Pearsall Smith gave "the Salvation Army a much needed stimulant for growth."[144] However, it is a matter of fact that the Army's breakthrough and extraordinary growth began in 1878 and followed on the change of

138. Ibid.
139. Ibid.
140. Salter, *Spirit and Intellect*, 102.
141. Booth, *Aggressive Christianity*, 85.
142. Dieter, *The Holiness Revival*, 47.
143. Kent, *Holding the Fort*, 329.
144. Ibid., 341.

Doctrine of Holiness

name. There was no breakthrough in growth or change in the Booths' emphasis on holiness following from the Brighton Convention. Norman Murdoch claims, "Between the time Caughey and the Palmers left England in the late 1860s, and the time Robert and Hannah Pearsall Smith came from Philadelphia in 1875 [sic], the Booths had slighted holiness teaching."[145] Murdoch offers no evidence for this singular assertion. It is contradicted by the fact that the Christian Mission began to hold special meetings for the promotion of holiness in 1870. In the first edition of the *East London Evangelist* published in October 1868, the editors William and Catherine Booth declared, "We also propose devoting a large portion of our space to the topic of Personal Holiness. The importance of this theme nor tongue nor pen can possibly overrate. Practical Godliness is the great want of this age [. . .] on the standard we propose to rear aloft, we hope to write in large and legible characters—HOLINESS TO THE LORD."[146]

That the Booths were firm in their holiness convictions prior to the Brighton Convention is evident from an account contained in Catherine's reminiscences.[147] In March 1874 the Whitechapel Hall was officially reopened following renovations. Catherine took part in the celebrations along with Brewin Grant,[148] Henry Varley,[149] and Robert Pearsall Smith. It would seem that because the Booths were known for their public stand on the doctrine of holiness Smith invited William for lunch. According to Catherine, they accepted the invitation so that William could test Smith's teaching and identify whether he might be a suitable ally. William's questions are not listed in Catherine's notes but Smith's responses are. Smith told William that "he believed what John Wesley preached and John Fletcher defended. William said that he thought it was not so understood."[150] Smith said he realized his theology was opposed to the Booths' and apparently suggested their shared experience of sanctification was more important than any theological differences. He illustrated this with an ill conceived story about tomato jam. Smith gave a friend who did not like tomatoes some tomato jam. His friend liked it, because he did not know what he was

---

145. Murdoch, *Origins of The Salvation Army*, 68.

146. *The East London Evangelist*, "Our Purpose."

147. Booth, *Reminiscences*, 149.

148. An Anglican clergyman popularly known for engaging in public apologetic debate.

149. A Plymouth Brethren evangelist with a national reputation.

150. Booth, *Reminiscences*, 149.

eating. Afterwards Smith told him he had been eating tomato jam. Smith said so it is with holiness. "William explained this to me," said Catherine, adding, "We both regretted it."[151] This is a tantalizingly incomplete section of the reminiscences. There appears to have been another meeting with Smith at which Catherine was present.[152] Catherine writes, "He [Smith] breakfasted with us. *What I said to him. My prediction.*"[153] The prediction is not included in the notes. It seems unlikely that it was positive. Catherine also notes that William attended the convention at Brighton, recognized its vast opportunity, and indicates that they were aware of "*the sudden collapse that followed.*"[154] The account is interesting for the light it sheds on the Booths' view of Pearsall Smith, for what it reveals of the Booths' connection to the wider Holiness Movement in 1874, and also for the evidence that their hard test for the authenticity of holiness teaching was that it conformed to the doctrine of Wesley and Fletcher.[155] The Booths were unlikely to have been impressed by Smith's testimony. Hannah Pearsall Smith described her husband's melodramatic experience:

> Suddenly from head to foot he had been shaken by what seemed like a magnetic thrill of heavenly delight, and floods of glory seemed to pour through him, soul and body, with the inward assurance that this was the longed-for Baptism of the Holy Spirit. The whole world seemed transformed to him, every leaf and blade of grass quivered with exquisite color, and heaven seemed to open out before him as a present blissful possession. Everybody looked beautiful to him, for he seemed to see the Divine Spirit within each one without regard to their outward seemings [sic]. This ecstasy lasted for several weeks.[156]

The experience of Hannah, when she received holiness teaching "calmly, and with intellectual delight," would have seemed more sensible, even comprehensible, to Catherine, than Robert's ecstatic experience.[157] The

---

151. Ibid.

152. Hannah Smith came to Europe a year after Robert. Pollock, *The Keswick Story*, 13.

153. Booth, *Reminiscences*, 149.

154. Ibid; After the Brighton Congress, faced with charges of sexual impropriety, Pearsall Smith resigned from all public work, cf. Roberts, "Evangelicalism and Scandal in Victorian England."

155. Booth, *Reminiscences*, 149.

156. Smith, *A Spiritual Autobiography*, 288–89.

157. Ibid., 289.

Booths published Hannah's address *The Joy of Obedience* in the November 1875 edition of their magazine.[158] On the subject of enthusiasm and the place of feelings in religion, Catherine wrote, "Whole hearted, thorough, out and out surrender to God [. . .] that, with or without feeling is the right thing, and *that* is the secret of our power [. . .] we have glorious feelings as the outcome; but the feeling is not the religion—the feeling is not the holiness."[159]

There were strong connections between the organizers of the Brighton Convention and the Booths. An association through Edmund Gardner Fishbourne has been noted. The *Christian Mission Magazine* reported: "The Higher Christian Life Conference" held at Oxford in 1874, "for the avowed purpose of waiting upon God for that baptism of divine power which would enable [Christians] to reach and maintain a higher standard of holiness;"[160] but no report of the Brighton Convention of 1875 appeared in the magazine. The issue in which a report might have appeared was dominated by news of the Mission's own Annual Conference, which would be sufficient reason for the omission. What William made of the Brighton Convention is not recorded. In so far as the occasion marked the emergence of the Keswick movement it marked a bifurcation of the Holiness Movement in Britain, with Keswick on one side and the Booths and The Salvation Army, together with those who would associate with the Wesleyan holiness Southport Convention, for example, on the other. A letter from Catherine to a friend, which Booth-Tucker dates to 1886, identifies one aspect of the cause of separation, although it also incidentally records the continuance of conversation across the wider Holiness Movement. Catherine's friend had espoused the "glorious truth" as Catherine understood it, and was opposed to the alternative view of their other "friends."[161] Catherine identified the source of their "friends'" error as wrongly "separating the consequences from the cause."[162] She spoke of an argument she had with Hanmer William Webb-Peploe, an Anglican clergyman who was one of the founding fathers of Keswick: "I had a long argument with Webb-Peploe on this same point. He admitted the indwelling of Christ, but he would not admit the consequent cleansing and power. As you say, this of course makes an excuse

---

158. Smith, *The Christian Mission Magazine*, "The Joy of Obedience."
159. Booth, *Godliness*, 124.
160. *The Christian Mission Magazine*, "The Higher Christian Life Conference."
161. Booth-Tucker, *Catherine Booth*, II:400.
162. Ibid.

for sin. It seems as though they could not detach the idea of creature merit from the state of being cleansed, whereas it is only while in this experience that we realise the entire nothingness of self and self-efforts."[163]

Ian Randall describes how, in 1895, Webb-Peploe "reaffirmed Keswick's distinctive doctrine of sanctification. The power of the Holy Spirit could counteract sin, he taught, but not eradicate it in the lives of believers."[164] The outraged reaction of Richard Reader Harris, barrister, and founder of the Pentecostal League of Prayer, was to offer "£100 to anyone who could prove from Scripture that sin must of necessity remain in the believer."[165]

But there were other differences besides those of doctrine. It is hardly controversial to suggest that the Keswick movement primarily directed its attention to the "churched" while the Booths were characteristically focused on the needs of the "unchurched" masses. Keswick was a somewhat upper-middle-class movement, while the Booths were gripped by the need of the working classes and the underclass. Bebbington suggests that "the setting was essential to the [Keswick] experience," and as evidence offers a report of the 1895 conference which claims that Keswick's lovely panorama, when gazed upon with sanctified and receptive eyes, has a cleansing and beautifying effect upon the soul.[166] The many thousands who regularly attended Christian Mission and then Salvation Army Friday night holiness meetings had to discover the romance of holiness in rather different surroundings. Numbered among the buildings William Booth rented in the early days of the Christian Mission were a stable, a carpenter's shop, a skittle alley, and a shed in Poplar, "between which and some stables and pig-sties there was only a wooden partition. The stench which oozed through the open cracks was enough to have poisoned us all."[167] According to Pamela Walker, Bebbington's identification of the Holiness Movement in England with romanticism is a consequence of his concentration on its upper-middle class advocates: "While Bebbington's interpretation may capture the spirit of those holiness advocates, when this doctrine took root and flourished in the urban working-class context of the Salvation Army, its meaning changed. For Salvationists, holiness required intense struggle with their own sinful nature and against the powerful enticements to sin that surrounded them.

163. Ibid.
164. Randall, "The Pentecostal League of Prayer," 185.
165. Ibid.
166. Bebbington, *Evangelicalism*, 168.
167. Booth-Tucker, *Catherine Booth*, I:424.

Doctrine of Holiness

That encounter with the Holy Spirit did not end in peace and repose. It made the convert into an evangelist ready to do battle with evil."[168]

J. C. Pollock records a casual remark overheard after the 1889 Keswick Convention, "People get their teaching at the Tent, but their blessing at The Salvation Army."[169] The throwaway comment, though unfair, indicates, perhaps, how the different emphases of Keswick and the Army were perceived, at least in the popular imagination. It also suggests that the Army continued to play a catalytic role within the wider Holiness Movement through the 1880s.

John Fletcher

It is possible that Catherine Booth's understanding of the work of the Holy Spirit in entire sanctification may derive more from John Fletcher than from John Wesley. The earliest suggestion that William and Catherine thought in pentecostal categories appears in a letter from William to Catherine written in March 1853. William is defending Methodism and revivalism: "I say, let me have the passions aroused and they will move the will. The church is full of light, full of knowledge and yet she is comparatively speaking inactive. We want action.[170] We want effort. We want deep feeling. We want a sense of the reality of eternal things, such a sense as shall move us to combined effort to save souls. Oh, for a breeze of the Holy Spirit to come upon the churches and lead us to combined effort to save souls."[171]

The first examples of Catherine using pentecostal language appear in her letters to William in July 1853.[172] Through the summer of 1853, when William and Catherine explored the possibility of William becoming a minister in the Methodist New Connexion, they read the rules and constitution of the New Connexion. In the doctrines of the New Connexion they would have read, "We believe [. . .] that it is our privilege to be fully sanctified in the name of our Lord Jesus Christ, and by the Spirit of our God."[173] This was not the beginning of the connection in Catherine's thought between

---

168. Walker, *Pulling the Devil's Kingdom Down*, 75.

169. Pollock, *The Keswick Story*, 77.

170. William has almost certainly used *want* in the sense of *lack*, i.e. "we *lack* action," etc., which abates the stridency just a little.

171. Booth and Booth, *Letters*, 82.

172. Ibid., 131.

173. Baggaly, *MNC Minutes*, 222. The New Connexion doctrines, edited and amplified, were adopted by The Salvation Army

sanctification and the baptism of the Holy Spirit, however. Catherine wrote to William in December 1853, "Tell [God] your will and desire is to be holy, leaving him to choose your employment and position, and ask him for the inward baptism of the Holy Ghost, that what you already desire may become the actual delight of your life. This was Fletcher's religion, and the main spring of Caughey's success."[174]

William and Catherine Booth therefore provide supporting evidence for Laurence Wood's contention that connecting entire sanctification with the baptism of the Holy Spirit was commonplace in Wesleyan circles before the full emergence of the nineteenth-century Holiness Movement, and that the application of pentecostal metaphors and imagery to Christian Perfection did not begin with Charles Finney, Phoebe Palmer or Asa Mahan, but with John Fletcher. Catherine Booth studied Fletcher's *Checks to Antinomianism* intensively, and there she would have discovered his association of Christian Perfection with being baptized or filled with the Holy Spirit.[175] In 1847 Catherine read the biography of Mary Bosanquet Fletcher, which included the following text from one of Mary Fletcher's sermons: "And will he approve lazy, dull seekers of that spiritual Canaan, that 'Baptism of the Spirit' to which every believer is expressly called? We often talk of the time when 'righteousness is to overspread the earth,' but this millennium must overspread our own heart, if we would see the face of God with joy. For the very end of our creation is, that we may become 'the habitation of God through the Spirit.'"[176]

By this time Catherine was almost certainly familiar with the journal of Miss Roe, better known by her married name Hester Ann Rogers.[177] In the September 1869 edition of the *East London Evangelist*, Catherine published extracts from Miss Roe's journal, which recorded an interview with John Fletcher in which Fletcher told Miss Roe that "all who enjoy perfect love" magnify God, "by speaking unto men, with the new heart of love and the new tongue of praise; as on the day of Pentecost."[178]

Catherine was familiar with the life and work of many other Methodists of an earlier generation, among them William Bramwell, Adam Clarke,

---

174. Booth and Booth, *Letters*, 186.

175. Bramwell-Booth, *Catherine Booth*, 28,326; Cf. Fletcher, *Works*, II:656.

176. Moore, *The Life of Mrs. Mary Fletcher*, 434.

177. Evidenced by Catherine's misspelling of Mrs. Rowe as Mrs. Roe in her diary of 1847.

178. Rogers, *The East London Evangelist*, "Perfect Love."

Doctrine of Holiness

and Richard Watson, who made the same association.[179] It is not necessary to agree with the most controversial aspect of Wood's thesis, that John Wesley himself was so persuaded by John Fletcher's reasoning that he too came to think of Christian Perfection in pentecostal terms, in order to conclude that Catherine Booth made this connection by virtue of her roots in Methodism and not through her later reading of Phoebe Palmer, Asa Mahan, or even William Arthur.

Randy Maddox took issue with some aspects of an earlier presentation of Wood's thesis. Maddox did not disagree that Wood had demonstrated a continuity of thought from Fletcher into nineteenth century Methodism, but presented in a response to Wood three models of the way in which Pentecost and Christian Perfection are connected in the writings of Wesley and Fletcher.[180] The first model Maddox calls the *Dispensations of Grace* model. Under this model Pentecost is thought of as "the decisive moment in salvation history when this greater gracious gift was poured out on the church, becoming available to all thereafter."[181] Under the terms of this model all Christians owe such spiritual life as they enjoy to the regenerating Spirit. It is not necessary that they were at the first Pentecost, or that they experience a personal Pentecost. Maddox finds this model in Wesley long before he met Fletcher.[182] The second model Maddox calls the *Pristine Church* model. This model advances the further polemical claim that "the disciples present at the first Pentecost were so open and responsive to the Spirit that they *unanimously* and *immediately* were transformed into *full* holiness of heart and life."[183] The purpose of this claim is to emphasize the fallen, feeble nature of the church subsequently, even though the same resources are available. Again Maddox believes this model, found in Wesley, does not derive from Fletcher. The third model Maddox calls the *Personal Recapitulation* model. Maddox regards this model as deriving from Fletcher and following from his view that the sequential dispensations of outpourings of grace in salvation history are recapitulated in the life of the believer, so as to "include a personal post-justification experience of the 'baptism of the Spirit.'"[184] Maddox was not persuaded by Wood's thesis in its earlier form that Wesley accepted the implications of this third model.

179. Wood, *Pentecost in early Methodism*, 174, 77, 90, 217, 84.
180. Maddox, "Wesley's Understanding of Christian Perfection," 79.
181. Ibid., 79–80.
182. Ibid., 80.
183. Ibid.
184. Ibid..

There is a qualitative difference between Maddox's three models. The first and last have rather more of the status of theological propositions, while the second is more of a polemical tool. All three models are found in the addresses of Catherine Booth. Catherine fully accepts the *Dispensations of Grace* model. That Catherine fully recognized the Holy Spirit's role in regeneration, in the gift of new life, and that she thought of the present age as the dispensation of the Spirit, has been noted. Catherine made frequent polemical use of the *Pristine Church* model. In the introduction to her address on *Aggressive Christianity*, Catherine draws a comparison between the lively expectations of the church's success a person might have if they could somehow blot from their minds "all knowledge of the history of Christianity, from the time of this Inauguration Service—from that Pentecostal Baptism" to the present day and their sad astonishment when they realized how little had been achieved by the church despite all that was promised and provided for at Pentecost.[185] Catherine compares the "gigantic and momentous results" achieved by the first generation of Christians with the relative failure of Christians to transform the world of the present day.[186] Catherine was not unhappy with the implications of the *Personal Recapitulation* model. In her address in *Aggressive Christianity* entitled *Filled with the Spirit*, Catherine declares, "It is as much the privilege of the youngest and weakest believer here to be filled with the Spirit;" and she continues, "This Pentecost is offered to all believers. It comes or it would come, in the experience of every believer, if he would have it. God wants you to have it. God calls you to it. Jesus Christ has bought it for you, and you may have it, and live in its power as much as these apostles did, if you will—every one of you."[187]

These differing ways of conceiving of the connection between Pentecost and Christian Perfection are naturally linked together in Catherine's thought, particularly the first and last. First, Pentecost is that singular and necessarily unrepeatable historical event when the Holy Spirit was poured out upon the disciples of Jesus in fulfillment of the prophecy of Joel. This Pentecost inaugurated a new dispensation, a new age of the Spirit.[188] As Wood argues, and Maddox accepts, Wesley and Fletcher were at one in this view. Howard Snyder summarizes Wesley's position: "Pentecostal grace, the

---

185. Booth, *Aggressive Christianity*, 1.
186. Ibid., 2.
187. Ibid., 149.
188. Booth, *Church & State*, 78–79.

Doctrine of Holiness

grace of God poured out by the Holy Spirit at Pentecost and, as Wesley says, 'Not on the day of Pentecost only,' but all down through history, is now our common inheritance. Now, by the Spirit, God pours out the grace that restores the image of God, gives the mind of Christ, enables Christians to 'walk as [Jesus] walked.'"[189] Second, Catherine believes, following Fletcher, precisely because the current dispensation is the age of the Spirit, it is the privilege of every believer to be filled with the Holy Spirit. This infilling of the Spirit is an indispensable necessity, the means by which the believer is enabled to live a holy life.

Donald Dayton identified a number of consequences of what he considered to be a paradigm shift in the teaching of the Holiness Movement through the nineteenth century.[190] However, the development of Catherine Booth's doctrine of sanctification calls the notion of a rapid paradigm shift into question, supporting a more gradualist interpretation. Although there is evidence of some development when the form and frequency of her pentecostal language and imagery is compared across the years, from Catherine's diary of 1847, through her correspondence of the 1850s and 1860s, to her addresses of the 1870s and 1880s, there is equally a strong continuity. Catherine's first sermon, preached on Whit Sunday 1861 was titled *Be Filled with the Spirit*. It was a theme she frequently preached on, and an address with the same title is one of the addresses delivered in the 1880s included in *Aggressive Christianity*. Catherine's use of pentecostal language derives from her Methodist background in general, and from John Fletcher in particular, and her understanding and use of such language and metaphor is closely aligned with Fletcher's.

CONCLUSION

An attempt has been made over two chapters of this book to identify the major influences upon Catherine Booth's doctrine of holiness, and the impact of these influences upon her thought. It has been seen that although Phoebe Palmer and William Boardman helped Catherine to enter into an experience of holiness, the form and content of her teaching remained Wesleyan not only in broad shape but also in detail. In particular Phoebe Palmer's innovations of the "shorter way" and "naked faith in the naked word" were not taken up by Catherine. The same pattern holds true for

---

189. Snyder, "The Babylonian Captivity of Wesleyan Theology," 14.
190. Dayton, "Mahan," 64–67.

those other writers and preachers with whom Catherine claimed an affinity. Catherine's strong emphasis on the importance of entire consecration was influenced by Finney and also to some extent by Mahan, but Catherine knowingly avoided Finney's heterodoxies, following Wesley whenever Finney departed from a broadly Wesleyan line. In so far as Catherine's application of pentecostal language went further than John Wesley's, the most influential figure was not Phoebe Palmer, nor Asa Mahan, nor even William Arthur, but John Fletcher, with whose writings Catherine was deeply familiar, and whose ideas were also mediated to her through Mary Bosanquet Fletcher, Hester Ann Rogers, and other preachers and writers in the Methodist tradition. In the same way that Finney's influence caused Catherine to emphasize, rather more than Wesley, certain features of her generally Wesleyan scheme, Thomas Upham deepened Catherine's understanding, bringing her to a more ecumenical appreciation of the doctrine, and affirming the devotional elements of sanctification, though not to the exclusion of the ethical. Catherine had no desire to be innovative in her doctrine. She judged others by their adherence to the teaching of Wesley and Fletcher. Consequently Catherine harbored a suspicion of those holiness teachers, such as Pearsall Smith, who may have emphasized the personal and experiential aspects of entire sanctification to the detriment of the ethical, relational and social character of the doctrine.

The unity and affinity Catherine claimed with Upham, Wesley, Fletcher, and Finney rests on the commonality of a number of distinctive themes. Although in contrast to Wesley and Fletcher, Upham and Finney were rooted in Calvinistic Presbyterianism, albeit in its moderated New Divinity form, for all of these writers a strong appreciation of the moral law, as love of God and humankind, lies close to the heart of their doctrine. Consequently their view of sanctification is at root ethical and relational as well as deeply devotional. Further, they each stress, against antinomianism, that human choice and action have a role to play in sanctification. Equally, each affirms that sanctification is God's work, impossible humanly speaking and only achievable through the full work of Christ and the Holy Spirit. In so far as Finney departs from this, Catherine departs from Finney. Each affirms that it is the privilege of all believers to be entirely sanctified, and that this privilege is the glory of the gospel. Finally, in all four, the social character of holiness results in a strong eschatological hope, the expectation that the outworking of the doctrine will lead to the triumph of the gospel in human history and a manifestation of the kingdom of God in human society.

An attempt has been made over three chapters of this book to outline and describe the underlying theology which gives form, consistency and coherence to the exhortations and writings of Catherine Booth. Her preferred manner of interpreting the atonement has been identified and its sources discussed, as has the shape of her soteriology, in the form of a comprehensive and identifiably Wesleyan *ordo salutis*; and finally the development of her doctrine of entire sanctification has been charted, an outline of that doctrine has been presented and its formative influences discussed. Catherine Booth's soteriology has been seen to be consistent and coherent, the bedrock on which her various exhortations and writings rest; or, to change metaphors, the skeletal structure they enflesh. A number of distinctive themes run consistently through Catherine Booth's doctrine of entire sanctification. However, these themes are present throughout her soteriology, and consequently it becomes possible to identify the inherent logic of Catherine Booth's Salvationism. Four major themes form the anchor points of Catherine's soteriology and are bound together in a logical progression.

The logic of Catherine Booth's Salvationism begins with the proposition that God is the loving Creator and Governor of all things. God governs the universe by means of natural law, but also by means of the moral law, which is enshrined in the great commandment, as love of God and humankind, a principle of disinterested benevolence. The moral law is present in the form of conscience in every human heart.

Secondly, for the world to be as God intended, people must be brought to obey the moral law. This cannot be achieved by force, as love requires a free response of the will. People must be brought to choose, to desire, to will to obey, and to be given the power to do so. This is to restore people to their original state, the image and likeness of God; that is, to Christian Perfection, which is perfect love, for God and humankind. This salvation or restoration is achieved, humanly speaking, by soul saving; that is by addressing conscience, an advocate for the moral law in every human heart. Soul saving is an active partnership with God the Holy Spirit who alone convicts people of their sins.

Through the atonement, thirdly, sins are forgiven, and through Pentecost people gain power over sin, the ability to fulfill the moral law, to love God and love people. Full salvation is achieved by "Blood and Fire." The significance of "Blood and Fire" goes beyond the identification of the particular work of Christ and the Spirit in the economy of salvation; the conjunction is of equal importance. The atonement justifies and restores, and justification is inseparable from the new birth in the Spirit. Holiness is the reception of Christ as a perfect Savior from sin. Salvationism rests on a complete and interlocking Christology and pneumatology.

Finally, this doctrine of full salvation is charged with hope for the world, for as people come to love God and to love one another as God loves them, the reign of God, the reign of universal benevolence and the moral law, begins. When this happens everywhere it signals the triumph of the gospel and the millennium begins.

There may be little that is unique or original in the logic of Catherine Booth's Salvationism—the ideas of her antecedents are apparent in every proposition—and yet the logic is not Wesley's, not Fletcher's, not Finney's, but Catherine's. The force of this logic has consequences, not least for ecclesiology. This is not a subjectivist or individualistic soteriology but one that is ethical and relational to the core with far-reaching consequences for the mission of the church in the world in the forms of its evangelism and engagement with society. Reflecting on the potential social impact of a Wesleyan doctrine of holiness, Mildred Bangs Wynkoop records the regretful comments of H. Orton Wiley, who interprets some remarks of "Dr. Dale, the theologian" to mean:

> That [John Wesley's] doctrine of perfect love and full devotement to God should have carried life to ever higher levels, and permeated like leaven the whole social structure. Instead of shrinking from politics, it should have purified them. It should have become creative in art and literature instead of distrusting these fields of endeavour. It should have permeated business and social life, instead of becoming content to merely attach a divine sanction to virtues already recognised. A religion flaming with divine love should have called into full play all the heroism and devotion of life.[191]

Catherine Booth's Salvationism embraces a full vision of God's grace and power, unlimited in its capacity to save and restore fallen humanity. Out of this vision emerges hope for the world and humankind, universal and personal, relational and individual, a hope for the restoration of harmony to women and men in all their relations—with God, within their own divided selves, with one another, and with the wider creation in all its diversity and glory. It is a vision of salvation for the whole wide world. It may not be so strange or paradoxical after all that the ecclesial form which Catherine's vision took shook the world.

191. Wynkoop, "Theological Roots," 81.

FIVE

The Church

Any enquiry into Catherine Booth's doctrine of the church encounters a deep paradox. The Salvation Army has always been a highly visible form of Christianity, if not the church, distinctive in its evangelistic expression, with its street meetings, brass bands, flags, and drums. Equally, from the beginning, the Army has been prominent in the public square, pressing for social reform, and responding to human need, not only in critical times of war, earthquake, famine and flood, but also as forming a vital part of the social infrastructure. This ecclesial experiment can be seen as William and Catherine Booth's great achievement and was recognized as such by contemporary commentators such as W. T. Stead, who wrote, "Of those who, in the last quarter of the nineteenth century have most notably influenced the religious life of England, there are few who can be compared with Mrs. Booth. [. . .] Her work was not the mere carrying on of an existing organization. She and her husband built up out of recruits gathered in the highways and byways of the land, what is to all intents and purposes a vast world-wide church."[1]

And yet, despite the evidence that this ecclesial experiment was the logical outcome of Catherine Booth's Salvationism, directly and through her influence on William, her ecclesiological legacy would appear to have been a lack of clarity and a deal of uncertainty concerning the fundamental nature and being of the movement she founded; and in its third century Salvationists often struggle to articulate the ecclesial identity of the organization to which they belong.

---

1. Stead, *Mrs. Booth*, 199.

Catherine Booth

VISIBLE CHURCH—INVISIBLE ECCLESIOLOGY?

In 1987 The Salvation Army published *Community in Mission*, a "Salvationist Ecclesiology," written by an American Salvation Army officer Philip Needham. General Eva Burrows wrote in the foreword, "For the first century of its history The Salvation Army was too busily involved in its evangelistic mission to pause and investigate, at any depth, exactly what its form and nature might be within the church universal. Content to respond to the directives of the Holy Spirit, we concentrated on our work in the world rather than on our role in the church. Such questions, however, need to be explored and have taken a significant place in Salvationist thinking in recent years."[2]

The fact that it took 122 years for the Army to publish a single volume devoted to ecclesiology appears to support General Burrows's conclusions and endorse the view of Roger Green, who writes, "While we acknowledge the theological awareness of William and Catherine Booth and others around them in many areas, we recognize too that they had a weak ecclesiology, and we still pay the price for that weakness even today."[3] Green argues William's ecclesiology was weak for two reasons. First, because of his postmillennial theology, which, Green argues, "does not comport well with a strong ecclesiology."[4] For Green, contemporary Salvationists cannot sustain such an eschatological hope, and it has no place in a contemporary ecclesiology. Second, Green claims that following the abortive conversations with the Church of England in the 1880s regarding a merger of the Army with that church, William chose to distance the Army from the institutional church. Furthermore, Green believes the Army's ecclesiology has failed to keep up with the Army's historical evolution from a sect to a church, sociologically understood.[5]

Addressing the first International Theology and Ethics Symposium, held in May 2001 in Canada, General John Larsson, then Chief of the Staff,[6]

2. Needham, *Community in Mission*.

3. Green, "Facing history," 29.

4 Ibid.

5. Cf. Roland Robertson in Wilson, *Patterns of Sectarianism*. Responding to this notion, Andrew Eason has argued that the Army has manifested the characteristics of both sect and church typologies throughout its history. Eason, "The Salvation Army in Late-Victorian Britain," 3–27.; Harold Hill has made a comprehensive and detailed exploration of every facet of this transition as it applies to officership. Hill, *Leadership in The Salvation Army*.

6. The title of the Army's international second-in-command.

made a similar claim, and gave a lead for future ecclesiological explorations: "For all of his genius, William Booth never tackled in his thinking, writing and speaking, the matter of Salvation Army ecclesiology. He might even have spluttered at the mere mention of such a phrase! To him—or at least to part of his mind—it was a contradiction in terms. But we now know and accept that we are an Army in transition—from a Movement to a church."[7]

In 2008 the Army published *The Salvation Army in the Body of Christ*, a brief ecclesiological statement that might be thought to represent the conclusion of this process of transition and the realization of a strong, coherent ecclesiology. Indeed the statement claimed, "Salvationism has moved on [...] from being a para-church evangelistic revival movement [...] to being a Christian church with a permanent mission to the unsaved and the marginalised."[8] Article 8 of the amplified statement declared, "WE BELIEVE that The Salvation Army is an international Christian church in permanent mission to the unconverted, and is an integral part of the Body of Christ like other Christian churches, and that the Army's local corps are local congregations like the local congregations of other Christian churches."[9]

However, it is noteworthy, first, that the declaration was made in the amplified rather than the summary statement, which simply said the Army "belongs to and is an expression of the Body of Christ on earth, the Church universal, and is a Christian denomination in permanent mission to the unconverted, called into and sustained in being by God";[10] and second, that the statement introduced the uncomfortable juxtaposition "denominational church,"[11] while equating the terms "denomination" and "church" without recognizing the circular logic thereby implied; and third, that no theological justification was offered for the application of the term to a denomination beyond that of common usage.

Session 9 of the companion study guide, which discusses Article 8, is titled "A permanent mission to the unconverted,"[12] which is how General Albert Orsborn, who declined to call the Army a church, described the

---

7. Larsson, "Salvationist Theology," 22.

8. The Salvation Army, *The Salvation Army in the Body of Christ: An Ecclesiological Statement*, 10–11.

9. Ibid., 10.

10. Ibid., 1.

11. Ibid., 9.

12. The Salvation Army, *The Salvation Army in the Body of Christ: Study Guide*, 53.

Army.[13] It was while Orsborn was General that the Army became a founding member of the World Council of Churches, which suggests that Orsborn's reluctance was not due to any lack of ecclesiological self-confidence or thoughtless anti-ecclesiasticism. Writing in *The Officer*, Orsborn confirmed the Army's claim "that we have within ourselves a corporate spiritual life, with its own authority, able to provide for our people all the services and rights exercised by a church towards its members,"[14] and continued:

> We are almost universally recognized as a religious denomination by governments [. . .] for convenience in designating our officers, they group us with the churches. That is as far as we wish to go in being known as a church. We are, and wish to remain, a movement for the revival of religion, a permanent mission to the unconverted, one of the world's greatest missionary societies; but not an establishment, not a sect, not a church, except that we are a part of the body of Christ called "The Church Militant" and we shall be there, by his grace, with "The Church Triumphant."[15]

What is still required therefore is an exploration of the Army's foundational ecclesiology which takes seriously its founders' reluctance to call The Salvation Army a church, a reluctance evident even in the Army's current international mission statement, which states, "The Salvation Army, an international movement, is an evangelical part of the universal Christian Church." This enquiry should bear in mind Howard Snyder's persuasive argument that "every ecclesial group [. . .] has an actual ecclesiology, whether implicit or explicit, articulated or unarticulated. Further, there is no theological or biblical reason to assume that an articulated ecclesiology is necessarily more coherent than or superior to an implicit one."[16] Equally, strong and weak are not necessarily synonymous with good and bad, in matters of ecclesiology.

---

13. Wiseman, *The Officer*, "Are We a Church?"
14. Orsborn, *The Officer*, "The World Council of Churches."
15. Ibid.
16. Howard Snyder, "The Marks of Evangelical Ecclesiology," in Stackhouse, *Evangelical Ecclesiology*, 81.

The Church

THE DEVELOPMENT OF CATHERINE BOOTH'S SALVATIONIST ECCLESIOLOGY

Catherine's interest in ecclesiology can be traced to the time when, forced to end her schooling by illness, she read the church histories of Mosheim and Neander. Although they were not contemporaries, Mosheim and Neander compete for the title "the father of modern Church history."[17]

Johann Lorenz Mosheim was born on 9 October 1693. His landmark work was *An Ecclesiastical History Ancient and Modern* of 1755. John Wesley published an abridged edition in 1781. Wesley found support for his primitivism in Mosheim and also used his working outline of church history, an outline which encouraged revivalism.[18] Mosheim divided the history of the church into centuries; within each century he divided the material into the external and internal history of the church. By the external history of the church Mosheim meant "all the occurrences and changes which have visibly befallen this sacred society."[19] By the internal history of Christianity Mosheim meant those "changes to which the Church in every age has been exposed, in regard to its distinguishing characteristics as a religious society."[20] This internal history Mosheim dealt with under five categories: the state of literature and science; church officers and government; religion and theology; rites and ceremonies; and lastly, heresies and schisms.[21] Thus Mosheim acknowledged the changing character of the church over the centuries as it responded to the pressures of religion, philosophy, and culture by resistance or assimilation. These changes, for Mosheim, whether for good or ill, were to a church and a faith which in their initial state were simple and pristine.[22] Mosheim encouraged Catherine Booth's primitivism and her ideas relating to the adaptation of measures.

Johann August Wilhelm Neander was born David Mendel, to Jewish parents, on 17 January 1789. He converted to Christianity in his youth, and his experience of the power of the gospel was such that "he wanted to present the history of Christ's Church as a living witness to this divine power, a witness that should speak, teach, admonish, and warn through all the

---

17. Buss, "Mosheim & Neander," 51.
18. Ibid., 55.
19. Mosheim and Maclaine, *Ecclesiastical History*, I:xv.
20. Ibid., I:xvi.
21. Buss, "Mosheim & Neander," 68.
22. Mosheim and Maclaine, *Ecclesiastical History*, I:88.

events involved in the development of the Christian Church."[23] In the introduction to his *General History of the Christian Religion and Church* Neander wrote, "It shall be our purpose to trace, from the small mustard-grain, through the course of the past centuries, lying open for our inspection, the growth of that mighty tree, which is destined to overshadow the earth, and under the branches of which all its people are to find a safe habitation."[24]

The separation in Neander's title between religion and church is accompanied by a division in his thought between the visible and the invisible church. These divisions represent distinctions rather than oppositions. Christianity as a religion is not limited to its manifestation as the visible church; and the visible church is always an imperfect realization of the invisible church.[25] Thus the organizations and the structures of the visible church are *adiaphora* to Neander.[26]

In the spring of 1854 Catherine wrote to William providing an outline for a sermon in which she summarized what she had learned from her readings in Christian history.[27]

> After the establishment of Christianity, when the pure and glorious light of the gospel shone on the primitive churches, *unfaithfulness* to the spiritual simplicity of Christ's doctrines caused the gathering of that cloud of error and superstition, which though at first not larger than a man's hand, gradually spread until it overwhelmed Christendom with its horrors and entombed the human mind in worse than Egyptian darkness. [. . .] By degrees the darkness became more and more dense, until at length we find the "lively oracles" chained to the altars of cathedrals. God's faithful witnesses mourned in dungeons or consigned to the stake, those earthly pandemoniums called inquisitions plying their hellish tortures in the name of the Lamb of God, and men calling themselves Christians, propagating their soul-destroying heresies by the aid of fire and sword.[28]

Catherine's interpretation of the "fall" of the church after the early period also points to the influence of John Wesley.[29]

23. Buss, "Mosheim & Neander," 135.
24. Neander, *General History*, I:1.
25. Buss, "Mosheim & Neander," 139.
26. Ibid., 140.
27. Booth and Booth, *Letters*, 138, 268.
28. Ibid., 217.
29. Collins, *Holy Love*, 240–41.

Kenneth Collins has identified the logical force of Wesley's ecclesiology as deriving from his soteriology: "The realization of such animating and life-changing graces as justification and regeneration, the movement from possibility to actualization, presupposes a community of saints that not only bears the gospel story through history but also forms the primary context for the instantiation of holy love in the newly transformed."[30] This deep connection between soteriology and ecclesiology is evident also in Catherine's writings and in the name *The Salvation Army*. The notion that the church is constituted by God's action in salvation and only secondarily by human action contextualizes the voluntarism identified with much evangelical ecclesiology. The priority of grace in Catherine Booth's soteriology, for which she is indebted to John Wesley, translates to a similar priority in ecclesiology and sets in perspective what might otherwise be viewed as the extreme voluntarism of The Salvation Army.

In his sermon *Of the Church*, published in 1786,[31] John Wesley notes the ambiguity of the word "church"; however, only as "a congregation or body of people united together in the service of God" will he allow its use in his sermon.[32] It is used properly, that is biblically, when applied to a gathering of two or three, to a family, to a congregation gathered together from across a town, or to the multiple congregations found in a large city or province. The plural "churches" may be applied to the dispersed congregations of a region; and in the singular it may mean "all the Christian congregations that are upon the face of the earth."[33] From a consideration of Paul's letter to the Ephesians Wesley provides "a clear unexceptionable answer to that question, 'What is the Church?'":[34] "The catholic or universal Church is, all the persons in the universe whom God hath so called out of the world as to entitle them to the preceding character; as to be 'one body,' united by 'one spirit'; having 'one faith, one hope, one baptism; one God and Father of all, who is above all, and through all, and in them all.'"[35]

---

30. Ibid., 237.

31. The date is critical following as it does on three events in 1784, the Deed of Declaration which established Methodist chapels under the jurisdiction of the annual conference; Wesley's ordination of two priests for the American colonies; and his revision of the Book of Common Prayer for North America. Rainey, "John Wesley's Ecclesiology," 421–22.

32. John Wesley, Sermon 74, "Of the Church," in Wesley, *Sermons*, 1–4, §7, III:46.

33. Ibid., §5, III:48.

34. Ibid., §14, III:50.

35. Ibid.

From this definition Wesley claims that any part of the universal church which inhabits any one kingdom or nation may be called a national church, as, for instance, the Church of England. A particular church may consist of any number of members, but whether "larger or smaller, the same idea is to be preserved. They are one body, and have one Spirit, one Lord, one hope, one faith, one baptism, one God and Father of all."[36]

Critically Wesley claims, "This account is exactly agreeable to the nineteenth Article of our Church, the Church of England."[37] However, equally critically, Wesley adds, "Only the Article includes a little more than the Apostle has expressed."[38] Quoting the Article, "The visible Church of Christ is a congregation of faithful men, in which the pure word of God is preached, and the sacraments be duly administered," Wesley notes that in the Latin translation "a congregational of faithful men" was rendered as *coetus credentium*, "a congregation of believers"; this Wesley takes to mean "men endued with *living faith*," and asserts that this interpretation keeps faith with the apostle's account.[39] For Wesley the Article speaks of the church universal and particular, and allows the question, "What is the Church of England?" to be answered: "It is that part, those members, of the universal church who are inhabitants of England. The Church of England is, that 'body' of men in England, in whom 'there is one Spirit, one hope, one Lord, one faith'; which have 'one baptism,' and 'one God and Father of all.' This and this alone is the Church of England, according to the doctrine of the Apostle."[40]

Wesley then considers that "remarkable addition" to the definition, "in which the pure word of God is preached, and the sacraments be duly administered";[41] to which he makes an equally remarkable response:

> I will not undertake to defend the accuracy of this definition. I dare not exclude from the church catholic all those congregations in which any unscriptural doctrines, which cannot be affirmed to be "the pure word of God," are sometimes, yea, frequently preached; neither all those congregations, in which the sacraments are not "duly administered." [. . .] Whoever they are that have "one Spirit,

---

36. Ibid.
37. Ibid., §16, III:51.
38. Ibid.
39. Ibid.
40. Ibid., §17, III:52.
41. Ibid., §18, III:52.

one hope, one Lord, one faith, one God and Father of all," I can easily bear with their holding wrong opinions, yea, and superstitious modes of worship. Nor would I, on these accounts, scruple still to include them within the pale of the catholic church; neither would I have any objection to receive them, if they desired it, as members of the Church of England.[42]

Wesley's view of the church is thus catholic in the sense that it is inclusive. Wesley refuses to exclude women and men with faith in Christ on account of their heterodoxy or heteropraxy, and includes them as individuals and as congregations within the church. Although Wesley specifically includes members of the Roman Catholic Church, his logic equally applies to dissenting congregations. The Article refers to the visible church, but Wesley's interpretation requires that a church which includes the faithful and regenerate, but excludes the faithless and unregenerate, must to some extent also be invisible. Collins identifies within the various levels of Wesley's definition of the church a "tension or conjunction" between the church as an institution and the church as a "living organism, the body of Christ."[43] That there is a tension rather than a separation suggests that for Wesley, although the institutional character of the church—so necessary to its visibility—is of its *esse*, the form it takes is of its *bene esse*. In his sermon *Catholic Spirit* Wesley expressed this view clearly, allowing for freedom in worship, government, the means of grace, and the sacraments.

> I dare not, therefore, presume to impose my mode of worship on any other. I believe it is truly primitive and apostolical: but my belief is no rule for another. I ask not, therefore, of him with whom I would unite in love, Are you of my church, of my congregation? Do you receive the same form of church government, and allow the same church officers, with me? [. . .] Nay, I ask not of you (as clear as I am in my own mind), whether you allow baptism and the Lord's supper at all. Let all these things stand by: we will talk of them, if need be, at a more convenient season, my only question at present is this, "Is thine heart right, as my heart is with thy heart?"[44]

For the Anglican and catholic Wesley, the church embraces Quakers as well as Anglicans, Methodists, Independents, and Roman Catholics. It is not that matters of order are *adiaphora* for Wesley, they are of the *bene esse*

42. Ibid., §19, III:52.
43. Collins, *Holy Love*, 240.
44. John Wesley, Sermon 39, "Catholic Spirit," in Wesley, *Sermons*, 1–4, §11, II:86–87.

of the church and therefore open to reform; indeed, for Wesley the purpose of Methodism "was not to form any new sect; but to reform the nation, particularly the Church, and to spread scriptural holiness over the land."[45]

If it is true, as Albert Outler has contended, that Wesley interpreted Article XIX "more comprehensively than its authors had ever intended,"[46] it might also be contended that Wesley's successors in Methodism interpreted Wesley with equal license, as Wesley insisted throughout his life that if the Methodists leave the Church of England, not only would he, Wesley, leave them, but God would leave them too.[47] Wesley's ecclesiological legacy has therefore not always been appreciated within Methodism, its problematic nature being apparent in Albert Outler's saying: "To the question, Is there a Wesleyan ecclesiology? The answer 'yes' is too much, the answer 'no' too little."[48] The ecclesial polity Wesley bequeathed to English Methodism reflected his ecclesiological convictions in so far as it only provided for Methodism's continuance as a reform movement within the Church of England. The orders and structures Wesley initiated provided for a reformation of the national church into a believers' church which respected the doctrine of the priesthood of all believers.[49] Wesley did not provide for the foundation of a Methodist Church of England. It is not surprising, therefore, that the development of Methodism's independent ecclesial identity strained its polity beyond breaking point. Catherine and William Booth were caught up in the consequent turbulence, which helped to form the creatively chaotic ecclesial context in which their movement was born.

Catherine's warm sympathy for Congregationalism was formed by her frequent attendance at Stockwell New Chapel and her regard (as noted earlier) for the ministry of David Thomas. Catherine copied his sermons and sent them to William, encouraged William to read his books, and proposed him as a model of preaching and ministerial excellence. David Thomas was born in Pembrokeshire in 1813 and came to Stockwell in 1844. He remained there until 1877, building a congregation consisting of "an ever widening circle of influential minds drawn from the political, legal,

---

45. John Wesley, "Minutes of Several Conversations", Q.3, in Wesley, *The Works of John Wesley*, VIII:299.

46. Wesley, *Sermons*, 1-4, III:74.

47. Rainey, "John Wesley's Ecclesiology," 432.

48. Outler, "Do Methodists Have a Doctrine of the Church?," 11.

49. David Rainey asserts that the Societies, Bands and Classes of Methodism were "consistent with the Protestant view of the priesthood of all believers." Rainey, "John Wesley's Ecclesiology," 434.

educational, and learned worlds, who gathered from far and near, attracted by the originality of his thinking and the freshness and charm of his commanding personality."[50] The Congregational Union associated Thomas with "the steady and unbroken progress in England" of what was termed "a religious evolution of which he himself was a conspicuous factor."[51] Thomas was a founder of the University of Wales, Aberystwyth, and a pioneer of *The Dial* newspaper. Nearly one hundred volumes of his writings were published during his lifetime and later published as his collected works. Thomas even inspired an extended piece of popular satirical invective, *The World of Cant*.[52] In *The Homilist*, an encyclopedic, scholarly compendium of support for preachers, which ran to forty volumes with an aggregate circulation of about 120,000 copies, all unattributed copy was by the editor, Thomas.[53] He had a significant, and so far largely unrecognized, influence on Catherine's development, although it was noted in his biography, "In the formation of the character of Mrs. Catherine Booth, the 'mother of the Salvation Army', he had a considerable share."[54] On 16 June 1855 David Thomas married William and Catherine. As General of The Salvation Army, William preached at Stockwell New Chapel. One of the members of the congregation was Wilson Carlile, who later became the founder of the Church Army.[55]

It is uncertain when Catherine first began to attend Stockwell Congregational Chapel.[56] Her enthusiasm for Congregationalism suggests it was some time before the summer of 1852. Booth-Tucker says she "frequently attended" the Congregational Chapel.[57] Catherine Bramwell-Booth claims, "The Reform Chapel was at rather a distance, and walking there was often beyond Catherine's strength, especially in bad weather."[58] However, Stockwell Congregational Chapel was no closer to 7 Russell Street, the

---

50. The Congregational Union, *Congregational Year Book* 1896, 237.

51. Ibid.

52. Bebbington, *Evangelicalism*, 130.

53. The Congregational Union, *Congregational Year Book* 1896, 293; Catherine read The Homilist, Booth and Booth, *Letters*, 293.

54. Stephen, *Dictionary of National Biography*, LVI:177–78.

55. Thomas, *Urijah Thomas*, 441.

56. Catherine Bramwell Booth has her hearing Thomas in July 1847. Bramwell-Booth, *Catherine Booth*, 45. Bennett shows this is a mistake. Booth, *Reminiscences*, 26.

57. Booth-Tucker, *Catherine Booth*, I:99.

58. Bramwell-Booth, *Catherine Booth*, 49.

Mumford home. The letters record William and Catherine's dissatisfaction with the reformers' services. In January 1853 William wrote, "I found the cause very low at Boston, but, after all has been said against them that can, I would rather worship with them than at Binfield House."[59] Catherine so distanced herself from the reformers in Brixton that William issued Catherine and Mrs. Mumford's quarterly tickets of membership from his chapel in Spalding.[60]

From Thomas, Catherine learned the persuasive power of reasoned argument, together with the importance of sound scholarship and exegesis lightly worn; and also a liberality, ecumenicity, and independence of spirit. Thomas was described as "a Broad Churchman," in "close theological sympathy" with other energetic, culturally engaged leaders of the church in Britain and America of a generous and evangelical spirit.[61] In *The Core of Creeds*, a publication of addresses given at the re-opening of Stockwell New Chapel, Thomas declared, "We have erected this sanctuary for the propagation of this idea. We this day dedicate it—not to the mummeries of any priesthood,—not to the perpetuity of religious form,—not to the eternal iteration of hoary creeds and worn out dogmas,—not to the purposes of sect or party,—but to the proclamation of the fact in its widest aspects, as well as particular relations, that there is a Redeeming God for fallen humanity—ONE MIGHTY TO SAVE."[62]

The different polities of Methodism and Congregationalism sparked a lively debate between William and Catherine in their correspondence. Writing to William in February 1853 Catherine expressed her dislike of the demands the circuit system placed upon its preachers and her preference for the Congregational system: "I like the independent system of a pastorate more and more. After all, it is the way to cultivate practical preaching and all other is mere cant."[63] One evening in March 1853, David Thomas visited the Mumford home after Catherine was taken ill during the Sunday morning service. They spoke of William's application to Cotton End. Thomas said, "I don't swallow their Calvinism. It has been left behind years ago." He added that "Calvinism was not a necessary condition," and "many

---

59. Booth and Booth, *Letters*, 48.
60. Ibid., 36.
61. Schaff, Jackson, and Herzog, *Encyclopedia of Living Divines*, 216.
62. Thomas, *The Core of Creeds*, 90.
63. Booth and Booth, *Letters*, 62.

of [Congregationalism's] best and most useful men were opposed to it."[64] Thomas assured Catherine and her mother that they would be welcomed as members of his church, and "expressed his detestation of the division of the Christian Church into sects and parties and his desire to recognise Christians only as such."[65] In her letter to William describing the visit, Catherine continued, "I sometimes think if a stranger were to read some of your letters, he would think you were waging war, either in your own mind or with me, between Independency and Methodism by your frequent contrasting of the two systems. But there is no need to do so with me. I have formed my own estimate of them both. I wish I could see the advantages peculiar to the two united in one. Perhaps the day is not far distant."[66]

Catherine appreciated the fervor, spirituality, and revivalism of Methodism. However, at the same time she regretted the disconnection between the preacher and his people, and the shallowness of the preaching, inherent, she believed, in the circuit system. Catherine also believed its polity encouraged authoritarianism, if not despotism. At Stockwell New Chapel Catherine experienced a successful model of Congregationalism with a dynamic minister supported by a congregation who lived out the priesthood of all believers and believed in the primacy of the local congregation as an expression of the visible church. Through March–April 1853, the debate waxed hot and strong. On the afternoon of 7 April, Catherine wrote to William, "I know your prejudices are strong and perhaps Methodism is the best field for you."[67] However, Catherine was not opposed to Methodism, and William was not blind to its faults. They were both equally dissatisfied with the Conference and the Reformers. Catherine wrote to William on 5 May:

> Let the hateful names of conference and reform sink into oblivion for a few days, and let us forget all religious distinctions. I wish from my heart we had done with them. [. . .] I truly feel for you in your struggles. Nevertheless I am thoroughly satisfied as to the rottenness of the foundations of conferencism and of its ultimate overthrow. All such systems will be overturned before real, undefiled Christianity prevails in the world. The very essence of Christ's religion is antagonistic to worldly polling and outward uniformity, and men may try and scheme and labour for ages to mould it after

---

64. Ibid., 83.
65. Ibid.
66. Ibid.
67. Ibid., 92.

their fashions and it will remain after all the simple, pure, beautiful thing which Christ left it.[68]

As a consequence of this dissatisfaction with the Reformers, through the summer of 1853 William and Catherine considered the possibility of William becoming a minister in the Methodist New Connexion. The Connexion, Methodism's first offshoot, "had its origin in a pure desire to introduce a more liberal system of church polity into Methodism, and to supply its people with every scriptural ordinance by the hands of their own ministers."[69] William and Catherine read the biography of the New Connexion's founder, Alexander Kilham, and studied its rules and constitution.[70] Kilham, born on 10 July 1762 at Epworth, and ordained in 1792, shared with many of Methodism's preachers grave concerns over matters of church polity. John Grundell summarizes their dissatisfaction:

> During the life of Mr. Wesley the Methodist mode of government was much disapproved, by many sensible people in the societies, who beheld in it, and in other parts of the high church policy connected with it, the latent but certain seeds of future strife and contention, which they foretold would finally cause a division in the societies: but as it was thought by some that this singular mode of government would end with Mr. Wesley's life, every attempt to alter it was considered as premature while he lived; thus their aversion to it was smothered in Mr. Wesley's last days, and they bore it as a temporary evil.[71]

Through a series of anonymous pamphlets, Kilham "argued that Methodists were *de facto* dissenters, and their preachers qualified to administer all Christian ordinances."[72] He eventually published a booklet entitled *The Progress of Liberty, amongst the people called Methodists*, which was a plea for freedom of conscience.[73] Kilham proposed: "Members should determine their own class leaders, the circuit meeting should approve any preacher proposed for the itinerary, circuits should appoint lay delegates to district meetings, district meetings should appoint lay delegates to the Conference of Preachers where these lay delegates, along with preachers,

68. Ibid., 102–3.
69. Baggaly, *MNC Minutes*, 11.
70. Booth and Booth, *Letters*, 111.
71. Kilham, *Life*, xvii–xviii.
72. Stephen, *Dictionary of National Biography*, XXXI:102.
73. Kilham, *Progress of Liberty*, 18–19.

would have jurisdiction over both spiritual and temporal affairs."[74] Consequently, Kilham was tried and expelled by Conference in 1796, and in 1797 together with his supporters, he formed The Methodist New Connexion.[75] The Connexion's second Annual Conference declared, "It was not from an affectation of singularity that determined us to proceed in supporting the rights and liberties of the people. [. . .] It was a conviction arising from scripture that all the members of Christ's body are one; and that the various officers of it should act by the general approbation and appointment of the people."[76]

Dr William Cooke, theologian and historian of the movement, set out the Connexion's core ecclesiological insight: the church of God is "a congregation of God's people, united together for Christian fellowship, the worship of God, and the celebration of religious ordinances."[77] The Connexion's polity, though not simply read out of the New Testament, was nevertheless an attempt to replicate the values and patterns of the apostolic community. Part III (on polity) of *A Digest of The Minutes, Institutions, Polity, etc. of the Methodist New Connexion* was introduced by a quotation from John Angell James, one of the founders of the Congregational Union in 1832, and the Evangelical Alliance in 1846.

> It will probably be contended by some, that the New Testament has laid down no specific form of Church Government, and that where we are left without a guide, it is useless to enquire if we are following his directions. If by this it be meant to say, that the Lord Jesus Christ has left us no apostolic precept or example, which is either directory for our practice, or obligatory upon our conscience, in the formation of Christian societies, nothing can be more erroneous. [. . .] It is true we shall search the New Testament in vain for either precedent or practice, which will support all the usages of our Churches, any otherwise than as those usages are deduced from the spirit and bearing of *general principles*.[78]

Catherine longed for a polity which reflected the simplicity of the New Testament church. "That system is false, be what it may, which needs

---

74. Shepherd, "From New Connexion Methodist," 91–107.

75. Stephen, *Dictionary of National Biography*, XXXI:102.

76. Minutes of the Methodist New Connexion, 1798, cited, Shepherd, "From New Connexion Methodist," 91–107.

77. Cooke, *A Catechism*, 72.

78. Baggaly, *MNC Minutes*, 175.

or engenders ponderous volumes of rules, minutes, laws and regulations, Model and Poll deeds. Jesus Christ will not acknowledge such weapons in his service."[79] She declared to William, "You know I am a thorough reformer."[80] She questioned, "Where is Christianity embodied? Oh, to help in some small degree to revive and enforce a practical, Christ-like Christianity. It is this alone which must save the world."[81]

THE SALVATION ARMY'S RELATIONSHIP TO THE CHURCH

In 1882 the Lower House of Convocation of the Church of England petitioned the House of Bishops to issue some instruction regarding the church's attitude towards The Salvation Army. A committee was formed to consider the question with Edward White Benson, Bishop of Truro, as chairman. Benson wrote to William Booth proposing talks regarding the relationship of the Army and the church and the possibility of some form of union. The churchmen who took part in the negotiations with Benson, who later became Archbishop of Canterbury, were Canon Brooke Foss Westcott of Westminster, afterwards Bishop of Durham; Joseph Barber Lightfoot, Bishop of Durham; Canon George Howard Wilkinson, who became Bishop of Truro and afterwards Bishop of St Andrews; and Randall Thomas Davidson, Chaplain to the Archbishop of Canterbury and the Dean of Windsor, a favorite of Queen Victoria and later Archbishop of Canterbury.[82] William Booth was willing "for the two organizations to run side by side, like banks of a river, with bridges thrown across over which the members could mutually pass and repass."[83]

The negotiations foundered over polity, although St John Ervine identifies the "temperamental antipathy" between Bramwell Booth and Randall Davidson, both forceful, opinionated, and relatively youthful as the "fundamental fact on which the discussion collapsed."[84] Far from disrupting the Army participants' interest in ecclesiological matters, as Roger Green implies,[85] the discussions caused Bramwell at least to reflect on them deeply,

79. Booth and Booth, *Letters*, 111.
80. Ibid., 149.
81. Ibid., 172.
82. Booth, *Echoes and Memories*.
83. Booth-Tucker, *Catherine Booth*, II:427.
84. Ervine, *God's Soldier*, I:609.
85. Green, "Facing history," 29.

The Church

and in *Echoes and Memories*, after describing the negotiations, he articulated his understanding of the Army's relationship to the church. Bramwell began by claiming that the Church of England was no more the church than the church at Jerusalem or Rome or the church of the Lutherans, Puritans, Calvinists, or Presbyterians.[86] He continued, it was the intention of Jesus to "gather out of the world a people composed of His true believing followers"; this necessitated the formation of a body or society "distinct from the world in life, in purpose, and in interests."[87] The consequence is the emergence of "a visible society—the Society spoken of in the Bible as the Church or Congregation."[88] Bramwell argued, "But as to the outward form which this Society should take, Jesus Christ gave no recorded instruction. It is impossible to believe, if He had intended any particular constitution or form of government to be essential to this Society—His Kingdom on earth—that He would not have left explicit directions with regard to it. Whereas on the whole matter He is entirely silent."[89] Just as there is only one Israel, so there is only one church, and Bramwell declared, "Of this, the Great Church of the Living God, we claim, and have ever claimed, that we of The Salvation Army are an integral part and element."[90] Bramwell saw in the Army's forms and methods many parallels with the apostolic church. He concluded with a carefully worded ecclesiological statement:

> We believe then that our Lord Jesus Christ has called us into His Church of the Redeemed, that our call has not been by man or the will of man, but by the Holy Spirit of God; that our Salvation is from Him, not by ceremonies or sacraments or ordinances of this period, or that, but by the pardoning life giving work of our Divine Saviour. We believe also that our system for extending the knowledge and power of His gospel, and of nurturing and governing the believing people gathered into our ranks, is as truly and fully in harmony with the spirit set forth and the principles laid down by Jesus Christ and His Apostles as those which have been adopted by our brethren of other times or of other folds.[91]

---

86. Booth, *Echoes and Memories*, 64.
87. Ibid.
88. Ibid., 64–65.
89. Ibid., 65.
90. Ibid.
91. Ibid., 67.

It is notable that in this statement Bramwell does not claim that the Army is "a church." Indeed, he claims, "It was not a Church after the fashion of the Churches but an Army that was aimed at."[92] He quotes George Scott Railton, "We are an Army of Soldiers of Christ, seeking no Church status, avoiding as we would the plague every denominational rut, in order perpetually to reach more and more of those who lie outside every Church boundary."[93] Railton was in turn echoing William Booth who declared, "It was not my intention to create another sect. [. . .] We are not a church. We are an Army, an army of salvation."[94]

Catherine Booth considers the Army's relationship to the church in *The Salvation Army in relation to the Church and State*. However, this book contains no definitive statement of the Army's ecclesial identity. There is no explicit claim that the Army is a church, or that it is part of the church, or that Salvation Army corps are churches; equally, they are not denied. However, the following statements can be supported from Catherine's writings in so far as they touch upon the doctrine of the church.

First, when Catherine refers to the church she is speaking of the worldwide community of the people of God, a community that transcends sectarian boundaries.[95] Bramwell declared, "We claim, and have ever claimed," that "we of The Salvation Army are an integral part and element" of "the Great Church of the Living God."[96] Bramwell implicitly included William and Catherine in this statement, and Catherine's use of the word "church" is consistent with Bramwell's claim that Salvationists are a part of the one true church composed of all believing followers of Christ. It is inconceivable, given the influence of Wesley and Methodism, David Thomas and Congregationalism, and Kilham and the reform movements in Methodism, that she might have thought otherwise.

Second, Catherine uses the plural form "the churches" as a synonym for the singular, in a meditated way,[97] in congruence with Wesley as well as her Congregationalist tendencies.[98] It can therefore be said that when Catherine refers to the churches, she is speaking of the diverse local

---

92. Ibid., 48.
93. Ibid; Cf. Railton, *Heathen England*, 143–44.
94. Nicol, *General Booth*, 85.
95. Booth, *Practical Religion*, 197; Booth, *Godliness*, 148.
96. Booth, *Echoes and Memories*, 65.
97. Booth, *Church & State*, 27–44.
98. Cf. Volf, *After our likeness*, 154–58.

congregations of all denominations. Once again, given her influences, it is inconceivable that Catherine did not think of local congregations of Salvationists as expressions of the visible church of Christ, although when she speaks for instance of "a further difference between us and the majority of the churches," the inferences are admittedly ambiguous.[99] When speaking of Christian Mission stations or Salvation Army corps, Catherine slipped easily into the language of Methodism referring to these local congregations as societies, thereby equating them. One of the few changes that William and Catherine made as they imported the polity of the Methodist New Connexion into the Christian Mission was to establish their local societies independently, instead of in circuits. Catherine saw in the Army the fresh expression of a primitive first generation Christianity: local congregations of believers mobilized in the mission of Christ, nothing less than a restoration of the New Testament church. The very choice of the name "corps" for the local congregation, the primary battlefield formation of any Army, indicates their priority as an expression of the church in Catherine and William's thought.[100]

Finally, Catherine's preferred expression for denominations is "sects," and in her view they are neither a theological nor practical necessity. Denominations are responsible for perpetuating ancient divisions, maintaining useless modes and measures, and sustaining worthless traditions. They are no more than historical forms of the church valid for a season; their failure to recognize their temporal relativity is harmful to the cause of Christ. "God," Catherine writes, "cares very little about our sectarian differences and divisions."[101] The Army has no ambition to become a sect and no intention to become another divisive "ism" within the church. The modes and measures employed by The Salvation Army belong not to the *esse* of the church but its *bene esse*. Consequently they are open to renewal and reform. They were intended as a provisional expression of an abiding New Testament principle—the adaptation of measures; the neglect of this principle was the primary cause of sectarianism and division within the church.[102]

---

99. Booth, *Church & State*, 38.

100. Harold Hill attributes this to the founders' haziness "about the precise application of military terms"; which is to miss the point—they used the terms as they wished. Hill, *Leadership in The Salvation Army*, 80.

101. Booth, *Church & State*, 29.

102. Booth, *Popular Christianity*, 95.

Why were the Army's founders so loath to call the Army a church? First, for Catherine, it would have been a denial of her inherited ecclesiology which believed in the one church made visible in the many local congregations of God's people. This ecclesiology had given birth in the past to unions and connexions and societies, and now to an Army. Second, it would have imported an undesirable ambiguity into the Army's ecclesial identity, with no agreement on what it meant to call a sect or denomination, a church; for Anglican and Roman Catholic believers their church was not "*a* church" but "*the* church." Third, it was unnecessary and dangerous: unnecessary, because "church" is far from being the only appropriate or biblical word that describes the people of God; dangerous, because it risked legitimizing sectarian divisions and establishing denominationalism and a privatized view of the church as the Army's practical ecclesiology, something which was particularly dangerous given the Army's authority structures. However, the Army's founders never thought the Army was *less* than "a church after the fashion of the churches."[103]

Thus, the refusal of Catherine and her co-founders to call The Salvation Army a church by no means reflected the weakness of their ecclesiology. It was instead an expression of their ecclesiology's very core, allowing the claim for freedom in *adiaphora*, and in matters of the *bene esse* of the church, and was precisely what made a fresh, dynamic and extravagant expression of the church possible.

THE FORM OF THE CHURCH IN CATHERINE BOOTH'S ECCLESIOLOGY

Catherine views the church from a four-fold perspective. The form and shape of the church is seen from a Christological, missiological, pneumatological, and eschatological perspective. These are not discrete categories; they are interconnected and overlap. In Catherine's thought these categories are prior to and determinative of ecclesiology, and the partial dissolution of ecclesiology within these categories explains the apparent elusiveness of her doctrine of the church.

The Church in Christological Perspective

Colin Gunton has identified "two interlocking factors in operation" when the Christological dimensions of ecclesiology are considered. The first is

---

103. Sandall, Wiggins, and Coutts, *History*, II:126.

historical: what was Jesus doing when he chose twelve disciples? Do the twelve represent a reconstituted Israel, and therefore the creation of a historical community? Alternatively, are the disciples the first of an order of clergy? The second factor is dogmatic: in what manner is the church "conceived to be patterned or moulded by the shape and direction of Jesus' life and its outcome"?[104]

Catherine, who did not conceive of orders of ministry as of the church's *esse*, believed that Jesus instituted a new community when he chose the twelve, a community in which Christ was incarnate in the lives of all his followers. The church is nothing less than "Jesus Christ come in the flesh AGAIN IN His people, living out before the world His principles, acting upon His precepts, living for the same objects for which He lived."[105] The "teeming thousands who never cross the threshold of church, chapel, or mission-hall, to whom all connected with religion is as an old song, a byword, and a reproach [. . .] need to be brought into contact with a living Christ in the characters and persons of His people."[106] The life and mission of the church must be a full expression, visible and tangible, of the life and mission of Christ:[107] "Christianity must come to them embodied in men and women, who are not ashamed to 'eat with publicans and sinners'; they must see it looking through their eyes, and speaking in loving accents through their tongues, sympathising with their sorrows, bearing their burdens, reproving their sins, instructing their ignorance, inspiring their hope, and wooing them to the fountain opened for sin and uncleanness."[108]

Regarding the second factor, the dogmatic, the manner in which the life of the church is patterned after the life of Christ, Gunton proposed that the church has too often emphasised the divine Christ rather than the human Jesus of Nazareth, and the ordering of its ecclesiology to a docetically tending Christology has had disastrous effects. Gunton questioned, "What kind of ecclesiology would derive from a greater stress on the fact that the ecclesiological significance of Jesus derives equally from the humanity of the incarnate?"[109] In her own way, Catherine too was exercised by this: "There are thousands talking about His 'second coming' who will

---

104. Gunton and Hardy, *On Being the Church*, 58–59.
105. Booth, *Godliness*, 42.
106. Booth, *Practical Religion*, 126–27.
107. Ibid., 127.
108. Ibid.
109. Gunton and Hardy, *On Being the Church*, 60.

neither see nor receive Him in the person of His humble and persecuted followers. Christ manifested in flesh, vulgar flesh, they cannot receive. No; they are looking for Him in the clouds! What a sensation there would be if He were to come again in a carpenter's coat! How many would recognise Him then I wonder?"[110]

Catherine continued, "Oh for grace always to see Him where he is to be seen. [. . .] Well, bless the Lord, I keep seeing Him risen again in the forms of drunkards and ruffians of all descriptions."[111] For Catherine, the self-evident humanity of the Army's converts, their frailty and humble origins, did not diminish but enhance their ability to mediate Christ to the world. Although Catherine never referred to her understanding of this Christological aspect of the church as sacramental, she does hold what might be understood as a sacramental view of the church; in the power of the Holy Spirit the church mediates the living Christ to the world. In fact this insight is deep rooted in the very heart of Salvationist spirituality and ecclesiology, memorably expressed in verse by General Albert Orsborn:

> My life must be Christ's broken bread,
> My love his outpoured wine,
> A cup o'erfilled, a table spread
> Beneath his name and sign.
> That other souls, refreshed and fed,
> May share his life through mine.[112]

The Church in Missiological Perspective

Second, for Catherine the church is inaugurated by Christ to fulfill and complete his mission. The church is not an end in itself, but a means to an end. Writing of the Great Commission Catherine asserts, "The vast obligations imposed on the people of God in this command have never yet been more than half realised. *Go ye*, not [to] build temples or churches, and wait for them to come to you, but *go ye*, run after them, seek them out and preach My Gospel to EVERY creature."[113] Catherine quotes Joseph Lightfoot, Bishop of Durham: "The Salvation Army has at least recalled us to the lost

---

110. Booth, *These Fifty Years*, 46.
111. Ibid.
112. Song 512, *SA Song Book*, 409.
113. Booth, *Practical Religion*, 193.

ideal of the work of the Church,—the universal compulsion of the souls of men."[114]

Catherine believed two biblical principles emerged out of this missiological perspective. The first was the principle of aggression. Self-evidently this principle is closely associated with the militant character of the movement as an Army. Catherine believed she had coined the term "aggressive Christianity" and that the major difference between the Army and the churches lay in this principle.[115] For Catherine, aggression means going to people, rather than attempting to attract them or merely interest them; it means persuading people, rather than simply proclaiming truth to them; it means addressing an embodied and encultured whole person, in whatever way is necessary to speak to their heart, soul, and mind.[116] It means accepting the commission given to the apostle Paul, "to open their eyes":[117] "They are indifferent, preoccupied, asleep in their sin and danger. I send thee as my Herald to arouse them, shake them, open their eyes, make them think, and realise the verity of eternal things!"[118]

Catherine's addresses are a demonstration of this principle. Her direct, forceful, expressions can seem overwhelming and unpleasant, and at times she seems to be almost pharisaically critical of other Christians. Catherine's manner of presentation and the audience's response are inevitably missing from the printed word. William Chisholm, a professional stenographer hired to record many of Catherine's addresses, described an occasion when she indicted the churches with a great list of failures and missed opportunities: "The counts of this indictment were heaped up with a force so cumulative, and with such a completeness in effect, that Mrs. Booth herself at last seemed overcome, and finally sat down in a flood of tears."[119] An address on *The Iniquity of State Regulated Vice*, delivered at Exeter Hall in February 1884, included, in published form, the audience reaction. The inclusion transforms the text. Catherine's passionate, strong words are frequently interrupted by loud cheers, applause, cries of "Hear, hear," and laughter. Exclamation marks which read as overstatement in cold print invariably predict an audience reaction and confirm her power to speak to the heart,

114. Booth, *Church & State*, 30.
115. Ibid., 73, 30.
116. Booth, *Aggressive Christianity*, 8–10.
117. Booth, *Practical Religion*, 193.
118. Ibid.
119. Booth, *These Fifty Years*, 39–40.

co-operate with the Spirit's convicting work, and recruit the conscience as her ally.[120] Self-evidently the principle of aggression can be misunderstood. An example demonstrates how gracious Catherine's aggressive Christianity could be in practice:

> One morning when she was journeying from the North of England, a young man was suddenly thrust into the compartment as the train was leaving York. His travelling kit was thrown in after him. On seeing Mrs. Booth alone he sat down and exclaimed under his breath, "--- the women!" After a little while she spoke to him about the influence of good women, and gradually drew from him a sad story of disappointment and failure. Before they reached King's Cross he had knelt with her before God, and he remained a friend for many years.[121]

It is not enough, for Catherine, simply to present the truths of the gospel. It is necessary "to persuade men" and "to make the soul realise and feel [the] message."[122] Not only has the Army "resuscitated this idea, but by the power of God [. . .] we have also raised a force of men and women who are now working it out."[123]

Catherine's second biblical principal was adaptation. We must, Catherine says, "adapt ourselves and our measures to the social and spiritual conditions of those whom we seek to benefit."[124] Searching the New Testament Catherine found only one "law" laid down in respect to the modes and measures the church may legitimately take—adaptation. Catherine quotes Paul, "I am made all things to all men, that I might by all means save some."[125] She continues, "The only law laid down in the New Testament for the prosecution of this aggressive warfare is the law of adaptation."[126] Not only modes and measures but the forms and structures of the church are relativised by this perspective. Catherine was encouraged in the formation of her views by her early reading of Mosheim. Buss summarizes Mosheim's view, "Unless mandated by Scripture, Church polity is also an *adiaphron*."[127]

120. Booth, "The Iniquity of State Regulated Vice."
121. Booth, *These Fifty Years*, 39.
122. Booth, *Church & State*, 31.
123. Ibid.
124. Booth, *Practical Religion*, 196.
125. 1 Corinthians 9:22
126. Booth, *Practical Religion*, 195.
127. Buss, "Mosheim & Neander," 105.

Consequently, Catherine believed the churches had made a grave error by failing to recognize the permanent continuing demands of the Great Commission and instead giving permanent significance to what should only ever have been temporary forms: "It is here, I conceive, that our Churches have fallen into such grievous mistakes with reference to the propagation of the Gospel in our own times. We have stood to our stereotyped forms, refusing to come down from the routine of our forefathers, although this routine has ceased to be attractive to the people, nay in many instances, the thing that drives them away."[128]

The Salvation Army's adoption of new measures is frequently attributed to the influence of Charles Finney.[129] However, although Finney was an apologist and exponent of measures such as the anxious seat, he largely adopted them from Methodism.[130] Although some, if not most, of these measures originated within American Methodism, through the influence of transatlantic revivalists such as the American Lorenzo Dow and British Methodists such as George Shadford they were enthusiastically adopted by British revivalists such as Isaac Marsden. From the year of his conversion in 1834, Marsden preached in the streets, markets, and public houses, before being called as a lay preacher in 1836.[131] His practice was to "conclude the service with a lively prayer-meeting. He would have plenty of singing, short and practical prayers, and he would insist on the use of the penitent form."[132] Isaac Marsden preceded William Booth in Methodist revivalism and was also a life-long friend and supporter, and this suggests that the Booths adopted the "new" measures, not through the indirect influence of Finney but because they saw them used by English Methodists. The Booths always referred to the penitent form or the mercy seat, never the "anxious seat."

Marsden was the cause of a serious disagreement between William and Catherine. In March 1853 Catherine wrote to William in Spalding, "As to that Isaac Marsden, he might be sincere, but exceedingly injudicious and violent. I would not attend one of his prayer meetings on any account. I don't believe the gospel needs such roaring and foaming to make it effective and to some minds it would make it appear ridiculous and bar them

---

128. Booth, *Practical Religion*, 196.

129. Cf. Walker, *Pulling the Devil's Kingdom Down*, 44–45.

130. Carwardine, *Transatlantic Revivalism*, 16.; cf. Carwardine, "The Second Great Awakening."

131. Taylor, *Isaac Marsden*, 38.

132. Ibid., 40.

against its reception forever."[133] However, William had almost been converted by the preaching of Marsden in Nottingham when he was 14 years old, and he fiercely defended the older man.[134] William's reply is missing, but Catherine acknowledged William's argument and repeated one of William's soul-piercing lines in a later letter: "If you cannot bear the hearty responses and alleluias of God's people, our fellowship will not be in prayer meetings."[135] Marsden lived to pour hot coals on Catherine. In the early days of the Christian Mission he worked voluntarily alongside William in the East End; he gave liberally to the work of the Army, distributed *The War Cry* among his friends, and the last thing he read before he died was the latest edition of the Army's newspaper.[136]

It was largely the methods of this older generation of Methodist revivalists that William and Catherine adopted in their revival ministry of the early 1860s, although they were open to fresh possibilities. In Walsall they encountered the "Hallelujah Bands." Catherine wrote in her *Reminiscences*, "Their meetings suddenly became a marvellous success. [. . .] Theatres, music halls, drill sheds, warehouses, circuses and old, unused chapels, in fact, buildings of all descriptions were utilized, but none could contain the multitudes who sought admission. [. . .] Drunkards, thieves, harlots, gamblers, infidels and church members alike scrambled to find admission, sat listening to messages of salvation, large numbers of them going forwards to the penitent form, Salvation Army fashion."[137] Catherine noted that William "watched the movement with considerable interest"; their methods shed light on how to reach the masses with the gospel.[138] From them Catherine and William learned the possibilities inherent in Spirit-inspired creativity when the gift of freedom in modes and measures is realized.[139]

The Church in Pneumatological Perspective

Third, for Catherine, the church is constituted and directed by the Holy Spirit as it works to fulfill Christ's commission. This third overlapping perspective also has the functional effect of relativising the historical forms

---

133. Booth and Booth, *Letters*, 87.
134. Taylor, *Isaac Marsden*, 152.
135. Booth and Booth, *Letters*, 91.
136. Taylor, *Isaac Marsden*, 151, 87.
137. Booth, *Reminiscences*, 71–72.
138. Ibid., 73.
139. Booth, *Church & State*, 51.

of the church.¹⁴⁰ Catherine believed the outpouring of the Spirit in and through The Salvation Army legitimized the new form the mission of the church had taken through the movement: "Everywhere, even in the thickest of the fight, God has given us the ear of the people, accompanying our testimony with the outpouring of the Blessed Spirit, working signs and wonders equal to anything recorded in the Acts of the Apostles."¹⁴¹ Indeed the Holy Spirit was responsible for the birth of this startling new form of the church. The Army grew "because of the Divine Life that was in it. We could not help it, even if we had desired to do so."¹⁴²

This recovery of the pneumatological formation of the church is a defining characteristic of the movement. Catherine writes, "A further difference between us, and the majority of the Churches is, the resuscitation of the SUPERNATURAL, of the DIVINE. *Here I think is our real power*":¹⁴³ "Ours is not a religion of intellect, of culture, of refinement, of creeds, or of ceremony or forms. We attach very little importance to any of these in themselves. We gladly take hold of some of these, and use them as mediums through which to convey the living energy of the Spirit; but the POWER IS IN THE LIFE, not in the form."¹⁴⁴

Catherine's familiarity with William Arthur's book *The Tongue of Fire* has been noted. Arthur described the baptism of the Holy Ghost as "the one and only source of [the church's] power."¹⁴⁵ God's holy fire in the church is the greatest need of the age.¹⁴⁶ Arthur believed that the nineteenth-century church was equipped humanly speaking "in such a degree and of such excellence as was never known in any other age":¹⁴⁷ "We want but a supreme and glorious baptism of fire to exhibit to the world such a spectacle as would raise ten thousands hallelujahs to the glory of our King. [. . .] Let but this baptism descend, and thousands of us [. . .] would then become mighty. Men would wonder at us, as if we had been made anew."¹⁴⁸ For such a church, the conversion of the whole world was a real possibility.¹⁴⁹

140. Ibid.
141. Ibid., 66.
142. Ibid., 34.
143. Ibid., 38.
144. Ibid., 38–39.
145. Arthur, *Tongue of Fire*, 297.
146. Ibid.
147. Ibid.
148. Ibid., 297–98.
149. Ibid., 333–42.

Arthur's book expressed ideas found in the writings of John Fletcher[150] and John Wesley. Fletcher looked for a "great Pentecostal display of the Spirit's glory [. . .] within and without."[151] He believed in a global Pentecost that would usher in the coming millennium, and that Methodism was the forerunner of the great pentecostal church of the coming age.[152] Wesley held the same expectations.[153] In his sermon of 1783, *The General Spread of the Gospel*, he looked forward to that day when "The grand Pentecost shall 'fully come', and 'devout men in every nation under heaven', however distant in place from each other, shall 'all be filled with the Holy Ghost.'"[154] As a consequence of this great outpouring of the Holy Spirit upon the church "will be accomplished all those glorious promises made to the Christian Church, which will not then be confined to this or that nation, but will include all the inhabitants of the earth."[155] Similarly, Catherine saw in the Army "the fulfilment of the prophecy of the last great ingathering of souls."[156] William Booth expressed the Army's fervent pentecostal prayer in song:

> Thou Christ of burning, cleansing flame,
> Send the fire!
> Thy blood bought gift today we claim,
> Send the fire!
> Look down and see this waiting host,
> Give us the promised Holy Ghost;
> We want another Pentecost,
> Send the fire![157]

According to Catherine, nothing less than a pentecostal baptism of the Holy Ghost can give the church power to "go and subjugate the world to Jesus."[158]

---

150. Cf. Streiff, *Reluctant Saint?*, 46.
151. Wood, *Pentecost in Early Methodism*, 146.
152. Ibid., 145–62.
153. Ibid., 163–207.
154. John Wesley, Sermon 63, "The General Spread of the Gospel," in Wesley, *Sermons, 1–4*, §20, II:494.
155. Ibid.
156. Booth, *Church & State*, 74.
157. Booth, *The War Cry*, "Another Song by the General: The Fire!"
158. Booth, *Aggressive Christianity*, 194.

The Church in Eschatological Perspective

For Catherine Booth, the church exists to reveal in community and realize in space and time the values of the kingdom of God. Consequently its historical forms, modes and measures are relativized in the light of Christ's coming kingdom on earth. She stated:

> Jesus Christ came to establish the *kingdom of God upon the earth*. [. . .] He intended this kingdom to be a literal kingdom, that is, as truly a kingdom as any of the kingdoms of this world, that he intended it to be a holy kingdom, a kingdom of righteousness, and consequently separate from, and above, all other kingdoms; that Christ spoke of his followers as a community, existing in the midst of another kingdom or community, having its own laws and principles and aims entirely distinct and separate from the world.[159]

Furthermore, although this kingdom may as yet only be partially realized in the community of the church, its full realization is assured as a future historical event, in continuity with and in fulfillment of the mission of the church in the present age: "If we could bring all men to love each other as brethren, there would be an end of Animosity, Despotism, Caste, National Hatred, And War; and peace and good-will would reign over the earth. This is God's ultimate idea for the world, this is the true millennium which is to come, towards which all real progress tends."[160]

Against those who failed to share her optimism and believed that the age of the church would not end in the triumph of the gospel, Catherine affirms, "You say, It will never be accomplished. How do you know? Don't tell me that the dispensation of the Spirit is going to end in this ignominious fashion. I don't believe it. I believe that the fullness of the Gentiles has to come in, and the remnant of Israel too. [. . .] How little we know of God's purposes, or of *how* they are to be accomplished!"[161]

Catherine was not dogmatic in her postmillennialism; she believed in the coming millennium and the triumph of the kingdom of God in history, but did not specify the time or manner of Christ's return. However, her optimistic view was undoubtedly characteristic of post- rather than premillennialism.[162] Catherine did not describe her eschatological vision

---

159. Booth, *Popular Christianity*, 86.
160. Booth, *Church & State*, 15.
161. Ibid., 78–79.
162. Underwood, "Millenarianism," 82–83.

in detail, but William did. Writing in *All The World* William subtitled his article on *The Millennium*, "The Ultimate Triumph of Salvation Army Principles." William identified three characteristics of "the good time coming."[163] First, the reign of God as King will be acknowledged throughout the world; second, the universal rule of God will result in obedience to all his laws; and third, love will hold universal sway, that is, "men will love God with all the heart, and each other as themselves, and they will make this manifest in all their outward conduct."[164] As a consequence happiness will overflow the earth.[165] So far, Catherine would surely have concurred. However, William's vision became extraordinarily concrete as he considered the consequences for London. The green spaces of Hyde Park would be roofed in, with towers climbing towards the stars, as a temple for the millions who would gather to worship God.[166] Denominational differences would disappear as people united in praise of the living God. Workhouses, courts, jails would empty as the churches filled.[167] Catherine might have been delighted by William's dream, but she never allowed her own imagination such a free rein.

The Booths' eschatology is, for Roger Green, a fundamental weakness in their ecclesiology, setting an unrealistic hope at the heart of their doctrine of the church: "Not only are we not postmillennialists (and who could possibly be a postmillennialist in the twentieth century?), but we do not have any particular millennial vision or historical goal that drives and motivates us as William Booth's postmillennialism drove the early Army."[168] Green may be correct in this last assertion; but the absence of an eschatological vision or historical goal in contemporary Salvationism is not necessarily to be celebrated, given the expectation of Jesus that his followers should pray every day for the coming of the kingdom of God on earth. Green continues, "We believe that the world is getting worse and that some day the Lord will return. Beyond that we do not say much."[169] However, that is to say a great deal. It is by no means *a priori* and necessarily true that "the world is getting worse"; but to debate the question is to miss the point, which is that for Christians in both the nineteenth and twenty-first centuries escha-

163. Booth, *All the World*, "The Millenium."
164. Ibid., 338.
165. Ibid., 340.
166. Ibid., 341.
167. Ibid.
168. Green, "Facing history," 29.
169. Ibid.

tology must be a matter of faith rather than sight, hope rather than fact. Green alleges that "postmillennialism [. . .] in large measure, along with the radical commitment of women in ministry," was the reason for "the tremendous growth both of The Christian Mission and of The Salvation Army," a growth, Green says, "we have not been able to sustain."[170] If Green is claiming the founders' eschatological hope was partially a cause of the Army's growth and the loss of that hope was a cause of the consequent decline, this would seem an argument for the recovery of a robust and renewed eschatological hope rather than the reverse.

Catherine's eschatology had deep roots. Fletcher and Wesley also believed in the coming millennium and the ultimate triumph of the kingdom.[171] For Miroslav Volf, an eschatological hope is an essential element in the nature of the church: "The church lives from something and toward something that is greater than itself," and that hope, in concrete form, offers hope of renewal for all creation.[172] "We come to recognize the fresh breath of God and the light of God that renew the creation only because there are communities called churches—communities that keep alive the memory of the crucified Messiah and the hope of the coming One."[173] The terrible contemporary realities experienced by Volf rendered that hope all the more necessary.[174]

Unlike William, Catherine was careful not to over-concretize her vision of the future reign of God. Consequently, and to the extent that her hope is the strongest possible expression of the church's prayer "Your kingdom come," her eschatology by no means renders her ecclesiology weak or irrelevant to the contemporary Salvationist. Jürgen Moltmann offers a fuller perspective:

> If we view history, with its conditions and potentialities, as an open system, we are bound to understand the kingdom of God in the liberating rule of God as a transforming power immanent in that system, and the rule of God in the kingdom of God as a future transcending the system. Without the counterpart of the future of the kingdom, which transcends the present system, the transforming power immanent in the system loses its orientation.

---

170. Ibid., 30–31.
171. Wood, *Pentecost in Early Methodism*, 145–62.
172. Volf, *After our Likeness*, x.
173. Ibid.
174. Ibid.

> Without the transformation immanent in the system the future transcending the system would become a powerless dream. That is why in actual practice the obedience to the will of God which transforms the world is inseparable from prayer for the coming of the kingdom.[175]

Albert Orsborn expressed the eschatological hope that yet burned in the hearts of Salvationists in a song written, poignantly, for the Army's International Congress of June 1914.

> Oh, for the time of Christ's completed mission,
> Throbs of is rapture reach us as we pray,
> Gleams of its glory, bursting on our vision,
> Urge us to labour, speed us on our way.
>
> *Jesus shall conquer, lift up the strain,*
> *Evil shall perish and righteousness shall reign.*[176]

Moltmann expressed the same idea in theological prose, with a Christian hope now tested in the crucible of two great wars: "The doxological anticipation of the beauty of the kingdom and active resistance to godless and inhuman relationships in history are related to one another and reinforce one another mutually."[177]

These four interwoven perspectives—the Christological, missiological, pneumatological and eschatological—lie at the heart of the ecclesiological vision that gave birth to The Salvation Army.

CONCLUSION

For Catherine, The Salvation Army was an integral part of the church; in an inclusive, non-partisan sense, the Army is the church. Raised up by God, inspired and guided by the Holy Spirit, the Army provided a sharp, aggressive, missional edge to the community of faith as it reached out to the lost. Catherine wrote, "We want the Salvation Army to be like Samson's foxes, going through the churches with a fire-brand, setting every true Christian on fire."[178] Any presumption implicit in this image must be resisted, but it remains an illuminating metaphor, representing the Army as a part of

---

175. Moltmann, *The Church in the Power of the Spirit*, 190.
176. Song 1/3, *SA Song Book*, 143.
177. Ibid.
178. Booth, *Church & State*, 75–76.

the church, not discrete and self-sufficient, but integrated and engaged, a catalyst for renewal as well as mission. The Army is not an established gathered sect, but a mobile force gathered at the edge of engagement, at the interface between the church and the world, the battle's front. Catherine Booth's firmly held, theologically grounded ecclesiology did not require an Army; however, it established the freedom in which an Army could emerge as an expression of the Body of Christ and resulted in an astonishing flourishing of creative, innovative mission.

SIX

Ministry

If the Army's doctrine of the church has caused confusion in its ranks over the years, then so equally has its doctrine of Christian ministry. Following the 1995 International Leaders' Conference, General Paul Rader commissioned the International Doctrine Council to address a recommendation "That the roles of officers and soldiers be defined and a theology of the priesthood of all believers be developed to encourage greater involvement in ministry."[1] The outcome of this recommendation was the publication in 2002 of a slim volume entitled *Servants Together* which established that at the root of the Army's understanding of ministry was, and always had been, a firm belief in the priesthood of all believers. *Servants Together* confirmed that there is no difference in status between soldiers and officers in The Salvation Army. They are servants—or ministers—together. However, in seeking at the same time to explain satisfactorily the distinction between officers and soldiers it served to confirm some deep ambiguities associated with the Army's polity.

It is not hard to find cause for ambiguity and miscomprehension. The doctrine of the priesthood of all believers has been at the heart of the Army's ecclesiology from the very beginning; yet at the same time, the division of the Army into hierarchical orders of ministry, the use of ranks and the unequal distribution of power, have given the Army's polity quite a different appearance. William Booth had to learn to laugh at the frequent accusations that he was a Pope: "They say that The Salvation Army is a despotism and a religious hierarchy, and that I am a despot, who dwells in a Lordly mansion, eating his food out of golden vessels and riding about in an expensive motor-car (Laughter and applause.) And they call me a Pope.

---

1. The Salvation Army International Doctrine Council, *Servants Together*, Foreword.

(Laughter.) And so I am! The word Pope means papa (laughter)—and I am your Papa!" (Cheers)."[2]

The recommendation of the Leaders' meeting in 1995 was evidence in itself that Salvationists have not always understood themselves to be *Servants Together*; and some of the changes made in the 2008 revised edition prove that matters have yet to be resolved. For example, chapter 9 in the 2002 edition is entitled *Team Ministry*, but in the 2008 edition it is entitled *Consultative Ministry*.

This chapter will consider, first, the development of Catherine Booth's own ministry; second, her writings on women's ministry; and third, the development of orders of ministry within the Army and the distribution of authority, in order to examine these critical ambiguities and possible contradictions in the Army's polity in the light of Catherine's experience, values and insights.

MINISTRY DEVELOPMENT

According to Pamela Walker, Catherine Booth "exemplified a new model of Christian womanhood, articulating a new approach to female ministry and creating an influential career as an evangelist. As well as formulating the Salvation Army's egalitarian policies, she served as an inspiration to thousands of young women who preached under the aegis of the organisation."[3]

In the summer of 1880 Catherine Booth conducted a campaign in which she spoke to capacity audiences at some of the largest venues in London's West End. When Catherine addressed the subject *Witnessing for Christ* she recalled her long personal failure to fulfill this commission. From her conversion in June 1846, Catherine confessed, "the Spirit of God had constantly been urging me into paths of usefulness and labour which seemed to me impossible."[4] Catherine resisted until Whit Sunday 1860, when she "felt the Spirit come upon me," and it was as if a voice challenged her to speak out for God.[5] Catherine's West End congregations included many from the upper classes; she was invited to address private gatherings of "lords and ladies" and minor royals.[6] Through 1880 Catherine was

---

2. Nicol, *General Booth*, 112.
3. Walker, *Pulling the Devil's Kingdom Down*, 8–9.
4. Booth, *Aggressive Christianity*, 136.
5. Ibid., 137–38.
6. Booth-Tucker, *Catherine Booth*, II:285.

"swamped with work,"[7] speaking to hundreds of thousands of people in more than sixty-two towns.[8] She had become one of the foremost evangelists, teachers, and apologists of her age.

In 1872, Catherine's "first public efforts [. . .] were in connection with feeding the hungry and starving poor."[9] Commenting on the place of evangelism and social action in mission, Catherine criticized the "cogent and plausible" but heartless arguments of social economists who said that if the poor would not work, they should not eat, and that it was wrong to relieve the poverty of the vicious, criminal, and idle classes. Against this Catherine set the example of the Father who makes the sun rise on the evil and the good, and the rain fall on the just and unjust, and the command of Jesus who said when you give a feast invite the poor, the maimed, the lame, the blind. Social action is foremost an expression of God's indiscriminate love for the world. However, "the enjoyment of the good things of this life" depends on "submission to God and obedience to His laws"; therefore, evangelism and social action go together, hand in hand.[10] This connection is evident in what Catherine calls, in *Church and State*, her "starting proposition, that if you can only resuscitate and energize the moral sense in a man, he will soon rectify himself in all the relations of life,"[11] and this is why she believed the Army was "carrying out the very HIGHEST PRINCIPLES OF MORAL AND SOCIAL REFORM."[12]

Roger Green introduces a degree of equivocation into Catherine's understanding of the relationship between evangelism and social action, particularly as manifested in the Darkest England scheme.[13] However, although Catherine did not advocate social action without evangelism, equally she was not in favor of evangelism without social action. The mission Christians were called to was identical to Christ's. The commission had been given to be as Christ in the world, "beautiful words, and yet how much they involve which few understand—'As Thou hast sent Me into the world, even so, send I them into the world.'"[14]

7. Ibid., II:288.
8. Ibid., II:309.
9. Booth, *Reminiscences*, 126.
10. Ibid., 126–27.
11. Booth, *Church & State*, 22.
12. Ibid., 25.
13. Green, *Catherine Booth*, 267–72.
14. Booth, *Aggressive Christianity*, 123.

In one of her addresses Catherine notoriously asked, "What does it matter if a man dies in the workhouse? If he dies on a doorstep covered with wounds like Lazarus—what does it matter if his soul is saved?"[15] Norman Murdoch and Ann Woodall conclude from this that Catherine's commitment to social action was compromised at best.[16] In his novel *Whitechapel*, Ian Porter gives Catherine's words to a sarcastic critic who despises the Army "because of its [. . .] indifference to the causes of poverty."[17] The context of Catherine's widely misrepresented words is an attack on that charity "which contemplates the earthy part of man in a superior degree to the spiritual part," as opposed to that which "always contemplates man in the entirety of his being, and always gives first importance to the soul."[18] Catherine pleads, "Don't misrepresent me and say I teach all of the one and none of the other. God forbid [. . .] real Christianity cares for body and soul."[19] The dilemma Catherine faces, as an evangelist committed to social action, revolves "around that great problem of infinite love, 'What is man profited, if he shall gain the whole world, and lose his own soul?'"[20]

Strong principles undergirded Catherine's actions, whether in managing the feeding programs of the Christian Mission, in her alliance with Josephine Butler and W. T. Stead in the 1885 crusade against sex-trafficking and in favor of raising the age of consent, or from her death bed participating in the creation of the Darkest England scheme, of which Stead wrote, "That The Salvation Army is entering upon a new development is probably due more to her than any single human being, and in its new social work we see the best and most enduring monument to the memory of a saintly woman."[21]

Norman Murdoch's opinion that "as its evangelistic program stagnated in the 1880s, social salvation replaced evangelism as the Army's mission" is not supported by the facts which show strong growth through these years, or by the integral place of social action within the Booths' understanding of

---

15. Booth, *Godliness*, 29.

16. Murdoch, "Frank Smith: Salvationist Socialist," 8; Woodall, *What Price the Poor?*, 165.

17. Porter, *Whitechapel*, 61.

18. Booth, *Godliness*, 27.

19. Ibid., 28.

20. Ibid., 28–29.

21. Stead, *The War Cry*, "The Late Mrs. Booth."

mission, rooted as it was in Methodism and revivalism.[22] Reflecting on the theological framework of early- to mid-century Methodist social concern, Tim Macquiban has argued, "The 'optimism of grace' which encouraged openness to all irrespective of condition broke through the societal expectations of a more discriminatory and harsher attitude to the poor in a way which released the spirit of reckless generosity found in Wesley and the early Methodists."[23] Macquiban has drawn a direct line between these Wesleyan expressions of social concern and the Army's mixture of personal and social salvation.[24] Timothy Smith has argued that revivalism characteristically "provoked increasing Christian interest not only in social problems, but in reforming the structures of society."[25] Revivalism and perfectionism became a "socially volatile" mix when combined with postmillennial expectations.[26] Catherine's temperance stance was predicated on the nature of alcohol as a social evil, and was not a manifestation of Victorian kill-joy prurience; the soldier's pledge was a statement of ethical commitment, not an arbitrary, individualistic, and gratuitous act of self-denial. Catherine's soteriology was ethical and social to the core; salvation leads inexorably to the transformation of society and to the reign of peace and righteousness, the saving of individual souls is but the necessary beginning of the war in which the Army is engaged.[27]

Catherine modeled a form of ministry that embraced evangelism and social action, and which demonstrated the right of women not only to preach but to lead, not only to serve but to rule. The intention of her *Reminiscences* was "to encourage women everywhere to rise up and go forth, speaking and working for Christ and for souls."[28]

FEMALE TEACHING

Catherine rehearsed her arguments for the equality of women in her correspondence with William in the early 1850s and in a long anonymous letter to David Thomas written on Sunday 22 April 1855, prompted by remarks

22. Murdoch, *Origins of The Salvation Army*, 147.
23. Macquiban, "Methodism and the Poor," 298–99.
24. Macquiban, "Soup and Salvation," 35.
25. Smith, *Revivalism and Social Reform*, 250–51.
26. Ibid., 225.
27. Kew, *Catherine Booth*, 129.; Murdoch, *Origins of The Salvation Army*, 165.
28. Booth, *Reminiscences*, 91.

Thomas made which she took to denigrate the place of women.[29] Writing to William on 1 January 1852 Catherine fired her first salvo. The light falling on the subject of women's equality was a happy omen for "English homes and England's future glory."[30] In her letter to Thomas she asked, "whether you have made the subject of women's equality as a *being* the matter of calm investigation and thought."[31] What most endears Christianity to Catherine's heart is "what it has done, and what it is destined to do, for my sex."[32] The three essential points of Catherine's argument for women's ministry are first, women were originally created equal with men; second, their subjection was part of the curse; third, in Christ the equality of women has been restored.[33] In April 1855 Catherine wrote a long letter to William on the same subject, though the content was quite different.[34] As Bennett says, "Both letters are remarkable."[35] William's response was mildly equivocal. He reserved full judgment for a later date. He was not immediately inclined to change his opinions. Although in qualities such as intellect he saw a woman as inferior, in other respects she is superior. He would not stop a woman preaching, but neither would he encourage it. He admitted he might be prejudiced, and he would quarrel with no means that might help the world's salvation.[36] In fact William was convinced long before Catherine that she should preach, and encouraged her to do so.

Why was Catherine so angry with Arthur Rees, the Sunderland minister who wrote against female ministry, when he was only expressing what so many others believed? The writer who eulogized Catherine in *The Banner* wrote "We English are by no means favourably disposed towards women who mount the platform or the pulpit."[37] Following Pamela Walker's analyis, it seems possible that Rees's association of revival excitement and female ministry in the creation of unnatural disorder may have been particularly galling to Catherine.[38] Catherine believed that, on the contrary,

29. Booth and Booth, *Letters*, 283; Booth, "Letter to David Thomas: 22 April 1855."
30. Booth and Booth, *Letters*, 47.
31. Booth-Tucker, *Catherine Booth*, I:83.
32. Ibid., I:85.
33. Ibid., I:83–86.
34. Booth and Booth, *Letters*, 283–86.
35. Ibid., 283.
36. Ibid., 287.
37. *The Banner*, "The Funeral of Mrs. Booth."
38. Cf. Walker, *Pulling the Devil's Kingdom Down*, 26; for Walker's analysis of Rees and Catherine's argument, see ibid., 24–31.

it was the sign of an unnatural disordered world that women were under-educated, their talents buried and their potential wasted. Catherine argued that women's ministry "could be sustained within a conventional gendered social order in an institutional church committed to vigorous soul saving."[39] Catherine's argument has a three-fold structure reflecting Rees's three main objections to female teaching.

The first objection was that it was unnatural and unfeminine. Rees claimed, "The sphere of women, even nature teaches us, is not the platform or the pulpit."[40] Catherine accuses Rees of confusing nature and custom; custom makes things appear to be natural which may be unnatural, and the reverse is also true.[41] Women have natural attributes, a graceful form and nature, winning manners, persuasive speech, and an emotional sensitivity which make them well suited for public speaking.[42] Even if it is granted that the natural sphere of women is the home and the kitchen, they should be no more confined to it than men to their sphere of working the ground.[43] Before the Fall, men and women were equal in nature, status, and power; both were created in the likeness of God. The word for woman in Hebrew, Greek and Latin, being the word used for man with a feminine ending, indicates that they are alike in all things apart from gender. The English words *male* and *female* operate similarly.[44] That the words of subjection, "he shall rule over thee," are part of the curse is proof of woman's natural equality. Even this subjection is limited, applying only to a wife in so far as such submission is "fit in the Lord."[45] Woman is an independent, responsible being, capable of understanding and obeying God's law.[46]

Rees's second objection was that female teaching was unscriptural.[47] Catherine discusses first 1 Corinthians 11:1–15 and Paul's prohibition of women praying or prophesying with their heads uncovered. This Catherine believes must refer to the prophesying predicted in Joel 2:28 and proclaimed by Peter in Acts 2:17. The only reasonable conclusion from these

---

39. Ibid., 31.
40. Rees, *Reasons*, 5.
41. Booth, *Female Teaching*, 3.
42. Ibid.
43. Ibid., 4.
44. Ibid., 5.
45. Ibid., 6.
46. Ibid.
47. Rees, *Reasons*, 6.

verses is that women did prophesy and teach in the primitive church and Paul is simply requiring compliance with local customs of propriety.[48] Next, Catherine turns to 1 Corinthians 14:34,35 where Paul requires women to be silent in the churches and forbids them to speak. This, Catherine argues, cannot refer to speaking as in 1 Corinthians 11 for which Paul has given explicit and full directions.[49] Following Adam Clarke, Catherine allows that it may refer not to speaking in devotional and religious settings but in the political and disciplinary assemblies of the church. However, for Catherine all hinges on the meaning of the Greek *lalein*, which she finds in various lexicons to be translated as to prattle, be loquacious, chatter, or babble.[50] Paul is therefore not imposing absolute silence on women in any of the assemblies.[51] What is forbidden is "a pertinacious, inquisitive, domineering, dogmatical kind of speaking, which while it is unbecoming in a man, is shameful and odious in a woman, and especially when that woman is in the church, and is speaking on the deep things of religion."[52] Catherine gives examples from Justin Martyr, Irenaeus, and Eusebius of gifted women who were distinguished in their love and zeal for the Lord.[53] She argues that if the passage is to be taken literally and out of context then Rees must submit to Paul's other directions, and allow his whole church to prophesy one by one, and sit still and listen while they do it, something she doubts he would allow.[54] Mary Magdalene's commission, Catherine argues, was not to deliver a private message, as Rees asserted,[55] but the first announcement of the glorious news to a lost world, as public as the situation demanded, and intended to be published to the ends of the earth; moreover Mary was commissioned to reveal the fact to the apostles and thus became their teacher.[56] Rees had argued, "as to the prophecy of Joel; I don't set prophecy against precept,"[57] but Catherine argues, "He makes God do so."[58] God promised

48. Booth, *Female Teaching*, 7–8.
49. Ibid., 9.
50. Ibid., 10.
51. Ibid., 11.
52. Ibid., 9.
53. Ibid., 12–13.
54. Ibid., 13.
55. Rees, *Reasons*, 12.
56. Booth, *Female Teaching*, 14.
57. Rees, *Reasons*, 12.
58. Booth, *Female Teaching*, 15.

Catherine Booth

to pour out his Spirit on all flesh, and that daughters as well as sons should prophesy. Rees says if they have the gift, they must not use it;[59] but God says they shall use it.[60] Catherine believes Paul's injunction that women must not teach[61] can only refer to domineering, disrespectful teaching.[62]

At this point in her argument Catherine widened her frame of reference to include Deborah, a prophet and judge, a woman of high authority, who was the military head over ten thousand men;[63] Huldah, the prophetess, who answered the king with the authority of the King of kings;[64] the great company of women prophets or women evangelists of Psalm 68, correctly translated, described by Hugo Grotius as a "great army of preaching women [...] or female conquerors";[65] and Miriam, classed with Moses and Aaron as a leader of the people.[66] Catherine continued from the New Testament, noting that Anna's speech was as public as Simeon's;[67] that on the day of Pentecost, women assembled with the disciples, tongues of fire rested on them all, the Holy Spirit filled them all, and all spoke as the Spirit gave utterance;[68] that Paul described men and women alike and precisely as his fellow laborers in the gospel;[69] that both Priscilla and Aquila were Paul's helpers;[70] that Junia was a noteworthy apostle as well as kin and fellow prisoner to Paul;[71] that Tryphena, Tryphosa, and Persis labored with Paul in the Lord;[72] and that Phoebe, a servant of the church at Chenchrea, was a deacon.[73] These women were examples of the ruling principle set out by Paul in Galatians 3:28, that all are one in Jesus Christ; there is neither Jew nor Greek, male nor female.[74]

59. Rees, *Reasons*, 12.
60. Booth, *Female Teaching*, 15.
61. 1 Timothy 2:12
62. Booth, *Female Teaching*, 16–17.
63. Judges 4:4–10
64. 2 Kings 22:12–20
65. Psalm 68:11; Booth, *Female Teaching*, 18.
66. Micah 6:4
67. Luke 2:37,38
68. Acts 1:14; 2:1, 4
69. Philippians 4:3
70. Romans 16:3–4
71. Romans 16:7
72. Romans 16:12
73. Romans 16:1
74. Booth, *Female Teaching*, 18–20, 21.

Rees's third objection was that God's sentence upon women was not cancelled, and they remain "in the present life [. . .] under a denser cloud of suffering and humiliation" than men.[75] Catherine responded that God did not subject woman to man as a being, but as a wife.[76] No unmarried or widowed woman is subject to any man; and as a wife "the ameliorating and exalting provisions of Christianity all but restore her to her original position"; for love is the law of marriage.[77] Rees has ignored the remedial effect of the religion of Christ which "recognises [a woman's] individuality, and raises her to the true dignity of her moral and intellectual nature."[78] Quoting Samuel Johnson and Aimé Martin, Catherine claims that woman is not man's intellectual inferior by nature, but as a consequence of a lack of training and education.[79] Rees claims that women's proper sphere is private, but "God says 'Them that honour me I will honour'";[80] and Jesus said of the Samaritan woman that wherever in the world the gospel was preached, what this woman had done would be told in memory of her.[81] Catherine continues with a roll call of twenty-three women of past and present, including Phoebe Palmer, Mary Fletcher, Elizabeth Hurrell, Sarah Mallet, Hester Ann Rogers, Elizabeth Fry, and Catherine Marsh, who with numberless others have contributed to the extension of the gospel.[82] Catherine concludes by questioning, "whether God really intended woman to bury her talents and influence as she now does? And whether the circumscribed sphere of woman's religious labours may not have something to do with the comparative non-success of the gospel in these latter days?"[83]

Catherine's pamphlet not only argues for female teaching, but, as the title of the third edition of her pamphlet confirms, also presents a justification for *Female Ministry*.[84] It is, however, notable that Catherine does not present a case for ordained female ministry; rather she presents a case for the equality of men and women under God in fulfilling the call of God to

---

75. Rees, *Reasons*, 14.
76. Booth, *Female Teaching*, 22.
77. Ibid.
78. Ibid., 23.
79. Ibid., 24.
80. Ibid., 25.
81. Ibid.
82. Ibid., 26–30.
83. Ibid., 32.
84. Booth, *Female Ministry*.

ministry which includes the charismatically gifted roles of apostle, prophet, evangelist, pastor, and teacher, and these roles are never considered by her to be exclusively fulfilled by any kind of order of ordained ministry. Catherine's illustrative examples are necessarily of women who were not ordained even where, in the examples of many Methodist women, their ministry was recognized by John Wesley. Catherine was never ordained or commissioned as a Salvation Army officer. In notices and announcements she was simply described as Mrs. Booth.

It perhaps cannot be said that *Female Teaching* is a feminist tract. However, although Olive Anderson rightly acknowledges that Catherine was "exceptionally radical in her views," she wrongly claims that Catherine "remained a firm believer in the subordination of women so far as their domestic and social position was concerned."[85] This is not the case, and it is inaccurate to state that "for [Catherine] 'true emancipation' meant simply emancipation in the Church."[86] *Female Teaching* offers more than an argument for female ministry, or the release of women into the work of the Church. This is evident in Catherine's discussion of the status of women before the Fall and of the extent of the benefits of Pentecost. Salvation, for Catherine, is the restoration of women to the image and likeness of God in Christ, which restores to women their natural equality with men in respect of nature, status, and authority, and creates the possibility of women achieving their potential not only in the sphere of the Church but also in the world. Anderson has also claimed that "the exercise by these women of this modicum of practical emancipation [. . .] contributed nothing to the spread of feminist ideas."[87] This might be compared with the conclusions of a reporter for the *Daily News* after Catherine's death:

> It has been remarked with justice that the Salvationists owe their rapid rise, and their astonishing success, to the very effective way in which they have testified to their belief in the spiritual and intellectual equality of the sexes. Promotion is by merit in the army, and not only promotion as between man and man, but as between Salvationists of either sex. Mrs. Booth was not only the devoted helpmate of "the General," she was his co-worker; and many of the most fruitful ideas in Army organization originated in her mind. In all the long history of religion there is not such instance as the Army affords of the absolute sinking of the disqualification of sex.

85. Anderson, "Women Preachers in Mid-Victorian Britain," 483.
86. Ibid.
87. Ibid., 484.

In honouring Mrs. Booth today the Salvationists testify in a peculiar manner to the strength of their hold on this great principle of progress. This alone has won them millions of the most devoted recruits.[88]

As a consequence of Catherine's commitment to female ministry the 1870 Constitution of the Christian Mission declared, "Godly women possessing the necessary gifts and qualifications shall be employed as preachers [. . .] and they shall be eligible for any office, and to speak and vote at all official meetings."[89] As Eason states, "This was a significant declaration, going far beyond the privileges given to the female preachers of past ages."[90] Similarly the introduction to the first edition of Orders and Regulations for The Salvation Army of 1878 declared, "As the Army refuses to make any difference between men and women as to rank, authority and duties, but opens the highest positions to women as well as to men, the words 'woman,' 'she,' 'her,' are scarcely ever used in orders—'man,' 'he,' 'his,' being always understood to mean a person of either sex, unless when it is evidently impossible."[91]

Given Catherine's positive example, her clear teaching, and the recognition she received, it is surprising that Eason identifies Catherine's legacy in respect of female ministry to have been "detrimental for the female officers who followed in [her] footsteps."[92] According to Eason, there were tensions between Catherine's promotion of female ministry and "her conservative views about sexual difference, motherhood and wifely submission."[93] Because Catherine "based her own preaching on a denial or deficiency of self rather than on her gifts and her right to utilize them," and "never took sufficient credit for her role in the founding of the Army," she devalued her own contribution to The Salvation Army.[94] Consequently, he maintains, "the public legacy that Catherine Booth left to Salvationist women was an ambiguous one."[95]

---

88. *Daily News*, "Mrs. Booth's Funeral."
89. The Christian Mission, "Minutes of the First Conference," Section 12.
90. Eason, *Women in God's Army*, 44.
91. Booth, *Orders and Regulations*, Part 1, i.
92. Eason, *Women in God's Army*, xiii.
93. Ibid.
94. Ibid., 110.
95. Ibid., 111.

Eason identifies four ways in which he considers Catherine undermined her own legacy. First, she refused to affirm her own abilities or acknowledge her own significance in order to protect "the fragile ego of her husband." Eason comments, "As Norman Murdoch has noted perceptively, Catherine's early success [. . .] was more than 'an insecure husband could cope with.'"[96] Murdoch's reasoning is based on partial quotations from two letters William wrote to Catherine in the autumn of 1864.[97] In the first William wrote, "You far exceed me in the influence you can command in a service";[98] in the second, "You heard how they pitched into my writing and praised yours. There, as elsewhere, I must decrease and you must increase!" However, Murdoch has ignored the context in which Begbie quoted these letters. In those difficult days when they faced an uncertain future, were often separated, struggled with finance and experienced failure as well as success, Begbie says, William "was sometimes called upon to encourage the drooping spirits of Catherine."[99] This is evident from other letters Begbie quotes and Murdoch ignores. In one William writes, "Cheer up. [. . .] All will be well. Whatever you do, don't be anxious."[100] In another he commiserates, "I cannot understand how they can possibly treat you and the work of God thus. If it had been me, I should have scarcely marvelled, but you—it is absolutely confounding."[101] In a letter written just before their move to London, addressed to "My dear little disconsolate Wife"[102]—disconsolate because some church had rejected her ministry—William continues, "Let us try again for the glory of God. The Lord is using me here and bringing up the Church."[103] In March 1865, when Catherine was experiencing better times, he wrote, "I am glad you had so good a meeting. [. . .] I could never stand in your way or prohibit your labouring when [. . .] you could do so much good. This I settled years ago."[104] Again alleging William's "frail ego," Murdoch quotes Catherine Bramwell Booth as saying that Catherine was "sensitive to the impression that her preaching was more praised than his

96. Ibid.
97. Murdoch, *Origins of The Salvation Army*, 37–38.
98. Booth and Booth, *Letters*, 346.
99. Begbie, *William Booth*, I:296.
100. Ibid., I:301.
101. Ibid., I:302.
102. Ibid., I:311.
103. Ibid., I:312.
104. Ibid., I:313.

Ministry

[William's]."[105] However, Catherine Bramwell Booth actually wrote, "She [Catherine] was sensitive, though not he [William]."[106]

The second charge Eason makes against Catherine is that because of her evangelical upbringing she had such a spirit of self-abnegation that she was unable "to take credit for anything she did."[107] In stark contrast to such a notion stand the letters Catherine wrote in the early days of her preaching ministry. To William she wrote on 13 September 1860, "If our means fail, I can get some money I am sure. I will get up some lectures and charge so much to come in, and with such an object in view I could do far beyond any thing I have yet done, and the people would come to hear me."[108] On 3 September she wrote, "I was at the Shore yesterday. Good congregation in the morning, and a precious season to myself, and as far as I could judge to everybody else. It was by far the best effort I have made. [. . .] At night the chapel was well filled, with extra forms and communion rails. Did very well, much better than at Bethesda, but not quite to my satisfaction."[109]

That it was in the context of a natural confidence in her own ability that she realized the danger of pride and the importance of self-denial is revealed later in the same letter, reporting the same occasion: "I had a very good test afforded me, by which to try my humility, by a good brother who could scarcely put three words together praying very earnestly that God would crown my labours, seeing that he could bless the weakest instruments in his service, etc. You will smile and so do I, but it did me good inasmuch as I made it then a probe for my heart and found that there was yet a good deal of self there."[110]

In *Female Teaching* Catherine had expressed the principle that self-denial is the way of self realization: "Our Lord links the joy with the suffering, the glory with the shame, the exaltation with the humiliation, the crown with the cross, the finding of life with the losing of it."[111] Diane Leclerc has argued that for John Wesley and Phoebe Palmer sin was not ultimately defined in Augustinian terms as pride, to which the antidote was a negative self-abnegation and a passive, submissive attitude to imposed social roles;

---

105. Murdoch, "Female Ministry," 359.
106. Bramwell-Booth, *Catherine Booth*, 236.
107. Eason, *Women in God's Army*, 111.
108. Booth and Booth, *Letters*, 329.
109. Ibid., 326.
110. Ibid.
111. Booth, *Female Teaching*, 25.

instead pride was conceived of as a form of idolatry to which the antidote is a positive consecration and devotion to God, and consequently the possibility of transcending conventional social roles; it was this reconfiguration which explains the release into ministry of so many women within the Holiness Movement.[112]

Eason's third charge is that Catherine continued to support feminine submission in marriage and maternal obligation in the home. Eason avers that Catherine believed wifely submission was governed by the law of love, but argues, "It did not mean much in daily life," and "merely put a benevolent face on patriarchy."[113] However, in *Female Teaching* Catherine argued that wifely submission was not part of God's initial design for the natural order but part of the curse, and by making love the law of marriage God had removed its sting.[114] In fact, such is the character of the perfect union of man and woman in marriage that, writing to William in late 1853 or early 1854, Catherine refers first to "the heads of the family" and, to make her meaning abundantly clear, to the "heads" of the household.[115] A small demonstration of this in the Booth household, a servant remembered, was that "the General never sat at the head of his table, when Mrs. Booth was present, but always beside her."[116]

Eason's fourth charge is that Catherine did not endorse a view of womanhood that sought to remove women from the domestic sphere.[117] It is true enough that Catherine continued in the domestic sphere as she ministered in the public sphere and defended that custom; but in *Female Teaching* she questioned "why woman should be confined exclusively to the kitchen and the distaff, any more than man to the field and the workshop?"[118] This is a rhetorical question with only one answer, which is, there is no reason why woman should be so confined. Susie Stanley has claimed, "Public preaching, in itself, undermines the assertion that Wesleyan/Holiness women preachers were traditionalists. Their preaching flagrantly challenged traditional notions of woman's sphere since the pulpit was the literal

---

112. Leclerc, *Singleness of Heart*.
113. Eason, *Women in God's Army*, 114–15.
114. Booth, *Female Teaching*, 22.
115. Booth and Booth, *Letters*, 200.
116. Begbie, *William Booth*, I:318.
117. Eason, *Women in God's Army*, 112–13.
118. Booth, *Female Teaching*, 4.

symbol of the male domain."[119] Pamela Walker has identified that the flaw in Eason's argument lies in his misinterpretation of the grounds on which equality between men and women might be claimed. It is anachronistic to require Victorians to deny feminine and masculine characteristics in their understanding of mutual respect, authority, and equality, or to expect Victorian women to deny their responsibility in the domestic sphere: "Eason measures The Salvation Army against a notion of equality that is abstract and timeless. His definition of equality would have been foreign to most Victorians." Walker concludes, "Because Eason does not fully appreciate the complexities of Victorian notions of gender, his claims to correct errors in the historiography cannot be sustained."[120]

And yet Eason's proposition, that there has been almost from the beginning a serious disjunction between the Army's rhetoric in support of female ministry and its implementation, is well founded. Barbara Robinson's reaction to Eason's book is unsurprising: "As I read, I found myself becoming increasingly angry, not with the author, but with the painful facts this book holds up for analysis. Eason is not telling us anything those of us who are denominational 'insiders' do not already know."[121] And it is true that Catherine was never formally integrated into the power structures of The Salvation Army; she was never ordained, never commissioned, held no rank or appointment, and did not therefore model a solution to the practical dilemma that has compromised the role of married women officers throughout the Army's history. The somewhat free, arbitrary, and ambiguous role of a leader's wife, at every level, in The Salvation Army may be fairly traced back to Catherine Booth. It is possible from her expressed views to suggest three tentative reasons for her choices. First, Catherine was always skeptical about the nature and claims of an ordained ministry and remained a congregationalist at heart; second, she was a reformer by nature and retained her suspicion of established power structures in the church; and third, she had no wish to play any part in the creation of a sect. However, in opposition to Eason's thesis that Catherine's role in practice contradicted her ecclesiology, these reasons can be seen to derive directly from it. They do raise more questions, however, which relate directly to what it means, or perhaps what it has come to mean, to be an officer, a minister of religion no less, in The Salvation Army.

119. Stanley, *Holy Boldness*, 20.
120. Walker, "Eason : Women," 976.
121. Robinson, "Andrew Mark Eason. Women in God's Army," 90.

ORDER AND AUTHORITY

On or soon after Sunday 15 December 1889, after Catherine had endured a night of excruciating pain, her family and closest friends gathered around her bedside as Catherine spoke what she thought would be her final words:[122]

> You are going to join hands with me. I cannot get hold of all your hands, so Emma will be one side and you, Pa, the other, and you must take hands all round like they do with the electric battery, and I shall feel I have got hold of you each till the light meets me on the other side, and then you can let me drop, safe in the arms of Jesus.[123] [. . .] Love one another, love one another. Stand fast together, and the Devil can sneer at the Booths.[124] [. . .] And now you who have joined hands with me. [. . .] Promise me that you will be faithful to The Salvation Army, faithful to those great principles on which it has been founded by God, faithful in hours of danger and temptation. Perhaps a time of great upheaval will come, when the world will do its best to injure you [. . .] promise me that you will be true [. . .] say it one at a time, that I may know your voices.[125]

First Bramwell, next Railton, and then Herbert promised. Catherine addressed Herbert, "When the trials come and the tempter approaches you, stick to Bramwell, and while there is love and unity the devil can curse away at the family as hard as he likes."[126] Catherine's words and actions were prescient. Ballington and Maude were the first to secede from the Army in February 1896, followed by Catherine and Arthur Booth-Clibborn in January 1902, and Herbert and Cornelie in February 1902. To compound the family's tragedy, Emma Booth-Tucker was killed in a train crash in Missouri in October 1903. After their mother's death, the younger Booths, raised by an autocrat to be autocrats, chafed under autocratic rule and as the high autocrat under whose dominion they suffered was more often than not their older brother Bramwell, they soon found the autocracy of the Army insufferable.[127] This was not only a Booth family problem however.

---

122. Compiled from Booth-Tucker and Bramwell's accounts, which are complementary and incomplete.
123. Booth-Tucker, *Catherine Booth*, II:449.
124. Booth, *On the Banks of the River*, 79.
125. Booth-Tucker, *Catherine Booth*, II:449.
126. Ibid., II:450.
127. Ervine, *God's Soldier*, II:745–49.

The secessions were the strongest evidence from within the movement that not all was well; they raised questions of order, authority, and the nature of ministry and pointed to an intractable dilemma at the heart of the Army's polity. It was not solved by the resignation of the Booths. It would lead inexorably to the events of 1929, the removal of General Bramwell Booth from office and the irreparable destruction of public confidence in the movement.[128]

In the immediate crisis Catherine's wisdom was sorely missed. For Catherine Booth the structures of the church, its orders of ministry, were of the *bene esse* of the church, and thus subject to the principle of adaptation. Adaptation had to be in keeping with biblical values, but even so the church enjoyed great freedom in this respect. Catherine wrote in *Church and State*, "Jesus Christ and his apostles left us free as air as to modes and measures, that we may provide the kind of organization most suited to the necessities of the age. There is not a hint of 'red-tapeism' in the whole of the New Testament. God does not care about the *forms* and modes, so that we have the living spirit in them; and all forms are but corpses when the spirit has gone out of them."[129]

The Christian Mission was ordered in a similar fashion to the Methodist New Connexion. William Booth was General Superintendent, and the full-time officers of the local societies were "evangelists." Ostensibly the Mission was ordered by a series of committees which answered to the Annual Conference. Robert Sandall described the Christian Mission's 1870 Constitution as a "self-denying ordinance" on William's part.[130] However, Glen Horridge has argued that from the first conference of 1870 onwards, whether consciously or not, William was tightening his control over the movement;[131] every constitutional change had that effect until by 1878, in the words of Alex Nicol, he had "authority to do with flesh and blood practically what he liked, send them where he thought best, dismiss them when he chose, and not even promise to give them remuneration, and a host of other drastic things."[132] Further evidence is provided by Gipsy Rodney Smith who claims that when he joined the Mission William was "popularly

---

128. For an account of these events cf. Larsson, *1929*.
129. Booth, *Church & State*, 51.
130. Sandall, Wiggins, and Coutts, *History*, I:178–79.
131. Horridge, *Salvation Army Origins*, 21–37.
132. Nicol, *General Booth*, 88.

referred to [...] as the Bishop,"[133] and although the Annual Conference included speeches and resolutions which were voted on, "it is certain that Mr. Booth was as absolute in his control of the Christian Mission as he now is [...] of The Salvation Army."[134]

Catherine's support for William's autocracy is hard to understand given her earlier convictions. On Tuesday 4 January 1853 William wrote to Catherine, describing how, rather unwisely, one of his supporters at Spalding had referred to him as "Superintendent."[135] Catherine's response was equally injudicious: "I believe all such authority unscriptural and anti-Christian. A conference Superintendent is as great a monstrosity as a popish priest, as far as he goes, and I should be sorry for anyone I hold dear to assume anything like it. A pastor, a minister, a father is what a preacher should be to his flock, not an authoritative ruler, but I know your views are like my own on that subject so I will say no more."[136]

According to W. T. Stead Catherine retained "a holy hatred of all despotic authority."[137] How can this be reconciled with the power that William took to himself as General of The Salvation Army? First, William's autocracy was moderated by his willingness to seek and accept counsel, not least from Catherine, according to Bramwell:

> In later years Mrs. Booth's help and counsel in the Cabinet of The Army was, of course, simply invaluable. Perhaps there, more than on the platform and more than in the Press, her influence on the Movement and on the world has been felt. In such an enterprise as this great War there daily arise questions of infinite moment which must be answered, and problems of the widest interest and importance must be solved. To these, with inflexible determination to find out what was *best*, and to help in *doing* it, Mrs. Booth could always be relied upon to address herself with marvellous wisdom and courage.[138]

There is evidence here that until 1890 at least the governance of The Salvation Army was rather more than a one man autocracy. Indeed, Catherine's passing reference to the conciliar nature of the Trinity in her address on

---

133. Smith, *Gipsy Smith*, 83.
134. Ibid., 83–84.
135. Booth and Booth, *Letters*, 49.
136. Ibid., 51.
137. Stead, *Mrs. Booth*, 204.
138. Booth, *On the Banks of the River*, 16.

the atonement suggests that the Army's conciliar form of leadership at the highest level sprang from its founders' deepest theological convictions.[139] Second, Catherine saw in William an apostolic gifting that enabled the ministry of the whole Body of Christ; the divine inspiration of the movement's organizational structure was a critical part of this conviction: "We tried committees, conferences, and all sorts of governments, showing how far we were (until God revealed it to us) from the grand military idea which is now proving such a wonderful power in organizing the converts for aggressive effort."[140]

From one perspective The Salvation Army was ruled by an autocratic General who required absolute obedience; but from another perspective the Army was ruled by a dream and inspired by a prophet. The women and men who followed William shared his vision; they saw him not as an autocrat, but as an apostle, a Spirit-anointed man of God. The working class women and men who joined this Army were not required to set aside past experiences of collective leadership: there was not an overabundance of workplace democracy in Victorian England.[141] They were used to hierarchy and autocracy, to playing their part in a system that got things done. Furthermore in its first ten years at least the Army was a meritocracy; when the Army was growing fast, there was no lack of freedom, no shortage of opportunity, no loss of responsibility. These first soldiers were expected to be leaders as well as followers, to speak out, suggest, and help find a better way. When Captain George Pollard, 20 years old, and Lieutenant Edward Wright, 19, set sail from Gravesend on 11 January 1882, charged by William to commence the work of The Salvation Army in New Zealand, uppermost in their thoughts would not have been resentment at the General's popish rule. They were having the time of their lives.[142]

Third, William's dominant leadership was hard won and moderated by mutual love and respect. W. T. Stead observed, "The authority of the General is exercised only by the continually renewed voluntary consent of his soldiers."[143] Gipsy Smith enjoyed the benefits of William's visionary leadership as well as experiencing the hard knocks of his autocratic style

---

139. Booth, *Life & Death*, 135–36.
140. Booth, *Church & State*, 68.
141. Horridge, *Salvation Army Origins*, 76–77.
142. Bradwell, *Fight the Good Fight*, 5–13.
143. Stead, *Mrs. Booth*, 204.

at first hand.[144] Smith's last word on William Booth says much: "I have the warmest feelings of love and admiration for General Booth. He gave me my first opportunity as an evangelist, and he put me in the way of an experience that has been invaluable to me. I think that William Booth is one of the grandest men that God ever gave the world. His treatment of me was always kind and fatherly."[145]

According to Booth-Tucker, William and Catherine's family life was the nurturing model for the development of the Army's sociality: "The General and Mrs. Booth had commenced within the narrow circle of their own home the work which had broadened out until it had included within its embrace the entire world."[146] The Booth household was in many ways typically Victorian; however, Catherine was not a typical Victorian wife. Writing to William one Sunday afternoon in the winter of 1853–54, Catherine included outlines for a series of sermons on the topic of home and family. Catherine referred to the benign rule of the "heads of the household," not the "head."[147] She wrote, "There must be discipline, but it must be the rule of love." She continued, "Love being the ruling power [. . .] will be felt to be irresistible, and [. . .] will yield a willing obedience. Love demands obedience only to such mandates as tend to the general good."[148] Booth-Tucker affirmed, "The Salvation Army was but an application of the same principles to a wider sphere," and drew attention to an unrecognized aspect of the nascent Salvation Army that derived from the complementary roles of William and Catherine as the movement's co-founders.

> The military idea was interwoven with that of the family. The one was the warp and the other was the woof. The two combined to give unity and cohesion to each other. The skeleton of the organisation, its bonework, so to speak, was composed of military rules and regulations, which of themselves would have been stiff, repulsive, valueless. But the warm filling up of family flesh and blood covered and beautified that which was in its turn indispensable to lend symmetry and strength to what would otherwise have been after all but a shapeless, heterogeneous, and comparatively useless mass. It is the attempted divorce of these two principles which God has so inextricably allied, that has bred so much confusion

144. Smith, *Gipsy Smith*, 112.
145. Ibid., 140.
146. Booth-Tucker, *Catherine Booth*, II:305.
147. Booth and Booth, *Letters*, 200.
148. Ibid., 200–201.

and failure in the religious world. "Order is Heaven's first law," and will be so to the end. But there must be something to order, or order of itself will be of little avail.[149]

To these notions of the order of the church as a family and as an Army, in *Church and State* Catherine added a third, that of a business. Applying this model to the church and illustrating by means of The Salvation Army, Catherine affirmed the importance of results, and the principle that "*we shall reap according as we sow*";[150] the need for efficiency, and for modes and measures that are simple and effective in achieving results, "that kind of organisation most suited to the necessities of the age";[151] the indispensability of hard work; and finally the spirit of enterprise, to which after "the presence of the Spirit of God" the success of the Army is most due.[152] For Catherine this is a participative not an autocratic model: "If you want to accomplish anything you call your heads of department together and plan how it is to be done; you set the best man to the best post, and make him responsible for carrying out your plans."[153] The Army's vision is of every Christian a soldier for Christ, engaged, mobilized: "Others besides clergymen, ministers, deacons, and elders can be used for the salvation of men."[154] And yet, unarguably, these three forms of sociality—an Army, a family, a business—can also be three of the most abusive forms of human sociality.

From 1878 to 1883 the Army experienced the most rapid phase of growth in its history—from 31 corps in Great Britain and Ireland in 1878 to 573 in December 1883.[155] During these years, the Army's centre of gravity was located in its soldiery, and consequently in the doctrine of the priesthood of all believers, understood as the battlefield commissioning of all Christ's followers. Catherine complained of organizations "compressing the life of their members, cramping it in, or throwing a wet blanket over it, not allowing it room for exercise and growth"; in contrast, "We give to every consecrated man, woman, and child liberty for the exercise of their

---

149. Booth-Tucker, *Catherine Booth*, II:305–6.
150. Booth, *Church & State*, 47.
151. Ibid., 51.
152. Ibid., 58.
153. Ibid., 51.
154. Ibid., 75.
155. Horridge, *Salvation Army Origins*, 38.

individual gifts to a far greater extent than we find anywhere else."[156] In an 1898 address reported in *The War Cry* William Booth addressed his soldiers:

> You cannot say you are not ordained. You were ordained when you signed Articles of War, under the blessed Flag. If not, I ordain every man, woman and child here present that has received the new life. I ordain you now. I cannot get at you to lay my hands upon you. I ordain you with the breath of my mouth. I tell you what your true business in the world is, and in the name of God I authorise you to go and do it. Go into all the world and preach the gospel to every creature![157]

But by 1898 the Army's centre of gravity had already shifted away from the soldiery. Its organizational structure of staff, field, and local officers is described in the 1878 Orders and Regulations. Certain ranks are associated with different levels, but titles such as Chief of Staff, Adjutant and Quartermaster appear at each level.[158] The titles may be arcane, but the structure is simple, as is the underlying theology. The essential difference between staff and field officers, and local officers is that the latter are not "wholly employed in the service."[159] There is no difference in status. The command, freedom, responsibility, obligation, and obedience exercised throughout the Army is different in scale but not different in kind; this is an ordering of the people of God by the people of God who are marshalling their resources for war. Railton quotes William, from an address to young officers:

> My conversion made me, in a moment, a preacher of the Gospel. The idea never dawned on me that any line was to be drawn between one who had nothing else to do but preach and a saved apprentice lad who only wanted "to spread through all the earth abroad" [. . .] the fame of our Saviour. I have lived, thank God, to witness the separation between layman and cleric become more and more obscured, and to see Jesus Christ's idea of changing in a moment ignorant fishermen into fishers of men nearer and nearer realisation.[160]

156. Booth, *All the World*, "Mrs. Booth's Address at the Exeter Hall Meeting, May 4th."
157. Booth, *The War Cry*, "What the General Expects of His Soldiers."
158. Booth, *Orders and Regulations*, Part 1, i.
159. Ibid.
160. Railton, *General Booth*, 17.

Ministry

Harold Hill has traced this emphasis running strongly through the early years. However, he has also demonstrated with a wealth of supporting evidence that the Army was subject to an inexorable process of clericalization.[161] Florence Booth, Bramwell's wife, was still affirming that the Army was raised up as a protest against the clericalization of the ministry of the church in the 1920s, and yet Hill notes, "At the same time as we have these very clear statements that The Salvation Army was an essentially lay movement, we find the development of an assumption that officers did enjoy a distinctive and special role—or status."[162] There are discordant notes in the 1878 Orders and Regulations. One section likening the people of God to a flock of sheep continues, "But the sheep will always be moved by the Devil to rebel against the shepherds, and to say, 'Why should not we have our own way?' This is why almost all religious bodies have come to be organised in a way providing for the direction of everything, and the selection of every officer by the votes of the sheep!"[163]

That such an important point might rest on such a cynical and poor exegesis is not encouraging. This argument demeans the sheep, elevates the shepherds, and separates them out in an implicitly clergy/laity divide, in a manner which devalues the notion that the people of God might have the mind of Christ. Here is the seeding of clericalization. Catherine believed that Christ was to be encountered in the form of converted thieves and drunkards; but perhaps Christ was only to be seen and not heard when encountered in such a form. Writing in *Echoes and Memories*, Bramwell expressed his understanding of what ministry in the Army had become, at least by 1925, "We humbly but firmly claim that we are in no way inferior, either to the saints who have gone before, or [. . .] the saints of the present [. . .] our Officers are, equally with them, ministers in the Church of God, having received diversities of gifts, but the one Spirit—endowed by His grace, assured of His guidance, confirmed by His Word, and commissioned by the Holy Ghost to represent Him to the whole world."[164]

This limited definition is nothing but problematic, in the light of the Army's pragmatic view of ministry and commitment to the priesthood and commissioning of all believers. Bramwell says nothing in this brief statement that until then could not have been predicated of any soldier in the

---

161. Cf. Hill, *Leadership in The Salvation Army*.
162. Ibid., 72.
163. Booth, *Orders and Regulations*, Part 1, 3.
164. Booth, *Echoes and Memories*, 67–68.

Army. Indeed, it could be argued that the genius of the Army lay in its corporate belief that every follower of Christ was graced, guided, and commissioned in just this way. In 1903 William wrote to Bramwell:

> More and more as I have wrestled with the [new] Regulations this week has it been borne in upon me that it is the Officer upon whom all depends. It has always been so. If Moses had not made a priesthood there would have been no Jewish nation. It was the priesthood of the Levites which kept them alive, saved them from their inherent rottenness, or at any rate from many of its consequences, and perpetuated the law which made them. Here is— where I think your great work for the next ten years will lie. No one can begin to do it like you.[165]

Ervine remarks, "This was a far different note from any that he had previously sounded. Priests had never previously been much esteemed by him who had a soldier's heart."[166] It was not priests but warriors who had raised the Army. Robertson concludes that William had come to "the conclusion that the priesthood of all believers, though already effectively dropped in practice, had to be attenuated as an ideal."[167] However this dislocation of the movement's centre of gravity was arrived at, it was not achieved by a process of theological reflection, and the consequence was inevitably to disengage the Army's ecclesiology from its polity.

CONCLUSION

Catherine Booth's view of Christian ministry was deeply egalitarian. At its heart lay the root insight of her soteriology, that salvation is nothing less than the restoration of women and men to the image and likeness of God in Christ. This was the basis of her feminism, and her claim that women had an equal responsibility and right with men to be ministers of the gospel. For Catherine, the call to mission and ministry was the common calling of all God's people. Christ's commission, "as the Father has sent me, so I am sending you," applies to all Christians, not to a select few.

In Catherine's lifetime the Army was effectively a meritocracy in which the principle of the priesthood of all believers applied to every member, regardless of rank, gender, or age, reflecting the Christological,

---

165. Begbie, *William Booth*, II:280–81.
166. Ervine, *God's Soldier*, II:777.
167. Robertson in Wilson, *Patterns of Sectarianism*, 80.

pneumatological, missiological, and eschatological imperatives of its ecclesiology. The Army's hierarchical structure was moderated in its effects by the movement's dual character as a family as well as an Army. The Army's leadership, safeguarded by Catherine's powerful influence in its innermost circles, was ultimately conciliar rather than autocratic.

SEVEN

The Sacraments

According to Bramwell Booth, Catherine Booth's views strongly influenced her husband William's decision in January 1883 to stop practicing the sacraments.[1] Moreover, it was by the robust expression of her views as the Army's primary apologist that Catherine consolidated what was probably intended by William to be a provisional decision.

This chapter will consider the historical development of the Army's position; Catherine Booth's own view of the sacraments; the formative influences upon her views; and her abiding influence upon the Army's non-sacramental position.

HISTORICAL DEVELOPMENT

At first the Christian Mission and the nascent Salvation Army followed in Methodist tradition and practiced the sacraments of baptism (for infants) and the Lord's Supper. William set out the rationale for his change of mind in an address to Officers subsequently published in *The War Cry*.[2] Four main points established the grounds for his decision. First, "the Sacraments are not conditions of Salvation"; second, "there is general division of opinion as to the proper mode of administering them"; third, "the introduction of them would create division and heart burning"; and fourth, "we are not professing to be a church, nor aiming at being one, but simply a force for aggressive Salvation purposes." Given these, William asked, "is it not wise for us to postpone any settlement of the question, to leave it over to some future day, when we shall have more light, and see more clearly our way before us?"[3]

---

1. Booth, *Echoes and Memories*, 192.
2. Booth, *The War Cry*, "The Sacraments."
3. Not numbered by Booth; ibid.

William added three provisions to his argument. First, "We do not prohibit our own people in any shape or form taking the sacraments"; second, "We will remember His love every hour of our lives, and continually feed on Him by faith"; and third, "We are agreed on the priority of the Baptism of the Holy Spirit."[4]

In 1895 William was interviewed by Henry Lunn for *The Review of the Churches*. On this occasion William added two new points. He questioned whether Jesus had himself instituted the sacraments, and raised the issue of ritualism. However he continued to insist "this with us is not a settled question," and he added, "We never declaim against the Sacraments; we never even state our own position. We are anxious not to destroy the confidence of Christian people in institutions which are helpful to them."[5]

William Booth's arguments were uncharacteristically reticent. Begbie claimed, "To the end of his days there were moments when he looked almost wistfully to the Sacrament of the Supper, and there were moments when he appears to have doubted, if only transiently, the wisdom of his decision."[6] It was Catherine who added steel to the argument.

Writing in 1925 Bramwell Booth summarized the arguments. He noted the question of baptism was not of great concern but that the Lord's Supper was an altogether different matter.[7] The genesis of the abandonment lay in Catherine's abhorrence of formalism.[8] William's approach was "utilitarian."[9] There was the practical "persistently troublesome" matter of whether alcoholic wine or some substitute should be used.[10] The use of alcoholic wine had proved to be a temptation to at least some saved drunkards, and non-alcoholic substitutes were unacceptable to sacramental purists. There was also the problem of who administered the sacrament.[11] The Army did not confer upon its officers the status of an ordained ministry or priesthood, but some congregations had refused to accept the sacrament from non-officer hands, and this also raised the thorny issue of women's

---

4. Ibid.
5. Lunn, "General Booth."
6. Begbie, *William Booth*, I:428.
7. Booth, *Echoes and Memories*, 191.
8. Ibid., 192.
9. Ibid., 193.
10. Ibid.
11. Ibid.

Catherine Booth

ministry. Lastly there was the problem of who was allowed to receive the sacrament.[12]

William was undoubtedly sincere when he protested that Salvationists never declaimed against the sacraments, and that the issue was not settled. However, Catherine was strident in her defense of the Army's position. Her views were more than utilitarian. William may have attempted to leave room for an alternative future position, but Catherine's passionate polemic effectively burnt the Army's bridges and cemented the Army's position as a non-sacramental movement within the church.

A NON-SACRAMENTAL SALVATIONIST

Catherine Booth was a fierce opponent of the sacraments because she believed they could be a hindrance to a true religion of the heart. The pragmatic reasons that led William to consider setting the matter of the sacraments to one side until some future date were as nothing compared to Catherine's forceful arguments against the continuance of sacramental practices. Catherine's robust opinions would surely have been another factor for the hard-pressed General to consider. Catherine's views regarding the sacraments were most fully expressed in her address *A Mock Salvation and a Real Deliverance from Sin*.[13] Catherine stated her conviction that lamentably "there are endless substitutions for salvation."[14] She identified these substitutions under four divisions: salvations of theory, salvations of ceremony, salvations of mere belief, and the salvation of unbelief.

Catherine launched her attack on the sacraments under the heading "salvations of ceremony," declaring, "Another mock salvation is presented in the shape of ceremonies and sacraments."[15] The main thrust of Catherine's argument was that the sacraments are a delusional substitute for the true ground of salvation, which is a heart delivered from sin by the redeeming work of Christ confirmed by the indwelling Holy Spirit.

Catherine claimed the sacraments were "only intended as outward signs of an inward spiritual reality."[16] According to the 1662 Book of Common Prayer, a sacrament is "an outward and visible sign of an inward and

---

12. Ibid.
13. Booth, *Popular Christianity*, 29–53.
14. Ibid., 34.
15. Ibid., 42.
16. Ibid.

spiritual grace."[17] However, Catherine claimed "these were *only* intended as" such. The Prayer Book definition continued that the sacraments are "a means whereby we receive the same, and a pledge to assure us thereof."[18] While Catherine did not deny that the sacraments are a "means of grace" she did plainly deny that they were anything more than signs. The sacraments are not effective in and of themselves. Catherine was denying the mechanism of an *opus operatum*. But she was also denying any other manner by which the sacraments might be indispensable to salvation. This was the fundamental ground on which Catherine made her protest against the sacraments.

Further, Catherine did not believe the practice of the sacraments to be definitive of the church. In this she was in disagreement with the Protestant Reformers Luther and Calvin as well as the Thirty-Nine Articles of the Church of England and, most importantly given her Methodist background, John Wesley. In his sermon *Of the Church* Wesley followed the Thirty-Nine Articles in defining the church as a believing people "among whom the pure word of God is preached, and the sacraments duly administered."[19]

Within the category of "sacrament," Catherine identified baptism, the Lord's Supper, and the ceremonials of ancient or modern churches.[20] Catherine apparently intended to include the sacraments of marriage, ordination, repentance, confirmation, and the anointing of the sick or last rites, though in particularly stating "modern churches" she left open the possibility of contemporary developments of the sacramental principle. By widening the scope of "sacrament" beyond the Lord's Supper and baptism, Catherine was implicitly denying to these two sacraments any privileged or definitive status.

Catherine next identified two groups who held to the delusion that they would be saved by virtue of their baptism. First, there were those who held to the "palpable delusion" of baptismal regeneration; but also, secondly, there were those "ordinary church and chapel going people" who held a less exalted view of the power of the ceremony to effect an imperceptible but real ontological change, but who still believed they would be saved because they had been baptized.[21]

---

17. HM Printing Office, *The Book of Common Prayer*, 288.
18. Ibid.
19. Wesley, *Sermons*, 1–4, §18, III:52.
20. Booth, *Popular Christianity*, 42.
21. Ibid.

The Church of England's Article XXV, with its affirmation of the sacraments as "sure witnesses and effectual signs," significantly falls short of a claim to *ex opere operato*, a claim which was to Catherine a "palpable delusion," given the large number of unregenerate yet baptized men and women who were attracted to Army meetings because of their desperate need of salvation.[22] For Catherine, the underlying principle at work was "an inveterate tendency [. . .] in the human heart to trust in outward forms instead of seeking the inward grace."[23] Where this was the case, Catherine argued, such forms were a hindrance rather than a help to that inner spiritual life which is the dynamic force of Christian experience. Where this was not the case, by implication Catherine appeared to accept the forms may be of some help. Her earlier statement that the sacraments were only outward signs would not then appear to discount them as means of grace. If in faith the inward grace is sought through the medium of the outward signs, then it might be found. But equally the grace can be found without the sign, and the sign does not inevitably convey the grace.

Catherine turned to the Old Testament for an illustration of this principle, this tendency to substitute a form for the real power, which she described as idolatry. She cited the example of the brass serpent raised by Moses for the healing of the people but later destroyed by Hezekiah when it became an object of idolatrous worship.[24] Catherine had nothing to say against forms per se, as "the bodies in which spiritual ideas and purposes are manifested," but "without LIFE they are useless and worse than useless."[25]

Circumcision was another example of a form "originally ordained by God" which, when substituted for inward righteousness, was rightly described by the apostle Paul as "nothing."[26] Catherine thought Paul would say the same of contemporary practices of the sacraments of baptism and the Lord's Supper. Even if Jesus Christ intended them as permanent institutions, Paul would count them as nothing compared to keeping the commandments of God, "such is the awful abuse to which these ceremonies have been subjected."[27] However, against this possibility Catherine averred there "are very strong arguments," citing "many most devoted and intel-

22. Ibid.
23. Ibid.
24. Ibid., 43.
25. Ibid.
26. Ibid., 44.
27. Ibid.

ligent Christians ever since the days of the apostle," and including "the 'Friends' of our own time."[28] According to Catherine, a line could be traced through history of those who had refused to accept that Christ intended the sacraments to be permanent institutions.

Catherine next turned her attention to those who affirmed the importance of the Lord's Supper and baptism, not as sacraments but as ordinances, ceremonies that must be observed because of their dominical institution. Against those who argued that she had "no authority to remit the Supper, because the Lord said we were to take it in remembrance of Him till He comes," Catherine offered a two-stage argument. First, Christ "left the taking of it at all perfectly discretional"; and second, its continuance depended upon how the promise of Christ's return was interpreted.[29] Catherine may possibly have based her claim that Christ left it to the discretion of his followers when, if ever, to take the Lord's Supper on a close interpretation of the words of Christ recorded in 1 Corinthians 11, which do not explicitly command a continuing practice. However, she did not explain any further this point. Catherine cited "'Friends,' and others of the most spiritual and deeply taught Christians of all times," who believed that Jesus was referring to "his coming at the end of the Jewish dispensation."[30] This comment confirms that underlying Catherine's view of the sacraments was a strong and distinctive realized eschatology. The Lord's return was connected to Pentecost and the gift of the Holy Spirit to the church. This was a more than a pneumatological perspective for it also answered Christological questions, such as how Christ continued to be present with his people; and it also answered eschatological questions regarding the nature and character of the present age. It led naturally on to questions of missiology, in regard to the expectations and provisions of Christ for Christian mission, and in turn to ecclesiology, regarding the character of this community called into mission in a pentecostal age.

For Catherine, then, it was not only pneumatology that was at the heart of the question of the sacraments. Catherine's concerns were also Christological and had to do with the Christian's experience of the presence of the risen Christ after his resurrection and ascension. Catherine began by placing the sacraments in a soteriological perspective. However, her views

---

28. Ibid.
29. Ibid., 45.
30. Ibid.

on the sacraments were bound up with her eschatology as well as her pneumatology, Christology, missiology, and ecclesiology.

Catherine turned next to Christ's words to the woman of Samaria. Christ's promise of an hour coming when "true worshippers shall worship the Father in spirit and in truth [. . .] could not have intended to teach that God could be more acceptably or profitably worshipped through any particular forms or ceremony than without such a form or ceremony."[31] The promise that "if a man love me, he will keep my words, and my Father will love him, and we (I and my Father) will come unto him, and make our *abode* with him" was not contingent on the "earthly medium of bread and wine." Nor was there a suggestion that by remembering Jesus, on whom "their thoughts were to be constantly concentrated," through this "medium" a communion with him might be established beyond and above that communion with him always and everywhere promised in this verse.[32] The promised well of water within was identified with the wine Christ promised to drink with his people in his Father's kingdom, wine which was "righteousness, *peace and joy*, in the Holy Ghost."[33] These were the true "sacraments"; if these were not enjoyed, all else was "Nehustan" (that is, like the bronze serpent).[34]

Catherine continued by claiming that if there were to be any binding forms in the new and spiritual kingdom, then the washing of feet enjoined by Christ should be included; however, regardless of Christ's injunction this particular form was generally neglected because of human pride and priestly assumption.[35]

From robust defense Catherine turned to attack. The undue value set upon the sacraments had been historically "one of the greatest hindrances to the extension of Christianity."[36] Catherine recalled a revival work "twenty-five years ago" where much was lost because of a controversy around water baptism.[37] For this reason the Army had shrunk from addressing the controversial matter of adult believers' baptism; Catherine found the wisdom of this decision confirmed by the apostle Paul's thanksgiving

31. Ibid.
32. Ibid.
33. Ibid., 46.
34. Ibid.
35. Ibid.
36. Ibid.
37. The 1859 Ulster Revival

that he baptized none of his early converts in Corinth because of similar controversy.[38]

Finally, Catherine asked, "What can be the value of imitating the marchings and vestments and songs of the ancient Jewish Church?"[39] The new focus of Catherine's attack was the Ritualist movement within the Church of England, which believed the church in its historical form was of divine origin, that it had maintained its tradition in continuity with and from apostolic times, and that liturgical renewal was the way to religious and national revival.[40] Catherine developed her views in a context of fierce controversy, in antithesis to other movements of renewal within the church, and they reflect the sharp divisions between radical evangelical and extreme liturgical programs for national and ecclesiological revival.[41] These themes were being played out on the national stage.

This section of Catherine's argument was especially censorious. She described participants in the sacraments as spiritually uncircumcised Philistines daring to place their hands on God's Ark by "anticipating the signs, ordinances, and alleluias of the Church Triumphant."[42] The celebrated event in March 1882 when more than 400 Salvationists marched from their citadel in York to take Holy Communion in St Peter's Holgate, with the blessing of Archbishop William Thomson, caused controversy within the Anglican church at the time, a controversy inflamed by the angry expressions of Ritualist clergy in York who described it as a "defamation."[43] The Ritualists differed from their predecessors in the Oxford Movement by lacking any general positive warmth towards evangelicals and by placing little emphasis on the validity or necessity of conversion. For Catherine, "the first qualification for participating in any spiritual exercises or ceremonies, is the *renewal of the heart* by the Holy Ghost."[44] A renewal of the church which aimed at the renewal of ceremonial practice rather than a reformation of the heart could lead only to "greater condemnation" and a "deeper hell."[45]

---

38. Booth, *Popular Christianity*, 47.
39. Ibid.
40. See Chadwick, *The Victorian Church*, I:212–21, II:308–27.
41. See Kent, *Holding the Fort*.
42. Booth, *Popular Christianity*, 47.
43. Coutts, *The Salvationists*, 72.
44. Booth, *Popular Christianity*, 47.
45. Ibid., 48.

FORMATIVE INFLUENCES

Catherine was a woman of independent spirit who was prepared to come to her own view even on matters as significant as church, ministry, and sacraments. However, it is possible to identify a number of theologians who made an important contribution to her views.

Augustus Neander

Catherine made her statements as they touched upon the sacramental history of the church with confident authority. Booth-Tucker wrote of Catherine's adolescent studies, "Her powerful mind fairly revelled in grappling with the deepest theological problems, nor was she satisfied with a mere superficial acquaintance with her subject," and he included the Lutheran historians Mosheim and Neander among the writers she studied at that time.[46] David Rightmire asserts, "These writings opened up the possibility of questioning the relationship between Christ, his Church, and the sacraments."[47]

Augustus Neander devoted the final section of the first volume of his *General History of Christian Religion and Church* to the subject of the sacraments. Neander wrote of the sacraments: "The *visible Church* required *visible* signs, for the spiritual facts on which its inward essence rests. Hence Christ, who meant to found a visible Church, instituted *two outward signs*, as symbols of the invisible fellowship between him, the *Head* of the spiritual body, and its members, the believers, and of the union of these members not only *with himself,* but *with one another.*"[48]

Neander described the sacraments as "outward signs of divine realities" and continued, "The connection of the moments represented by these outward signs with the whole of the Christian life, the union of the inward and divine things with the outward transactions, were present to the lively Christian feelings of the early believers; but it was here a source of great practical mischief—just as we observed in the case of the doctrine concerning the Church—that men neglected duly to separate and distinguish in their conceptions, what was connected together in their feelings."[49]

---

46. Booth-Tucker, *Catherine Booth*, I:28.
47. Rightmire, *Sacraments*, 62.
48. Neander, *General History*, I: 414.
49. Ibid., I: 415.

The Sacraments

This failure to conceptually separate the outward and inward aspect of the sacraments led to a mistaken view of the necessity of the outward sign and to a misguided valuation of the importance of infant baptism.

> But when now, on the one hand, the doctrine of the corruption and guilt, cleaving to human nature in consequence of the first transgression, was reduced to a more precise and systematic form, and on the other, from the want of duly distinguishing between what is outward and what is inward in baptism, (the baptism by water and the baptism by the Spirit,) the error became more firmly established that without external baptism no one could be delivered from the inherent guilt, could be saved from the everlasting punishment that threatened him, or raised to eternal life; and when the notion of a magical influence, a charm connected with the sacraments continually gained ground, the theory was finally evolved of the *unconditional necessity of infant baptism*.[50]

Neander baldly described the mechanism that establishes this necessity, the *opus operatum,* as a "false notion." He narrated the sad case of a converted heretic who pleaded with his bishop to baptize him again. Because the bishop believed in the *opus operatum* of the poor man's heretical baptism, he refused; however, the man "found it impossible to overcome his scruples and regain his tranquillity."[51] Neander concluded, "So destructive to peace of conscience were the effects of such tenacious adherence to outward things, of not knowing how to rise with freedom to those things of the Spirit, which the inward man apprehends by faith!"[52]

The doctrine of *opus operatum* bound the sign and that which is signified inextricably together. Neander did not present an alternative means of binding the sign to that which is signified, and thus presented the possibility that it was possible to have one without the other. It was possible, therefore, to be baptized and not saved; and to be saved and not baptized. This separation of the outward sign from the inward grace, which rendered one independent of the other, even inconsequential to the other, was the mechanism at the heart of Catherine's apologetic, and Catherine fully shared Neander's views of the corruption of the pure, primitive church through the course of history.

---

50. Ibid., I: 427.
51. Ibid., I: 441.
52. Ibid.

John Wesley

Catherine's opinions can only be attributed to the influence of Wesley by means of a tendentious interpretation of his views. For Wesley the Lord's Supper was a convicting and converting ordinance.[53] The sacraments were "means of grace," "the *ordinary* channels whereby [God] might convey to men preventing, justifying, or sanctifying grace."[54] Wesley wrote to John Smith, "I have not studied the writings of the Quakers enough [. . .] to say precisely what they mean by 'perceptible inspiration,' and whether their account of it be right or wrong. And I am not curious to know, since between me and them there is a great gulf fixed. The sacraments of Baptism and the Lord's Supper keep us at a wide distance from each other, insomuch that, according to the view of things I have now I should as soon commence deist as Quaker."[55]

Even so, some commentators find inconsistencies in Wesley's thought regarding the sacraments. Maddox writes in an article defending the integrity of Wesley's theology, "It seems fair to say that Wesley never constantly developed the implications of his radical reaffirmation of grace in 1738 for the doctrine of the sacraments. This is particularly true in regard to the issue of infant baptism."[56]

Until his death Wesley encouraged Methodists to attend church and partake in communion. He followed the Thirty-Nine Articles in defining the church as a believing people "among whom the pure word of God is preached, and the sacraments duly administered."[57] However, Wesley notably declined to "defend the accuracy of this definition," refusing to exclude from the church those congregations in which "unscriptural doctrines" are taught, as well as those congregations in which the sacraments are not "duly administered." "Whoever they are that have 'one Spirit, one hope, one Lord, one faith, one God and Father of all,'" Wesley declared, he could "easily bear" with their "wrong opinions" and "superstitious modes of worship," and he would not object to "receive them, if they desired it, as members of the Church of England."[58] From this one source Catherine could have

---

53. Wesley, *Journals and Diaries*, 18–24, XIX:158.
54. John Wesley, Sermon 16, "The Means of Grace," in Wesley, *Sermons*, 1–4, §II.1, I:381.
55. John Wesley, Letter to John Smith (25 June 1746), Baker, *Letters II*, 203.
56. Maddox, "Responsible Grace," 17.
57. Wesley, *Sermons*, 1–4, §18, III:52.
58. Ibid., §19, III:52.

claimed that from Wesley, despite Wesley, she had learned that it was not the practice of the sacraments which united the people of God but a common experience of life in the Spirit.[59]

Ole Borgen holds a high view of the consistency and integrity of John Wesley's sacramental theology. He states in his thesis, "John Wesley's theology is unitive. He has one unified doctrine of the sacraments, comprising Baptism and the Lord's Supper, which forms an integral part of the greater unitive structure."[60] Borgen constantly affirms the consistency of Wesley's views; where other commentators see flux in Wesley's view of the sacraments, Borgen allows, at worst, for a progressive development. However, Borgen allows that some difficulty attends Wesley's comments regarding the relationship between baptism and regeneration in his sermon "The New Birth." According to Wesley, "Baptism is not the new birth: they are not one and the same thing";[61] and he explains, "For what can be more plain than that the one is an external, the other an internal work? That the one is a visible, the other an invisible thing, and therefore different from each other: the one being an act of man, purifying the body, the other a change wrought by God in the soul, so that the former is just as distinguishable from the latter, as the soul from the body, or water from the Holy Ghost."[62]

In Borgen's words, "Wesley carries this argument one step further, expressing the possibility of the two parts of the sacrament being actually torn apart."[63] According to Wesley, "As the new birth is not the same thing with baptism, so it does not always accompany baptism; they do not constantly go together. A man may possibly be 'born of water' and yet not be 'born of the Spirit.' There may sometimes be the outward sign where there is not the inward grace."[64]

Thus Wesley apparently separates the sign from the signified. In proceeding Wesley appears to retract somewhat from this view in regard to infant baptism and to restore its efficacy, at least as Borgen understands him:

> I do not now speak with regard to infants: it is certain, our Church supposes that all who are baptised in their infancy are at the same time born again. And it is allowed that the whole office for the

---

59. Ibid.
60. Borgen, *John Wesley on the Sacraments*, 47.
61. John Wesley, Sermon 45, "The New Birth," in Wesley, *Sermons*, 1–4, §iv.1, II:196.
62. Ibid., §iv.1, II:197.
63. Borgen, *John Wesley on the Sacraments*, 153.
64. Wesley, Sermon 45, "The New Birth," in Wesley, *Sermons*, 1–4, §iv.2, II:197.

baptism of Infants proceeds upon this supposition. Nor is it an objection of any weight against this that we cannot comprehend how this work can be wrought in infants. For neither can we comprehend *how* it is wrought in a person of riper years. But whatever be the case with infants, it is sure all of riper years who are baptized are not at the same time born again. "The tree is known by its fruits."[65]

However, Wesley's phrasing in this passage is curious. The phrase "it is certain our Church supposes" does not necessarily reflect a sense of certainty on Wesley's part. That infants are born again when they are baptized may be for Wesley, it seems, not a certainty but a supposition. As for adults, Wesley is certain that "all of riper years who are baptized are not at the same time born again."[66]

It remains, however, that this supposition is supposed by the Church of England, and therefore for Wesley remains authoritative. According to Rob Staples, "Much confusion has prevailed among students of Wesley in the attempt to understand his view of the relationship between baptism and the new birth."[67] Staples asserts firmly that Wesley believed, "Infants are born again in baptism."[68] According to Albert Outler, Wesley made a "mild allowance for the doctrine of baptismal generation," while also placing a heavy stress "on conversion as a conscious adult experience of regeneration."[69]

It is certain that Catherine Booth was not a close disciple of Wesley in her expressed view of the sacraments. Nevertheless, the underlying theological position in regard to the necessary efficacy of the sacraments is not dissimilar. Catherine held that the sacraments were not a necessary means of salvation. John Wesley may have agreed. However, he would not have agreed with Catherine that the sacraments were only signs. There is a rich middle ground between these two alternatives which Catherine did not acknowledge.

---

65. Ibid.
66. Ibid.
67. Staples, *Outward Sign and Inward Grace*, 183.
68. Ibid., 184.
69. Outler, *John Wesley*, 318.

The Sacraments

Methodism

The immediate historical context of Catherine's views regarding the sacraments is crucial. The only reference W. T. Stead makes to the sacraments in his biography of Catherine is in connection with his assertion that "conversion is the pivot of the Salvation Army":[70] "Some churches emphasize [conversion] more than others. Some smother it under such trappings of formalities that no one save God, and least of all the individual himself, can see whether or not there has been a definite turning away from the old life and a not less definite and decisive entering upon the new. Baptism, confirmation, admission to church membership, and all manner of similar ceremonies, are but the outward and visible sign of inward change."[71]

It is evident that Stead, not a Salvationist, has some sympathy with Catherine's line of thought in regard to the sacraments, and as a popular commentator is expressing a not uncommon view. What appears today to have been an entirely bold, radical, and controversial move was not necessarily perceived as such in its immediate context.

Whether or not there are inconsistencies within Wesley's own thought, it is a matter of fact that in its sacramental practice, or more precisely its lack of it, nineteenth-century Methodism failed to live up to the high sacramental standards of its founder. The consequence of Wesley's determination not to create a Methodist Church with its own rank of ordained ministers, alongside his insistence that Methodists should be encouraged to partake of communion in their parish church, was that, in the words of T. H. Barratt, Methodists "have paid a sad price for the pathetic loyalty of their fathers to their old, unkindly mother [. . .] and [. . .] those four years of prohibition, followed by the restrictions of 1795 created a tradition which went far to annul the teaching and example of John Wesley and sowed seeds of which we reap the harvest even to this day."[72]

Wesley's strictures that the Lord's Supper should not be celebrated in Methodist chapels at the same time and in competition with the parish church meant that the Lord's Supper was commonly held in Methodist chapels during the evening service, and the central focus for Methodists in their Sunday morning service became the ministry of the word rather than the breaking of bread. The consequence in practice for many Methodists

---

70. Stead, *Mrs. Booth*, 34.

71. Ibid.

72. Barratt, The London Quarterly Review (July 1923), cited in Bowmer, *The Lord's Supper in Methodism*, 22.

was that effectively they became uninterested in this means of grace. At the same time Wesley's writings urging the importance and necessity of faithful attendance at Holy Communion were dismissed as the expressions of an earlier "High Church" phase of his thought.[73]

It is not possible to attribute a direct line of theological influence to Catherine's mentors and teachers within Methodism. The movement remained firmly sacramental in its theological expressions. Dr William Cooke wrote in his handbook of Christian Theology, "The Divine authority of this ordinance [The Lord's Supper] is so clear and decisive as to place it almost beyond the possibility of controversy, the dissentients being so few in number as to form but a trifling exception to its universal recognition."[74] Cooke lacked the prescience that one of his former students was about to radically change that state of affairs.

Through the early decades of the century it was commonplace for the Methodist Conference to urge upon their people the necessity of regular and faithful attendance at communion. Bowmer cites the Pastoral Letter of 1837, which greatly regretted the neglect of communion by many Methodists, and the disorderly, irreverent, and thoughtless behavior of many communicants.[75] Two letters to *The Wesleyan Times* also help to illuminate the context. On 17 July 1865 "A lover of the sacrament" wrote to complain that the London first circuit had passed a resolution making attendance at the sacrament the test of membership. The writer confessed that he had "not taken the sacrament for many years" and knew of a congregation where half the members never took communion because "intoxicating wine" was used at the Lord's Table. He declared, "The class meeting is the correct test of membership."[76] This prompted a response from another correspondent, James Russell, "a Methodist of fifty years standing" who was also deeply grieved at this "anti-Methodistical resolution," for someone who attends the sacrament may be spiritually dead, and "no one besides himself knows anything about it."[77]

Bowmer records the efforts made by Conference to encourage faithful participation in the sacrament and concludes, "By the end of the nineteenth century, the Wesleyan Conference was doing what it could to ensure that

---

73. Parris, *John Wesley's Doctrine of the Sacraments*, 34.
74. Cooke, *Christian Theology*, 678.
75. Bowmer, *The Lord's Supper in Methodism*, 25.
76. A Lover of the Sacrament, *The Wesleyan Times*, "Church Membership."
77. Russell, *The Wesleyan Times*, "Test of Membership."

The Sacraments

its people not only honoured the Lord's Supper, but also understood its meaning."[78] However, long before this achievement the Booths had left the Methodist movement.

The Holiness Movement

In an article on the sacraments published in the *Historical Dictionary of The Salvation Army* David Rightmire affirms:

> Holiness theology was [...] central to the implicit devaluation of the sacraments within The SA and the consequent shaping of the movement's non-sacramental position. [...] The SA, as part of the 19th century holiness revival, subordinated its sacramental theology to pneumatological priorities. From this perspective, it was through the experience of entire sanctification within the total process of salvation that the believer has direct communion with God through the fullness of Christ's spiritual presence in the heart. Consequently, the real presence of Christ is mediated to the believer through the sanctifying work of the Holy Spirit apart from outward forms.[79]

As Rightmire observes, William and Catherine Booth were not influenced by the Holiness Movement as it were from the outside. They and the Army they founded were fully part of it.

Within Catherine's apologetic the influence of the Holiness Movement is clear, in her contention that the wine Christ promises to drink with us in his Father's kingdom is wine which is "righteousness, *peace and joy*, in the Holy Ghost";[80] and in her view that when Jesus referred to his return he was referring to the events of the resurrection, the ascension, and Pentecost. In Catherine's theology, post-resurrection and post-ascension, the Christian's experience of the risen Christ is achieved through a personal Pentecost rather than through the breaking of bread. The influence of William Boardman, Phoebe Palmer, and Charles Finney upon Catherine has been charted. Catherine was indebted to these American teachers of holiness in her personal experience of sanctification. However, her antecedents within Methodism must also be recognized. The influences of John Wesley and particularly John Fletcher are apparent throughout her thought. According to Patrick Streiff, "Throughout his life, Fletcher's view of the future

---

78. Bowmer, *The Lord's Supper in Methodism*, 29.
79. Rightmire in Merritt, *Historical Dictionary of The Salvation Army*, 489.
80. Booth, *Popular Christianity*, 46.

was marked by the expectation of a new, more comprehensive operation of God's grace, but for the later Fletcher, with his pneumatological preoccupations, apocalyptic gave way more and more to the expectation of a new Pentecost and a church of the Spirit."[81]

Catherine's early reading of Fletcher created fertile ground into which the teaching of the Holiness Movement fell. However, in turn William and Catherine influenced and shaped the course of the Holiness Movement, not only in their homeland.

Catherine's views were not forged in an environment of active and appreciative sacramentalism. Her context within early nineteenth-century Methodism predisposed her towards a low valuation of the significance of baptism and the Lord's Supper. Her reading of Wesley and her teachers within Methodism confirmed to her that the sacraments were not essential means of salvation. From her reading of church history Catherine came to believe that the sacramental rites in their traditional and historical form were not an element within primitive Christianity.

Her experiences within the Holiness Movement confirmed to her that the presence of God within the experience of the believer was consequent upon a pentecostal baptism of the Holy Spirit rather than the mediating effect of the sacraments. Regeneration was indispensable to this experience but was achieved not through infant or believer's baptism but by means of repentance and faith and a spiritual re-birth. These things which she learned first from her understanding of Methodism were confirmed to her personally by her own experiences and by the impact of her revival ministry.

CATHERINE BOOTH'S INFLUENCE ASSESSED

Two writers have considered the influence of Catherine Booth upon the formation of the Army's view of the sacraments in their examination of the underlying reasons for the Army's discontinuation of sacramental practices.

Roger Green

Roger Green tends to discount the importance of Catherine's influence on the move to non-sacramentalism. Instead Green associates the Army's discontinuation of the sacraments with the discussions held with Anglican bishops in 1882 regarding the possibility that the Army might be in some

---

81. Streiff, *Reluctant saint?*, 46.

way enfolded into that church.[82] The lengthy negotiations self-evidently came to nothing.

Bramwell Booth identified one of the most serious difficulties: "To the more straight-laced negotiators the accredited position which the women officers already occupied in the Army presented serious difficulty."[83] According to Pamela Walker: "The Salvation Army was the first instance of English women giving communion as part of the official, regular work of a sect. It was a singularly shocking act."[84] Catherine would never have accepted any curtailing of the ministry of women within the Army, where women were given equal standing with men in every aspect of ministry: "The Salvation Army initially instructed all officers, men and women to offer communion monthly. Challenged to explain why women were permitted to perform this sacred ritual, George Scott Railton wrote, 'In this, as in everything else, the Lord's own principle there being "neither male nor female" in Christ Jesus is fully acted upon.'"[85]

It might be thought that when discussions with the Church of England closed, the matter of the sacraments would be closed again. It is therefore unclear why Roger Green should suggest that "all this talk about union caused the Army finally to focus on resolving the question."[86]

It is unlikely that the reason the Army decided its officers, male and female, would never again administer the sacraments was because the Church of England challenged the right of its officers to do so. Reasoning of this kind was out of character for both William and Catherine. Had the Archbishop of Canterbury demanded that no Salvation Army officer should ever again administer the Lord's Supper, it is possible that Salvation Army officers would still be doing so today. The twin driving forces were the persistently troublesome practical problems on which William Booth was being called to decide and, more importantly, Catherine Booth's deepening theological concerns. This is confirmed by Bramwell Booth.

> A sense of misgiving, however, arose, and made itself more evident with the growing work. I think that this misgiving was experienced first of all by Catherine Booth. She had a deep horror of anything which might tend to substitute in the minds of the

---

82. Green, *Catherine Booth*, 236–40.
83. Booth, *Echoes and Memories*, 62.
84. Walker, *Pulling the Devil's Kingdom Down*, 123.
85. Ibid., 122–23.
86. Green, *Catherine Booth*, 236.

people some outward act or compliance for the fruits of practical Holiness. Her knowledge of the low tone of the spiritual life in the churches, gained as a result of her friendship with many religious people and their leaders, made her look with dread upon the possibility that our people, most of whom were very ignorant and simple, might come in time to lean upon some outward ceremonial instead of upon the work of the Holy Spirit as witnessed in a change of heart and life.[87]

David Rightmire

In *Sacraments and The Salvation Army: Pneumatological Foundations* David Rightmire attempts to trace the historical roots of the Army's non-sacramentalism.[88] Rightmire summarizes his thesis: "The Salvation Army's abandonment of the sacraments is theologically grounded in its pneumatological priority and the practical orientation of its missiology. Subsequent sacramental self-understanding has failed not only to recognize the explicit connections between William Booth's sacramental practise and his holiness theology, but also to recognize the need for a re-evaluation of sacramental theology in the light of certain pneumatological shifts within the Army."[89]

Rightmire's claim that the abandonment was theologically grounded distinguishes him from those commentators who believe William Booth's pragmatism was the decisive factor.[90] And although he identifies William as responsible for the move, he also acknowledges, "Catherine Booth's influence on the theological development of the Army should not be underestimated."[91]

Rightmire attempts to trace one source of the Army's pneumatological priority to the sixteenth- and seventeenth-century Spiritualists, whom he considers the progenitors of Quakerism.[92] Rightmire claims that sixteenth-century radical reformers such as Thomas Muntzer, Melchior Hoffman, Caspar Schwenkfield, and Menno Simons "held views that sought to protect the spiritual nature of Christ from contamination with sinful human

---

87. Booth, *Echoes and Memories*, 202.
88. Rightmire, *Sacraments*.
89. Ibid., ix.
90. Ibid., 122–25.
91. Ibid., 60.
92. Spiritualism, in this context, refers to a movement associated with Anabaptism within the radical reformation.

The Sacraments

flesh. Thus these men emphasized the heavenly or celestial flesh of Christ. Rather than trying to explain the historical manifestation of the divine substance, the Spiritualists stressed in docetic fashion, the spiritual presence of Christ in the believer. Men such as Jacob Boehme (1575–1624) spoke of the irrelevancy of ecclesial, creedal and sacramental forms in the light of a mystical communion with the spiritual Christ."[93]

According to Rightmire, for the Spiritualists the sacraments were external ceremonies which could never mediate spiritual realities. Instead they promoted a spiritual communion, to be enjoyed as a continuous experience not dependent on external forms. Rightmire claims this "spiritualistic understanding of the sacraments crossed the English Channel from Europe in the sixteenth century."[94] Not least through the Collegiants and their book *The Light of the Candlestick*, this Spiritualism passed into Quaker thought: "What is particularly relevant is the affinity of *The Light of the Candlestick* and the Quaker theory of religious knowledge as expressed in terms of the 'Inner Light.'"[95]

In turn, according to Rightmire, the Quakers influenced the Army's founders. Rightmire claims, "In addition to the participation of some Quakers in the Christian Mission, Catherine Booth served to mediate Quaker theology to her husband," although, he admits, "The extent of her agreement with their theology is not explicitly stated."[96] Rightmire provides no source for his assertion, though it could be noted that in *Popular Christianity* Catherine names the Friends as allies.[97] The link that Rightmire forges between the Army's founders and their "Spiritualist forebears" leads him to characterize the Army's non-sacramentalism as dualistic and docetic: "Although holding to a Chalcedonian Christology in his [William Booth's] doctrinal statement, his spiritualized sacramental theology points in the direction of docetism, with its denial of the mediation of the spiritual through the material."[98] He concludes, "The docetic implications of Salvation Army non-sacramental theology are easily discernible."[99]

---

93. Rightmire, *Sacraments*, 103.
94. Ibid., 106.
95. Ibid., 107.
96. Ibid., 120.
97. Booth, *Popular Christianity*, 44.
98. Rightmire, *Sacraments*, 174.
99. Ibid., 267.

The supposed affinities between Spiritualist and Salvationist thought are only one strand of Rightmire's thesis. The strongest influence on the Army's pneumatology came from the Holiness Movement: "Of chief importance to this study, however, is the relationship between Booth's position on the sacraments and the pneumatological concerns of the late nineteenth century of which he was a part. The implicit and explicit influences of Booth's holiness theology on his decision to abandon sacramental practise establish the pneumatological foundations of Salvation Army non-sacramental theology."[100]

Rightmire's thesis has proved persuasive.[101] Valtanen follows Rightmire and concludes, "Given that the present Army places far less emphasis on the Holy Spirit, one may ask whether the original reason for rejecting the sacraments has almost disappeared."[102] Rightmire argues that the Army's understanding of the doctrine of holiness and its pneumatological position has indeed changed. He concludes, "It would seem, therefore, that if the Army's holiness position has changed, its sacramental theology needs to be re-evaluated in the light of its shifting pneumatological foundations."[103]

Rightmire thus identifies a connection between two of the Army's historical theological distinctives: its doctrine of holiness and its non-sacramentalism. However, Rightmire overstates the influence of the Quakers upon the Army. The strongest evidence for this influence he can uncover lies in Quaker thought being "part of the theological milieu of the day."[104] He admits, "In terms of actual theological influence, the evidence is inferential. The Founder's decision to de-sacramentalize the Army at the very least found precedent in the Quaker position."[105] As for the influence of the Spiritualists, Rightmire is reduced in the end to claiming, "Affinities between Spiritualist and Salvation Army sacramental theology do exist, though the degree of influence is not clear."[106] Rightmire acknowledges that Edward McKinley "views the influence of the Quakers as secondary and corroborative in the developing of a Salvation Army theology."[107] Right-

---

100. Ibid., xi.

101. Rightmire's conclusions have become literally definitive in that his contribution *Sacraments* to *The Historical Dictionary of The Salvation Army* is a précis of his thesis.

102. Valtanen, "Catherine Booth," 206.

103. Rightmire, *Sacraments*, 267.

104. Ibid., 118.

105. Ibid., 120.

106. Ibid., 118.

107. Ibid., 123.

mire's failure to identify anything but a tenuous inferential link serves to strengthen McKinley's case.

Furthermore, any comparison between Quaker and Salvationist theology would have to take into account the strong differences. The Army and the Quakers lie at far extremes in regard to patterns of ministry, organizational structure, worship and the expression of Christian mission, and whether for good or ill the Army replaced the ancient ceremonies of the Church with a set of substitute ceremonies. Rightmire claims, "It is obvious that Salvation Army non-sacramental practice is based on a spiritualized understanding of divine revelation."[108] However, in contrast to Quaker understandings of revelation which grant to the Inner Light prior authority over biblical revelation, the first article of the Army's doctrines states, "We believe that the Scriptures of the Old and New Testament were given by inspiration of God and that they only constitute the divine rule of Christian faith and practice."[109]

It is also significant that Rightmire discounts the Army's social mission, the strongest evidence that the movement's theology is neither docetic nor dualist. Rightmire wrote in justification of his approach, "In dealing with the founding of the Army, the concerns emphasized are those felt to be relevant to the focus of this inquiry. As a result, there is a conscious de-emphasis on the Army's social work—an area that has been over-emphasized in the secondary literature."[110]

However, whether or not the Army's social work has or has not been overemphasized is beside the point. It evidently derives from the passionate heart of the Army's theology. It is logically incoherent to ignore the Army's highly materialistic response to the needs of the world in a thesis that argues that the Army's gospel is over-spiritualized. W. T. Stead, discussing Catherine's socialism, instances a strong expression of the Salvationist's earthly gospel: "'I was thinking,' she remarked, 'as I was passing the Royal Exchange, and saw on the top, "The earth is the Lord's and the fullness thereof," how many believed it who walked beneath its shadow. I wonder what any one would be thought of were he practically to recognise the fact.

---

108. Ibid., 196.

109. In one of the few changes to the doctrines of the Methodist New Connexion made by the Army's founders this affirmation of scriptural authority was given first place in the Army's doctrines.

110. Rightmire, *Sacraments*, xi.

"Oh!" they would say, "he's not fit for his post—you'll have to take him away; he's a little affected in the head"."[111]

Stead claims, "Every Salvationist is a soldier enlisted in a holy war against all that is opposed to God's will in the existing order."[112] Stead was imprisoned for his part in the Maiden Tribute affair. He knew from personal experience how earthy the warfare theology of the Army could be. In its own self-understanding the Army's social work has often been expressed as one of the ways in which it has sought to fulfill the injunctions it reads into the biblical narratives concerning the sacramental acts.[113]

Rightmire also fails to do justice to the taproot of Salvationism within Methodism. Even if some degree of influence upon Salvationism from Quakerism present within the Victorian milieu is granted, and even if it is accepted that the Holiness Movement exercised an influence upon the thought of the Army's founders, what was influenced was a spirituality inherited from Fletcher and Wesley.

Moreover, Rightmire disregards the possibility that there might be a valid critique of the sacramental principle at the heart of the Army's move to non-sacramentalism. Rightmire asserts, "In examining Booth's sacramental thought, this work employs the sacramental theology of John Wesley as the operative standard for such discussion."[114] Rightmire believes that in departing from this "standard," the Army's founders departed from a stable and orthodox theology. However, the nature of Wesley's sacramentalism is not undisputed, and the form and content of sacramental theology in general is far from agreed. In the mid-twentieth century, from a Reformed perspective, Donald M. Baillie wrote, "We do not possess a theology of the Sacraments. Whatever we may have done in other departments of Christian truth in the way of thinking out a theology for the twentieth century, we have not thought out for our time, this vital part of our faith and practice."[115] From a Roman Catholic perspective, Hans Küng expressed a similar dissatisfaction with the state of theology in regard to the sacraments. "Are we afraid of questions?" Küng asked. "We have to face the fact that the

---

111. Stead, *Mrs. Booth*, 186.
112. Ibid., 187.
113. Coutts, *Bread for My Neighbour*, 44.
114. Rightmire, *Sacraments*, ix.
115. Baillie, *Sacraments*, X?

sacraments have not yet been discussed with that open and sober understanding which has marked ecumenical discussion in so many fields."[116]

Further, Rightmire assumes that the pneumatological emphases he perceives within the Army's theology are unbalanced rather than corrective. The theological context for understanding the sacraments within the Western church has been Augustinian, and Augustine has also provided the dominant model for the doctrine of the Trinity and correspondingly the dominant context of thought for pneumatology within the West. Recent writers on the Trinity have noted weaknesses in Augustine's theology in these areas. The "Achilles' heel," as Colin Gunton describes it, of Augustine's psychological model of the Trinity is his conception of the Spirit. His attempt to make the Trinity fit the procrustean bed of memory, understanding, and will, means that "three essential features of the economy scarcely feature."[117] The first missing feature is the eschatological dimension; that is, the role of the Spirit to realize, in time, the conditions of the age to come. Augustine's eschatology is essentially dualistic, requiring a choice between this world and the next. The second missing element is the conception of the Spirit as realizing the conditions of the age to come, particularly through the creation of community. In the theology of Augustine the church is beginning to be seen as an institution mediating grace to the individual rather than a community formed on the model of the inter-Trinitarian relations. Thirdly Gunton suggests that the conception of love suggested by Augustine's conception of the Trinity is not of the kind suggested by the incarnation; that is, love as love for the other as other. It therefore dissolves the notion of true otherness within the Trinity, and "the overall result is that because the doctrine of the Spirit has inadequate hypostatic weight in Augustine, the father of Western theology also lacks the means to give personal distinctiveness to the being of the Spirit in the inner Trinity."[118]

The re-emphasis on pneumatology in and through Wesley and his successors in the Holiness Movement and The Salvation Army can therefore be seen as a corrective towards an orthodox Trinitarianism. Catherine introduced an eschatological perspective as well as a pneumatological perspective into her apologetic and thereby introduces two of the missing three features that Gunton identifies.

---

116. Küng, *Sacraments*.
117. Gunton, *The Promise of Trinitarian Theology*, 50.
118. Ibid., 51.

CONCLUSION

Catherine's influence upon Salvationist non-sacramentalism was formative and definitive. Over the years her firm line was followed and the apparently provisional nature of William Booth's initial decision was forgotten. The Army's non-sacramentalism became consolidated by many articles and books.[119]

In 1982 the Word Council of Churches' Commission on Faith and Order published a discussion paper, *Baptism, Eucharist and Ministry*, which sought to encourage a debate concerning the relationship of the churches' understanding and practices of the sacraments and ministry to their mission.[120] The Army's response, *One Faith, One Church*, concluded: "We have to reject an increasingly literalistic interpretation of the sacraments, fearing a resultant tendency to ritualism and a movement away from apostolic simplicity."[121]

The use of the word "increasingly" in this statement suggests a significant feature of the debate. Despite the strength with which Salvationists have made their non-sacramental arguments, the Army is just as much on its own in this as it was in 1883.[122] And the debate has waxed rather than waned over recent years among Salvationists. In response to these and associated concerns General Paul Rader convened in March 1996 an *International Spiritual Life Commission* "to review the ways in which The Salvation Army cultivates and sustains the spiritual life of its people."[123] Although the Commission was given a broad brief, the spur to its creation was concern among Salvationists worldwide regarding the official position on the sacraments.

Ultimately the Commission reaffirmed the Army's position. However, it underlined that position as one of freedom. The Commission recognized that simply to defend the claim that the sacraments are not essential to salvation was to establish a negative rather than a positive argument at the heart of its apologetic. The Commission also gave permission for an exploration of the *significance* of the biblical signs of baptism and the Lord's

---

119. See, for example, Dean, *The Sacraments—The Salvationist's Viewpoint*; Kew, *Closer Communion*.

120. World Council of Churches, *Baptism, Eucharist, and Ministry*.

121. The Salvation Army, *One Faith, One Church*, 63.

122. If not more so. At least in the USA, many Quaker congregations practise the sacraments within their worship.

123. Street and International Spiritual Life Commission, *Called to be God's people*, vii.

Supper, attempting in this way to move the Army on to the fertile middle ground between the sacraments as mere signs and as essential means of salvation.

The Commission's call for the Army to rejoice in its freedom in these matters, and to express its position positively rather than negatively, derived directly from Catherine. Catherine wrote in *Aggressive Christianity*: "While the Gospel message is laid down with unerring exactness, we are left at perfect freedom to adapt our measures and modes of bringing it to bear upon men to the circumstances, times, and conditions in which we live—free as air."[124] However, the Spiritual Life Commission failed to settle the matter. Alan Satterlee summarized the continuing situation:

> The mixed opinions of Salvationists themselves prove that the question of the Sacraments is not yet settled. There are those who resist the addition of the Sacraments because it would partially dilute what makes the Army unique and compromise the high ground of salvation by faith alone. But the danger might be that we become traditional in a non-traditional position, not willing to investigate the merits offered by those whose opinions differ. Most Salvationists are somewhere in the middle, perhaps wistful about the ceremonies but too committed to the overall message of the Army to let it drive them away.[125]

The Army finds itself today as a broadly conservative part of the church paradoxically cleaving to a radical stance on what a majority of Christians today believe to be an essential characteristic of the church.

Catherine's rhetoric in the Army's first significant apologetic for its non-sacramental position forced the Army into a radical position in regard to the sacraments that has become uncharacteristic of its doctrinal stance generally. In her apologetic in *Popular Christianity* Catherine established a dichotomy between the sacraments as mere sign and therefore optional, and as a means of salvation and therefore essential, which proved definitive, and beyond which her successors in the Army have struggled to move. However, John Wesley did not believe the sacraments were mere signs nor did he believe they were means of salvation. His views were forged on the middle ground. The Spiritual Life Commission attempted to move the Army back on to this middle ground. However, the Army has struggled to build or secure a new position on the argument from freedom, which was

---

124. Booth, *Aggressive Christianity*, 50.
125. Satterlee, *Turning Points*, 56–57.

provided by Catherine; not least because the argument for Christian freedom cuts both ways. Any freedom which the church has to dispose with these signs in the cause of mission must equally be a freedom to explore their continuing relevance and significance.

EIGHT

Conclusion

Krista Valtanen argued in her doctoral thesis examining the theology of Catherine Booth's exhortations, "Beside Booth's expressed theology, there is a strong implied theology that this study has not been able to capture in its entirety. In reality, it seems that Booth's expressed theology is driven by her implied theology."[1] The aim of this study has been to discover and lay bare that implied theology, conceived of as the underlying structure of Catherine Booth's Salvationist spirituality, in order to examine and analyze its characteristic features, identify its sources and consider the extent of its abiding influence. This has been attempted by means of a detailed examination of the primary sources, and in particular by a close reading of those addresses delivered between 1879 and 1887 in which Catherine expressed the ideas she developed over her lifetime.

A SUMMARY OF FINDINGS

In chapter two, Catherine's doctrine of the atonement was examined. It was argued that her expressions of distaste for some substitutionary theories of the atonement reflected her espousal of aspects of a moral government scheme of redemption. This in turn reflected her high view of the moral law and her belief that the atonement was a full expression of God's love and justice, by means of which men and women were both justified and sanctified. These concerns were also evident in Catherine's *ordo salutis* in which justification and sanctification provided the twin focal points, and which was dominated by the overarching theme of the full restoration of men and women in the image and likeness of God in Christ. This chapter argued that Catherine's *ordo salutis* represented a full-orbed scheme of salvation in

---

1. Valtanen, "Catherine Booth," 271.

which conviction, repentance, faith, justification, regeneration, obedience, consecration, entire sanctification, and final glorification all found their place. A nuanced understanding of prevenient grace was evident which reflected the overriding influence of John Wesley and his successors over that of Charles Finney.

Critical to Catherine Booth's soteriology, with its grand theme of restoration, was the Wesleyan doctrine of entire sanctification, the means by which men and women, justified freely in Christ, are recreated in the likeness of Christ. In chapter three, Catherine's personal experience of sanctification was examined, and the influence of Phoebe Palmer and others explored. It was argued from a careful reading of Catherine's work that Palmer was not as influential for Catherine as others have suggested. In chapter four, Catherine's mature teaching of the doctrine was compared with John Wesley's and the influence of other holiness teachers, such as Charles Finney and John Fletcher, was considered. It was concluded that John Wesley and John Fletcher were the dominant influences upon Catherine's teaching, and that Fletcher was the main source of Catherine's pentecostal and postmillennialist emphases. Catherine stressed the social, moral, and ethical aspects of entire sanctification without denying or undervaluing its experiential or devotional character.

At this point it became possible to identify the four major themes that provided the anchor points for Catherine's soteriology. The logic of Catherine's Salvationism begins, firstly, with the proposition that God, the loving creator of all things, governs the universe by means of the natural law and the moral law. Secondly, for the world to be as God intends, people must be brought to desire to obey the moral law and be given the power to do so. This is to restore people to their original state, the image and likeness of God, conceived of as perfect love of God and humankind. Thirdly, this is achieved through the atonement and through Pentecost, by means of which people are justified, their sins are forgiven, and sanctified, empowered to live a life of love. Fourth, and finally, as people come to love God and love one another, the reign of God begins, a reign that will culminate in history, in the Millennium. Because this soteriological vision has social and personal dimensions, the logic of Catherine Booth's Salvationism has ecclesiological consequences.

Chapter five examined the development of Catherine Booth's ecclesiology, noting that Catherine was influenced by the Lutheran historians Mosheim and Neander, as well as by John Wesley and his successors in

Methodism. She also absorbed ideas from the Congregationalist minister David Thomas, an influence that has not been recognized. She moved towards an ecclesiology which differentiated between the *esse* and *bene esse* of the church, recognizing the institutional character of the church to be of its *esse*, but the forms of its institution to be of its *bene esse* and therefore open to reform and renewal. The Salvation Army was conceived of in Catherine's thinking as a living part of the one church of Jesus Christ, with its congregations considered to be churches, but the permanent validity of its forms, order, modes, and measures was denied. Also denied was that the Army, in itself, constituted a church in any theological sense. Catherine viewed the church from a four-fold perspective. From a Christological perspective, the church was an incarnational expression of the life and mission of Christ. From a missiological perspective, the church was not an end in itself, but a means to an end, that being the fulfillment and completion of the mission of Christ. From a pneumatological perspective, the church was constituted and directed by the Holy Spirit, and only by a pentecostal empowerment could the church achieve its great purpose. From an eschatological perspective, although the kingdom of God may as yet only be partially realized in the community of the church, its realization as a future historical event, the Millennium, in continuity with and in fulfillment of the mission of the church in the present age, was assured. Each of these perspectives had the effect of relativizing the forms the church took in history and cleared the way for the emergence of the church in a radically new form—The Salvation Army.

Chapter six considered the development of Catherine Booth's own ministry, her writings on female ministry, and her contribution to the development of orders of ministry and the distribution of authority and power within The Salvation Army. It was argued that Catherine's feminism was interconnected with her Salvationism, that the root concept which ensured the equality of men and women in life and ministry was the restoration of women and men to the image and likeness of God. Thus salvation released women from the consequences of the Fall and restored them to their original equality with men. The vestigial remnants of the curse in the subjugation of women to men in marriage were moderated by the character of marriage as a covenant of love. Catherine defended women's right to preach the gospel as the responsibility incumbent on all Christians to respond to the great commission. She made no division between lay and clerical orders within the church. Her guiding principle was the priesthood, and ministry, of all believers. Thus the total mobilization of the people of God in the mission of God reflected her contribution to The Salvation Army's emerging order, rather more than the emergence of an autocratic hierarchy.

Catherine Booth's contribution to The Salvation Army's position on the sacraments was explored in chapter seven. Catherine argued that the sacraments could be a dangerous substitute for true religion. Her primary objection was that the sacraments were presented as a means of salvation, when, in her view, they were not. Christians were free to choose whether or not to celebrate the sacraments. For Catherine, bound up with the issue of the sacraments were eschatological questions concerning the nature of Christ's promised return; Christological questions concerning Christ's continuing presence with his people; missiological questions concerning the nature of Christ's engagement with the world; and pneumatological questions concerning the mediation of grace. In her view, the sacraments were necessary to none of these things. Catherine believed in the sacramentality of a common human life, although she used the language of holiness, rather than sacrament, to describe this life.

Catherine's polemics, rooted in a mid- to late-nineteenth-century context, consolidated the Army's non-sacramental position. Catherine's argument for freedom ultimately cuts both ways: the freedom claimed to dispose of these signs in the cause of culturally relevant mission must equally be a freedom to explore their continuing significance. However, by her polarization of the argument and failure to recognize any mid-point between the sacraments as essential means or mere signs, Catherine failed to provide the ground for any such exploration.

THE SIGNIFICANCE OF THIS STUDY

Pamela Walker has argued, "The Salvation Army has received scant attention from scholars. Its place in Victorian working-class communities, its relationship to the women's movement, its innovative use of popular and commercial culture, and its integration of Methodism, revivalism and holiness have not been explored."[2]

This neglect has extended to the Army's founders, and certainly more to Catherine than to William Booth. Because of this neglect not much more has been said of the Army's founding theology than that it was an amalgam of "Methodism, revivalism and holiness."[3] Consequently, even though it

2. Walker, *Pulling the Devil's Kingdom Down*, 3.
3. Ibid.

Conclusion

has been recognized that Catherine Booth was the intellectual driving force of the movement, through whom its grand ideas were first formed, who became its primary apologist and who shaped its self-understanding, her theology has not been properly investigated, either in outline or in detail, and the unfortunate consequence has been that she has all too frequently been misunderstood.

The detailed outline of the structure and content of Catherine Booth's core theology offered in this book allows various misunderstandings to be identified and corrected, and various apparent anomalies to be resolved. Roger Green questioned Catherine Booth's understanding of her Wesleyan heritage, and argued that "for all her reading and native intelligence, Catherine did not have Wesley's comprehensive depth or theological vision." Green claimed that Catherine did not "deal with many of the finer details of Wesley's theology," and concluded that Catherine did not "demonstrate a command of these and other detailed and precise theological issues."[4] However, this study has revealed that Catherine did in fact have a nuanced understanding of her Wesleyan heritage and that her addresses reveal a strong grasp of "detailed and precise theological issues." Among these were the antinomian dangers inherent in an understanding of the imputation of Christ's active obedience in a substitutionary theory of the atonement, and the significance of prevenient grace for the claim that men and women, totally depraved by reason of the Fall, may yet choose to respond to the offer of salvation in Christ. John Kent claimed that William and Catherine Booth completely accepted Phoebe Palmer's revivalist holiness doctrine, with its altar theology and shorter way, and co-opted it as their own Salvationist doctrine.[5] However, this study has marshaled evidence to show that despite her appreciation for Palmer, in structure and detail Catherine's mature teaching of the doctrine was more an interpretation and contemporary restatement of the holiness teaching of John Wesley and John Fletcher.

On the issue of the sacraments, a subject much debated in Army studies, Robert Rightmire suggested in respect of the Army's view that "Catherine Booth served to mediate Quaker theology to her husband."[6] By this means, Rightmire attempted to forge a link between the Army's founders and the sixteenth-century "Spiritualists," which led him to describe the Army's non-sacramentalism as dualistic and docetic and a "denial of

---

4. Green, *Catherine Booth*, 101–2.
5. Kent, *Holding the Fort*, 326.
6. Rightmire, *Sacraments*, 120.

the mediation of the spiritual through the material."[7] However, this study has demonstrated that Catherine Booth's theology was social, moral, and ethical at its very core; that at its heart lay the notion of the enfleshment, or incarnation, of Christ and his gospel in the earthy, day-to-day lives of working class men and women, an idea which, far from denying the mediation of the spiritual through the material, affirmed the sacramentality of common life.

As a consequence of an inadequate understanding of Salvationism's grand ideas, certain features of its expression in the life and ministry of Catherine and William Booth and the movement they founded have been regarded as sometimes puzzling anomalies. In Norman Murdoch's opinion, it was "as its evangelistic program stagnated" that "social salvation replaced evangelism as the Army's mission"; until then the Booths were fixated on saving souls.[8] However, this study has revealed the integral relationship between the social and evangelistic aspects of Christian mission in the understanding of Catherine Booth, a relationship that reflects the holistic character of Christ's commission—"as the Father has sent me so I am sending you"—and the character of the church as a vehicle for prevenient grace, by means of an active demonstration of God's compassion for suffering humanity. Various features of Catherine Booth's Salvationism, such as her millennialism and feminism, can now be seen to derive directly from a coherent and consistent implicit theology, and consequently to be connected together in her thinking.

The development of Catherine Booth's ideas has been placed in a rich intellectual context, taking in the liberal and evangelical ideas of contemporaries such as David Thomas, including detailed examination of revivalists such as Charles Finney and the works of John Wesley and John Fletcher, and also analyzing the ideas of philosophers such as Joseph Butler. Many, if not most of these formational influences upon Catherine's intellectual and theological framework have not previously been examined in a rigorous academic way. Although the various formative influences upon Catherine's thought have been identified, with these influences often found to be present in the expressed or implicit detail of her doctrine, what has been revealed is a construction which, in its shape and structure and internal logic, is unique to Catherine Booth.

7. Ibid., 174.
8. Murdoch, *Origins of The Salvation Army*, 147.

Conclusion

The form of Catherine Booth's Salvationism establishes the logical connection between many of the distinctive characteristics of contemporary as well as historical Salvationism. However some important features in its structure play little or no part in modern Salvationism. Mrs. General Carpenter wrote in 1940, "So much of her beliefs, methods and teaching was built into its early super-structure that [. . .] the Army mother still speaks and unconsciously guides her great family."[9] However, after Catherine Booth's death Salvationism continued to evolve. Further research is required into the development of Salvationism after 1890 if the differences between the emphases of Catherine Booth's Salvationism and that of The Salvation Army today are to be better understood.

It might be argued that Catherine Booth's soteriology fits rather better with some reconstructions of the Holiness Movement's history than with others. Some adjustments to the historiography may be required, and this work has not been attempted in this study.

THE WIDER CONTRIBUTION OF THIS STUDY

As Roy Hattersley conducted his preliminary research into Catherine Booth, he quickly came to the opinion that "she had possessed the potential to be one of the most extraordinary women of the nineteenth century."[10] Subsequently he felt he had done her less than justice, and that she "*was* the most extraordinary woman of the nineteenth century."[11] Catherine Booth was recognized as one of the pre-eminent evangelists and revivalists of her age. This study sheds new light on the theology of a seminal but neglected figure in the mid to late nineteenth century Holiness Movement. Catherine and William Booth may well have been the most significant British evangelists at work in what Orr has called the Second Evangelical Awakening. This study has revealed for the first time the structure and contours of the theology that undergirded Catherine Booth's revival messages and exhortations.

Catherine Booth was also a powerful advocate of social reform. This study has laid bare the intellectual and theological connections between the evangelism and social activism of Catherine Booth, and provided an

---

9. Carpenter, *The Officers' Review*, "Catherine Booth's Influence on The Salvation Army."

10. Hattersley, "A Biographer Forever".

11. Ibid.

explanation for the emergence of The Salvation Army as an advocate for social reform and innovative provider of social care at a national and global level.

In addition, Catherine Booth was an effective campaigner for the rights of women. This study has demonstrated that Catherine Booth's feminism and Salvationism were interlocked, and that at the heart of both was her belief that in the restoration of the image of God to women and men in salvation the consequences of the Fall were reversed. Catherine was not simply an advocate for women's right to preach the gospel; in consequence of her theological convictions she was an advocate for the equality of women in all areas of life. Furthermore, Catherine Booth emerges as a significant figure from the Victorian era, a British theologian and church leader, with a rare if not unique intellectual and theological perspective—that of a woman.

Finally, Catherine Booth was recognized as the co-founder, with her husband William, of The Salvation Army. Catherine Booth was the visionary thinker whose ideas inspired the movement's radical departures from churchly norms, and the principal architect of the Army's theology. This study has revealed the depth of that founding theology and, for the first time, charted its formative influences, and described its shape and structure.

CONCLUSION

1890 was a watershed in the history of The Salvation Army. With the death of Catherine Booth and the launch of the Darkest England scheme, the movement began a new chapter. The years 1889–90 also marked the end of the Army's dramatic and explosive growth in its homeland. The recovery of Catherine Booth's intellectual legacy poses the questions: how "terrible and irreparable" did her premature loss to the movement she co-founded prove to be; and how beneficial to the Army's future development might the recovery and re-examination of that legacy be?

Bibliography

PRIMARY SOURCES.

Catherine Booth's Writings

Books

Booth, Catherine. *The Diary and the Reminiscences of Catherine Booth.* Edited by David Malcolm Bennett. Brisbane: Camp Hill, 2005.
———. *Female Ministry; or, Woman's Right to Preach the Gospel.* London: Morgan & Chase, 1870.
———. *Female Teaching; or, the Rev. A. A. Rees Versus Mrs. Palmer, Being a Reply to a Pamphlet by the above Gentleman on the Sunderland Revival.* Second, enlarged ed. London: G. J. Stevenson, 1861.
———. *Holiness: Being an Address Delivered in St. James' Hall, Piccadilly, London.* London: The Salvation Army, 1887.
———. *The Holy Ghost: An Address.* Toronto: Salvation Temple, 1885.
———. *Life and Death: Being Reports of Addresses Delivered in London.* London: Salvation Army Book Stores, 1883.
———. *Papers on Aggressive Christianity.* London: Partridge, 1881.
———. *Papers on Godliness.* London: Partridge, 1882.
———. *Papers on Practical Religion.* London: Partridge, 1878.
———. *Popular Christianity: A Series of Lectures.* London: Salvation Army Book Depot, 1887.
———. *The Salvation Army in Relation to the Church and State, and Other Addresses; with an Appendix on the So-Called Secret Book.* London: Partridge, 1883.

Articles

Booth, Catherine. "The Kingdom of Christ (I)." *All the World*, August 1885.
———. "The Kingdom of Christ (II)." *All the World*, September 1885.
———. "The Iniquity of State Regulated Vice." London: Dyer Brothers, 1884.
———. "Mrs Booth's Address at the Exeter Hall Meeting, May 4th." *All the World*, June 1887.
———. "Mrs Booth's Last Public Address." *The War Cry*, 18 October 1890.
———. "Mrs Booth's Latest Address." *All the World*, March 1890.
———. "Our Commission." *All the World*, April 1885.
———. "Reflections on the Jubilee Year." *All the World*, December 1887.
———. "Spiritual Bondage." *All the World*, December 1886.

Bibliography

———. "Spreading Salvation." *All the World*, July 1888.
———. "Taking Sides." *All the World*, June 1886.

Letters

Booth, Catherine. "2nd Letter to Her Mother: From Brighton, 1847." In *Booth Papers*. London: British Library.
———. "Letter to David Thomas: 22 April 1855." In *Catherine Booth Papers*: The Salvation Army International Heritage Centre.
———. "Letter to Her Parents: 16 September 1859." In *Booth Papers*: The British Library.
———. "Letter to Her Parents: 25 December 1859." In *Booth Papers*. London: British Library.
———. "Letter to Her Parents: 24 September 1860." In *Booth Papers*. London: British Library.
———. "Letter to Her Parents: 21 January 1861." In *Booth Papers*. London: British Library.
———. "Letter to Her Parents: 11 February 1861." In *Booth Papers*. London: British Library.
Booth, Catherine, and William Booth. *The Letters of William and Catherine Booth— (Founders of the Salvation Army) Extracted from the Booth Papers in the British Library and Other Sources*. Edited by David Malcolm Bennett Brisbane: Camp Hill, 2003.

Readers

Bramwell-Booth, Catherine, editor. *The Highway of Our God: Selections from the Army Mother's Writings*. London: Salvationist Publishing & Supplies, 1954.

Salvation Army Books and Pamphlets

Moyles, Robert Gordon. *A Bibliography of Salvation Army Literature in English (1865–1987)*. Texts and Studies in Religion. Lewiston: Mellen, 1988.
Booth, Bramwell. *Servants of All: A Brief Review of the Call, Character, and Labours of Officers of the Salvation Army*. 4 ed. London: The Salvation Army Book Department, 1914.
Booth, Florence Eleanor. *Powers of Salvation Army Officers*. London: Salvationist Publishing & Supplies, 1923.
Booth, William. *The General's Letters, 1885: Being a Reprint from "the War Cry" of Letters to Soldiers and Friends Scattered throughout the World*. London: Salvationist Publishing and Supplies, 1886.
———. *In Darkest England and the Way Out*. London: The Salvation Army, 1890.
———. *International Staff Council Addresses*. Staff Council : International Congress 1904. London: The Salvation Army Book Department, 1904.
———. *Orders and Regulations for Staff Officers*. London: The Salvation Army International Headquarters, 1904.
———. *Orders and Regulations for the Salvation Army*. Vol. Part 1, London: The Salvation Army, 1878.
———. *Salvation Soldiery: A Series of Addresses on the Requirements of Jesus Christ's Service*. London: The Salvation Army International Headquarters, 1890.

Bibliography

———, editor. *The Salvation War 1885*. London: Salvation Army Book Depot, 1885.
Booth, William Bramwell. *Echoes and Memories*. London: Hodder & Stoughton, 1925.
———. *On the Banks of the River: Being a Brief History of the Last Days on Earth of Mrs. General Booth*. Red Hot Library. 2nd ed. London: Salvationist Publishing and Supplies, 1900.
———. *These Fifty Years*. London: Cassell, 1929.
Carpenter, Minnie, Lindsay Rowell, and William Bramwell Booth. *Some Notable Officers of the Salvation Army*. London: Salvationist Publishing and Supplies, 1927.
Railton, George Scott. *Heathen England, and What to Do for It: Being a Description of the Utterly Godless Condition of the Vast Majority of the English Nation*. London: S. W. Partridge, 1878.

Salvation Army Newspapers and Periodicals

"The Higher Christian Life Conference at Oxford." *The Christian Mission Magazine*, October 1874.
"Mrs Phoebe Palmer." *The Christian Mission Magazine*, January 1875.
"Our Purpose." *The East London Evangelist*, October 1868.
"The War Congress." *The Christian Mission Magazine*, October 1878.
Booth, Evangeline. "My Mother." *The Officers' Review*, October–December 1940.
Booth, Florence Eleanor. "The Army Mother as I Knew Her." *The Officers' Review*, October–December 1940.
Booth, William. "All Things New: A New Year's Message from the New World." *All the World*, January 1895.
———. "Another Song by the General: The Fire!" *The War Cry*, 14 April 1894.
———. "Hallelujah Bands." *The Christian Mission Magazine*, July 1877.
———. "The Millennium: The Ultimate Triumph of Salvation Army Principles." *All the World*, August 1890.
———. "Our New Name." *The Salvationist*, 1 January 1879.
———. "The Sacraments." *The War Cry*, 17 January 1883.
———. "Salvation for Both Worlds: A Retrospect." *All the World*, January 1889.
———. "What the General Expects of His Soldiers." *The War Cry*, 22 January 1898.
Bramwell-Booth, Catherine. "Catherine Booth." *The Officers' Review*, October–December 1940.
Carpenter, Minnie Lindsay Rowell. "Catherine Booth's Influence on the Salvation Army." *The Officers' Review*, October–December 1940.
Gauntlett, Sidney Carvosso. "Catherine Booth, Defender of the Faith: Review of "Catherine Booth Och Salvationismen" by Laura Petri." *The Officer*, January 1929, 55–64.
Higgins, Mrs General, et al. "The Army Mother: Memories and Tributes." *The Officers' Review*, October–December 1940.
Railton, George Scott. "Mrs Booth." *The War Cry*, 18 September 1890.
Rogers, Hester Ann. "Perfect Love." *The East London Evangelist*, September 1869, 177–80.
Smith, Frank. "The Battle-Cry of the Social Reform Wing." *All the World*, August 1890.
Smith, Hannah Whitall. "The Joy of Obedience." *The Christian Mission Magazine*, November 1875.
Stead, William T. "The Late Mrs Booth." *The War Cry*, 11 October 1890.
Unsworth, Madge. "Wielder of a Mighty Pen." *The Officers' Review*, October–December 1940.

Bibliography

Upham, Thomas. "The Kingdom of God Is Within You." *The Christian Mission Magazine*, July 1870.
Van de Werken, Joanna. "Mother of Nations." *The Officers' Review*, October–December 1940.

Other Newspapers and Magazines

"The Funeral of Mrs Booth." *The Times*, 15 October 1890.
"The Funeral of Mrs Booth." *The Banner*, 17 October 1890.
"Funeral of Mrs Booth: The Service at Olympia." *The Times*, 14 October 1890.
"The Funeral of the Late Mrs Booth: A Remarkable Ceremony." *Manchester Guardian*, 15 October 1890.
"The Late Mrs Booth: A Salvation Army Funeral Service." *Manchester Guardian*, 14 October 1890.
"The London Homeopathic Hospital." *Illustrated London News*, 17 April 1858.
"Memorial Notices." *The Manchester Guardian*, 6 October 1890.
"Mrs Booth." *Manchester Guardian*, 14 October 1890.
"Mrs Booth." *Methodist Times*, 9 October 1890.
"Mrs Booth: The Life of Catherine Booth." *The Manchester Guardian*, 16 December 1892.
"Mrs. Booth's Funeral." *Daily News*, 13 October 1890.
"Revival Intelligence: Albion Street, Rotherhithe." *The Wesleyan Times*, 13 March 1865.
"Revival Intelligence: Mrs Booth's Revival Services in London: Concluding Notice." *The Wesleyan Times*, 10 April 1865.
"Revival Intelligence: Mrs. Booth Amongst Lodging-House Females." *The Wesleyan Times*, 27 March 1865, 197.
"Revival Intelligence: Mrs. Booth's Revival Services in London (from the Gospel Guide)." *The Wesleyan Times*, 3 April 1865.
A Lover of the Sacrament. "Church Membership." *The Wesleyan Times*, 17 July 1865.
B. E. "Revival Services." *The Wesleyan Times*, 17 April 1865.
Galileo, B. A. "The Great Propitiation." *The Homilist*, 1865–68, xvii:352; xviii:51–56, 112–15, 72–76, 234–37, 90–94, 349–55; xix:52–56, 108–14, 74–79, 229–37, 88–97, 354–56; xx:55–56, 235–37, 94–97; xxi:110–17; xxii:81–86, 373–78.
Lunn, Henry S. "General Booth." *The Review of the Churches*, 1895.
Russell, James. "Test of Membership." *The Wesleyan Times*, 31 July 1865.
Stead, William T. "Mrs Booth." *Northern Echo*, Monday 6 October 1890.

Biographical Writings

Beecher, Lyman. *Autobiography, Correspondence, etc. of Lyman Beecher*. Edited by Charles Beecher. 2 vols. New York: Harper, 1864.
Begbie, Harold. *The Life of General William Booth, the Founder of the Salvation Army*. 2 vols. London: Macmillan, 1920.
Booth-Tucker, Frederick St George de Latour. *The Life of Catherine Booth: The Mother of the Salvation Army*. 2 vols. London: The Salvation Army, 1892.
Bramwell-Booth, Catherine. *Catherine Booth: The Story of Her Loves*. London: Hodder & Stoughton, 1970.

Chappell, Jennie. *Four Noble Women and Their Work: Sketches of the Life-Work of Frances Willard, Agnes Weston, Sister Dora and Catherine Booth*. London: Partridge, 1898.
Duff, Mildred. *Catherine Booth: A Sketch*. London: The Salvation Army Book Dept., 1901.
Ervine, St John G. *God's Soldier: General William Booth*. 2 vols. New York: Macmillan, 1935.
Finney, Charles Grandison. *Memoirs of Rev Charles G Finney*. New York: Barnes, 1876.
Hall, Clarence. *Samuel Logan Brengle: Portrait of a Prophet*. New York: The Salvation Army National Headquarters, 1933.
Hulme, Samuel. *Memoir of the Rev. William Cooke, D.D*. London: C. D. Ward, 1886.
Kilham, Alexander. *The Life of Mr. Alexander Kilham, Methodist Preacher, Who Was Expelled from the Conference, or Society of Methodist Preachers: To Which Are Added, Extracts of Letters, (in Favour of Reform,) Written by a Number of Preachers to Mr. Kilham*. Nottingham, UK: Sutton, 1799.
Mahan, Asa. *Autobiography Intellectual, Moral and Spiritual*. London: Woolmer, 1882.
Moore, Henry. *The Life of Mrs Mary Fletcher: Consort and Relict of the Rev John Fletcher, Vicar of Madeley*. London: Wesleyan Methodist Book Room, 1817.
Nicol, Alex M. *General Booth and the Salvation Army*. London: Herbert and Daniel, 1911.
Ottman, F. C. *Herbert Booth: A Biography*. New York: Doubleday, 1928.
Railton, George S. *General Booth*. 3rd ed. London: Hodder and Stoughton, 1913.
Schaff, Philip, et al. *Encyclopedia of Living Divines and Christian Workers of All Demonminations in Europe and America*. Edinburgh: T. & T. Clark, 1887.
Smith, Gipsy. *Gipsy Smith His Life and Work: By Himself*. London: National Council of The Evangelical Free Churches, 1903.
Stead, William T. *Mrs Booth of the Salvation Army*. London: Nisbet, 1900.
Stephen, Leslie. *Dictionary of National Biography, 1885–1900*. Edited by Sydney Lee. 63 & IV vols. London: Elder Smith, 1898.
Taylor, John. *Reminiscences of Isaac Marsden, of Doncaster*. London: Woolmer, 1883.
Thomas, David Morgan. *Urijah Rees Thomas: His Life and Work*. London: Hodder and Stoughton, 1902.
Wheatley, Richard. *The Life and Letters of Mrs. Phoebe Palmer*. New York: Palmer, 1876.

Books and Pamphlets

Allen, Ralph W, and Daniel Wise, editors. *Helps to a Life of Holiness and Usefulness, or Revival Miscellanies: Selected from the Works of the Rev. James Caughey*. Boston: Magee, 1852.
Arthur, William. *The Tongue of Fire; or, the True Power of Christianity*. London: Wesleyan Methodist Book-Room, 1885.
Baggaly, William. *A Digest of the Minutes, Institutions, Polity, Doctrines, Ordinances, and Literature, of the Methodist New Connexion*. London: Cooke, 1862.
Baker, Frank, editor. *Letters II*. Vol. 26, The Bicentennial Edition of the Works of John Wesley. Nashville: Abingdon, 1976.
Barnes, Albert. *The Atonement: In Its Relations to Law and Moral Government*. Philadelphia: Lindsay and Blakiston, 1860.
———. "Introductory Essay." In *The Analogy of Religion*. New York: Newman and Ivison, 1858.
———. *Notes Explanatory and Practical, on the Second Epistle to the Corinthians and the Epistle to the Galatians*. New York: Franklin, 1840.

Bibliography

Boardman, William Edwin. *The Higher Christian Life.* London: Nisbet, 1860.
Booth, Abraham. *The Reign of Grace: From Its Rise to Its Consummation.* Leeds, UK: Wright, 1768.
Booth-Tucker, Frederick St George de Latour, editor. *The Successful Soul Winner: A Summary of Finney's Revival Lectures.* London: Salvationist Publishing and Supplies, 1926.
Butler, Joseph. *The Analogy of Religion, Natural and Revealed, to the Constitution and Course of Nature.* 20th ed. New York: Newman and Ivison, 1858.
Cooke, William. *A Catechism: Embracing the Most Important Doctrines of Christianity, Designed for the Use of Schools, Families, and Bible Classes.* London: Methodist New Connexion Book-Room, 1851.
———. *Christian Theology: Its Doctrines and Ordinances Explained and Defended.* London: Hamilton, 1879.
Finney, Charles Grandison. *Lectures on Revivals of Religion.* New York: Leavitt, Lord, 1835.
———. *Lectures on Systematic Theology: Revised, Enlarged and Partly Re-Written by the Author.* London: Tegg, 1851.
———. *Lectures to Professing Christians.* New York: Taylor, 1837.
———. *Sermons on Gospel Themes.* Oberlin, OH: Goodrich, 1876. microform.
———. *Sermons on Important Subjects.* 3rd ed. New York: Taylor, 1836.
———. *Views of Sanctification.* Toronto: Willard Tract Depository, 1877.
Fletcher, John. *The Works of the Reverend John Fletcher.* 4 vols. Salem, OH: Schmul, 1974.
Grotius, Hugo. *A Defence of the Catholic Faith Concerning the Satisfaction of Christ against Faustus Socinus.* Translated by Frank Hugh Foster. Andover, MA: Draper, 1889.
HM Printing Office. *The Book of Common Prayer.* London: Eyre & Spottiswood, 1892.
Kilham, Alexander. *The Progress of Liberty, Amongst the People Called Methodists: To Which Is Added, the Outlines of a Constitution, Humbly Recommended to the Serious Consideration of the Preachers and People, Late in Connection with Mr. Wesley.* Alnwick, UK: Catnach, 1795.
Lightfoot, Joseph B. *The Christian Ministry.* London: Macmillan, 1901.
Mahan, Asa. *The Baptism of the Holy Ghost.* New York: Hughes, 1870.
———. *Scripture Doctrine of Christian Perfection.* Boston: King, 1839.
Miley, John. *The Atonement in Christ.* New York: Phillips and Hunt, 1879.
Mosheim, Johann Lorenz, and Archibald Maclaine. *An Ecclesiastical History: Ancient and Modern, from the Birth of Christ, to the Beginning of the Eighteenth Century.* 4 vols. London: Cadell, 1826.
Neander, Augustus. *General History of the Christian Religion and Church.* Translated by Joseph Torrey. 7 vols. Edinburgh: T. & T. Clark, 1851.
Palmer, Phoebe. *Present to My Christian Friend on Entire Devotion to God.* London: Heylin, 1857.
———. *The Promise of the Father: A Neglected Specialty of the Last Days.* New York: Palmer, 1872.
Payne, George. *Lectures on Divine Sovereignty, Election, the Atonement, Justification, and Regeneration.* London: Gladding, 1836.
Rees, Arthur Augustus. *Reasons for Not Co-Operating in the Alleged "Sunderland Revivals": In an Address to His Congregation.* Sunderland, UK: Hills, 1859.
Rowe, Elisabeth. *Devout Exercises of the Heart in Meditation and Soliloquy, Prayer and Praise.* London: Watts, 1738.

Shaw, George Bernard. *Major Barbara, with an Essay as First Aid to Critics.* New York: Brantano's, 1917.
Smith, Hannah Whitall. *The Unselfishness of God and How I Discovered It: A Spiritual Autobiography.* London: Revell, 1903.
Thomas, David. *The Core of Creeds, or St. Peter's Keys.* London: Ward, 1850.
Watson, Richard. *Theological Institutes: Or, a View of the Evidences, Doctrines, Morals, and Institutions of Christianity.* 4 vols. London: Mason, 1841.
Wesley, John. *Journals and Diaries.* The Bicentennial Edition of the Works of John Wesley. Edited by Reginald W Ward and Richard P. Heitzenrater. Vols. 18–24, Nashville: Abingdon, 1990.
———. *The Letters of the Rev John Wesley.* Edited by John Telford. Standard ed. 8 vols. London: Epworth, 1931.
———. "A Plain Account of Christian Perfection." Chap. XXIX In *The Works of John Wesley,* edited by Thomas Jackson, 366–448. 1872, London: Wesleyan Methodist Book Room. Reprint. Kansas City: Beacon Hill, 1978.
———. *Sermons.* The Bicentennial Edition of the Works of John Wesley. Edited by Albert C. Outler. Vol. 1–4. Nashville: Abingdon, 1984–87.
———. *The Works of John Wesley.* Edited by Thomas Jackson. 14 vols. 1872, London: Wesleyan Methodist Book Room. Reprint. Kansas City: Beacon Hill, 1978.
The Song Book of the Salvation Army. London: International Headquarters, 1986.

Reports and Other Documents

The Christian Mission. "Minutes of the First Conference." London, June 1870.
The Congregational Union. *The Congregational Year Book for 1896: Containing the Proceedings of the Congregational Union of (Churches in) England and Wales and the Confederated Societies.* London: The Congregational Union of England and Wales, 1896.
The Salvation Army. *One Faith, One Church.* London: The Salvation Army, 1990.
———. *The Salvation Army in the Body of Christ: An Ecclesiological Statement.* London: Salvation Books, 2008.
———. *The Salvation Army in the Body of Christ: Study Guide.* London: Salvation Books, 2010.
———. *Salvation Story: Salvationist Handbook of Doctrine.* London: The Salvation Army International Headquarters, 1998.
The Salvation Army International Doctrine Council. *Servants Together: The Ministry of the Whole People of God.* London: The Salvation Army International Headquarters, 2002.
World Council of Churches. *Baptism, Eucharist, and Ministry.* Faith and Order Paper. Geneva: World Council of Churches, 1982.

SECONDARY SOURCES

Books and Pamphlets

Baillie, Donald. *The Theology of the Sacraments.* London: Faber and Faber, 1957.
Barrett, C. K. *Church, Ministry, and Sacraments in the New Testament.* Exeter, UK: Paternoster, 1985.

Bibliography

Barth, Markus. *Rediscovering the Lord's Supper: Communion with Israel, with Christ, and among the Guests.* Atlanta: John Knox, 1988.
Baxendale, David A. "Salvationism." In *Historical Dictionary of the Salvation Army*, edited by John G. Merritt. 500–501. Lanham, MD: Scarecrow, 2006.
Bebbington, David W. *Evangelicalism in Modern Britain.* London: Unwin, Hyman, 1989.
———. *Holiness in Nineteenth-Century England.* Didsbury Lectures. Carlisle, UK: Paternoster, 2000.
Bennett, David Malcolm. *The Altar Call: Its Origins and Present Usage.* Lanham, MD.: University Press of America, 2000.
———. *The General: William Booth.* 2 vols. Longwood FL: Xulon, 2003.
Borgen, Ole E. *John Wesley on the Sacraments: A Theological Study.* Nashville: Abingdon, 1972.
Bovey, Nigel. *The Mercy Seat Revisited.* London: The Salvation Army United Kingdom Territory, 2010.
Bowmer, John Coates. *The Lord's Supper in Methodism, 1791–1960.* London: Epworth, 1961.
Bradwell, Cyril R. *Fight the Good Fight: The Story of the Salvation Army in New Zealand, 1883–1983.* Wellington, NZ: Reed, 1982.
Carwardine, Richard. *Transatlantic Revivalism: Popular Evangelicalism in Britain and America 1790–1865.* Studies in Evangelical History and Thought. Milton Keynes, UK: Paternoster, 2006.
Chadwick, Owen. *The Victorian Church.* 2nd ed. 2 vols. SCM, 1987.
Chiles, Robert Eugene. *Theological Transition in American Methodism: 1790–1935.* Nashville: Abingdon, 1965.
Clifton, Shaw. *New Love: Thinking Aloud about Practical Holiness.* Wellington, NZ: Flag, 2004.
———. *Who Are These Salvationists?* Alexandria, VA: Crest, 1999.
Clouse, Robert G., editor. *The Meaning of the Millennium: Four Views.* Downers Grove, IL: InterVarsity, 1977.
Collier, Richard. *The General Next to God: The Story of William Booth and the Salvation Army.* London: Collins, 1965.
Collins, Kenneth J. *The Scripture Way of Salvation: The Heart of John Wesley's Theology.* Nashville: Abingdon, 1997.
———. *The Theology of John Wesley: Holy Love and the Shape of Grace.* Nashville: Abingdon, 2007.
Cooper, Catherine Fales, and Jeremy Gregory, editors. *Revival and Resurgence in Christian History*, Vol. 44. Woodbridge, UK: Boydell, 2008.
Coutts, Frederick. *Bread for My Neighbour: An Appreciation of the Social Action and Influence of William Booth.* London: Hodder and Stoughton, 1978.
———. *No Discharge in This War.* London: Hodder and Stoughton, 1975.
Coutts, John James. *The Salvationists.* London: Mowbrays, 1978.
Currie, Robert. *Methodism Divided: A Study in the Sociology of Ecumenicalism.* London: Faber and Faber, 1968.
Davies, Rupert, et al., editors. *A History of the Methodist Church in Great Britain.* 4 vols. Vol. 2. London: Epworth, 1978.
Dean, Harry. *The Sacraments: The Salvationist's Viewpoint.* London: Salvationist Publishing and Supplies, 1960.

Dieter, Melvin E. *The Holiness Revival of the Nineteenth Century*. Studies in Evangelicalism. 2nd ed. Lanham, MD: Scarecrow, 1996.

Dieter, Melvin E., et al., editors. *Five Views on Sanctification*. Grand Rapids: Zondervan, 1996.

Eason, Andrew Mark. *Women in God's Army: Gender and Equality in the Early Salvation Army*. Studies in Women and Religion. Waterloo, Ontario: Wilfrid Laurier University Press, 2003.

Fairbank, Jenty. *Booth's Boots: The Beginnings of Salvation Army Social Work*. 3rd ed. London: The Salvation Army, 1987.

———. *William and Catherine Booth: God's Soldiers*. London: Hodder and Stoughton, 1974.

Faragher, Christine. *Other Voices: Exploring the Contemplative in Salvationist Spirituality*. Melbourne: Salvo, 2010.

Foster, Frank Hugh. "A Brief Introductory Sketch of the History of the Grotian Theory of the Atonement." In *A Defence of the Catholic Faith Concerning the Satisfaction of Christ against Faustus Socinus*, xii–lvii. Andover, MA: Draper, 1889.

Friedrichs, Hulda. *The Romance of the Salvation Army*. London: Cassell, 1907.

Green, Roger J. *Catherine Booth: A Biography of the Co-Founder of the Salvation Army*. Crowborough, UK: Monarch, 1997.

———. *The Life and Ministry of William Booth: Founder of the Salvation Army*. Nashville: Abingdon, 2005.

———. *War on Two Fronts: The Redemptive Theology of William Booth*. Atlanta: Salvation Army Supplies, 1989.

Gresham, John Leroy. *Charles G. Finney's Doctrine of the Baptism of the Holy Spirit*. Peabody, MA: Hendrickson, 1987.

Grider, J. Kenneth. *A Wesleyan–Holiness Theology*. Kansas City, MO: Beacon Hill, 1994.

Gunton, Colin E. *The Actuality of Atonement: A Study of Metaphor, Rationality and the Christian Tradition*. Edinburgh: T. & T. Clark, 1988.

———. *The Promise of Trinitarian Theology*. Edinburgh: T. & T. Clark, 1991.

Gunton, Colin E., and Daniel W. Hardy. *On Being the Church: Essays on the Christian Community*. Edinburgh: T. & T. Clark, 1989.

Hardman, Keith J. *Charles Grandison Finney 1792–1875: Revivalist and Reformer*. Grand Rapids: Baker, 1990.

Hattersley, Roy. *Blood and Fire: The Story of William and Catherine Booth and Their Salvation Army*. London: Little, Brown, 1999.

Heath, Elaine A. *Naked Faith: The Mystical Theology of Phoebe Palmer*. Cambridge: Clarke, 2010.

Heitzenrater, Richard P. *Wesley and the People Called Methodists*. Nashville: Abingdon, 1995.

Hill, Harold Ivor Winston. *Leadership in the Salvation Army: A Case Study in Clericalisation*. Studies in Christian History and Thought. Milton Keynes, UK: Paternoster, 2006.

Horridge, Glenn K. *The Salvation Army: Origins and Early Days 1865–1900*. Godalming, UK: Ammonite, 1993.

Kent, John. *Holding the Fort: Studies in Victorian Revivalism*. London: Epworth, 1978.

Kew, Clifford W, editor. *Catherine Booth: Her Continuing Relevance: A Collection of Essays*. London: The Salvation Army, 1990.

———. *Closer Communion: The Sacraments in Scripture and History*. London: Salvationist Publishing and Supplies, 1980.

Bibliography

Küng, Hans. *The Sacraments: An Ecumenical Dilemma*. Concilium Theology in the Age of Renewal. Ecumenical Theology. New York: Paulist, 1967.

Larsen, Timothy. *A People of One Book: The Bible and the Victorians*. Oxford: Oxford University Press, 2011.

Larsson, John. *1929: A Crisis That Shaped the Salvation Army's Future*. London: The Salvation Army, 2009.

Leclerc, Diane. *Singleness of Heart: Gender, Sin, and Holiness in Historical Perspective*. Pietist and Wesleyan Studies. Lanham, MD: Scarecrow, 2001.

Leech, Kenneth. *The Eye of the Storm: Spiritual Resources for the Pursuit of Justice*. London: Dartman, Longman & Todd, 1992.

Ludwig, Charles. *Mother of an Army: The Story of Catherine Booth*. London: Kingsway, 1988.

Lunn, Brian. *Salvation Dynasty*. London: Hodge, 1936.

Madden, Edward H., and James E. Hamilton. *Freedom and Grace: The Life of Asa Mahan*. Studies in Evangelicalism. Metuchen, NJ: Scarecrow, 1982.

Maddox, Randy L. *Responsible Grace: John Wesley's Practical Theology*. Nashville: Abingdon, 1994.

Marshall, I. Howard. *Last Supper and Lord's Supper*. The Didsbury Lectures. Carlisle, UK: Paternoster, 1980.

McGonigle, Herbert Boyd. *John Wesley's Doctrine of Prevenient Grace*. The Wesley Fellowship, 1995.

———. *Sufficient Saving Grace: John Wesley's Evangelical Arminianism*. Studies in Evangelical History and Thought. Milton Keynes, UK: Paternoster, 2001.

McGrath, Alister E. *Christian Spirituality: An Introduction*. Oxford: Blackwell, 1999.

McIntyre, John. *The Shape of Soteriology: Studies in the Doctrine of the Death of Christ*. Edinburgh: T. & T. Clark, 1992.

McLoughlin, William G. *Modern Revivalism: Charles Grandison Finney to Billy Graham*. New York: Ronald, 1959.

Meeks, M. Douglas, editor. *The Portion of the Poor: Good News to the Poor in the Wesleyan Tradition*. Nashville, TN: Kingswood, 1995.

———, editor. *Wesleyan Perspectives on the New Creation*. Nashville: Kingswood, 2004.

Merritt, John G., editor. *Historical Dictionary of the Salvation Army*. Lanham, MD: Scarecrow, 2006.

Metcalf, William. *The Salvationist and the Sacraments*. London: The Salvation Army, 1965.

Moltmann, Jürgen. *The Church in the Power of the Spirit: A Contribution of Messianic Ecclesiology*. Translated by Margaret Kohl. London: SCM, 1977.

Mossner, Ernest Campbell. *Bishop Butler and the Age of Reason: A Study in the History of Thought*. New York: Macmillan, 1936.

Moyles, Robert Gordon. *The Salvation Army and the Public*. Edmonton: AGM, 2000.

Murdoch, Norman H. "Frank Smith: Salvationist Socialist." In *National Salvation Army Social Services Conference*. Orlando, FL. Unpublished, 2003.

———. *Origins of the Salvation Army*. Knoxville, TN: University of Tennessee Press, 1994.

Needham, Philip. *Community in Mission: A Salvationist Ecclesiology*. London: The Salvation Army International Headquarters, 1987.

Noll, Mark A., et al. *Evangelicalism: Comparative Studies of Popular Protestantism in North America, the British Isles, and Beyond 1700-1900*. Religion in America Series. New York: Oxford University Press, 1994.

Bibliography

Orr, James Edwin. *The Fervent Prayer: The Worldwide Impact of the Great Awakening of 1858.* Chicago: Moody, 1974.

———. *The Second Evangelical Awakening: An Account of the Second Worldwide Evangelical Revival Beginning in the Mid-Nineteenth Century.* First popular ed. London: Marshall, Morgan & Scott, 1955.

Outler, Albert. "Do Methodists Have a Doctrine of the Church?" In *The Doctrine of the Church*, edited by Dow Kirkpatrick, 11-28. New York: Abingdon, 1964.

———. *John Wesley.* Library of Protestant Thought. New York: Oxford University Press, 1964.

Palmer, Phoebe. *Phoebe Palmer: Selected Writings.* Edited by Thomas C. Oden. Mahwah, NJ: Paulist, 1988.

Parris, John Roland. *John Wesley's Doctrine of the Sacraments.* London: Epworth, 1963.

Parsons, Gerald, editor. *Religion in Victorian Britain: I Traditions.* Manchester: Manchester University Press, 1988.

———, editor. *Religion in Victorian Britain: II Controversies.* Manchester: Manchester University Press, 1988.

Penelhum, Terence. *Butler.* The Arguments of the Philosophers. London: Routledge & Kegan Paul, 1985.

Pollock, J. C. *The Keswick Story: The Authorised History of the Keswick Convention.* London: Hodder and Stoughton, 1964.

Porter, Ian. *Whitechapel.* Bloomington, IN: AuthorHouse, 2009.

Rack, Henry D. *Reasonable Enthusiast.* 3rd ed. London: Epworth, 1989.

Radford, David. "Catherine Mumford: Notes on Life in Boston, Lincolnshire." Unpublished, 2011.

———. "Notes on 'a Fenland Ministry': William Booth's First Appointment, Spalding, Lincolnshire." Unpublished, 2011.

Randall, Ian M. *Evangelical Experiences: A Study in the Spirituality of English Evangelicalism 1918-1939.* Studies in Evangelical History and Thought. Carlisle, UK: Paternoster, 1999.

———. *Spirituality and Social Change: The Contribution of F. B. Meyer (1847-1929).* Studies in Evangelical History and Thought. Carlisle, UK: Paternoster, 2003.

Raser, Harold E. *Phoebe Palmer: Her Life and Thought.* Lewiston, NY: Mellen, 1987.

Read, Harry. "Salvationism." In *Hallmarks of the Salvation Army*, edited by Henry Gariepy and Stephen Court, 7-11. Melbourne: Salvo Publishing, 2009.

Read, John. "Spirituality and Spiritual Formation." In *Historical Dictionary of the Salvation Army*, edited by John G. Merritt, 553-57. Lanham, MD: Scarecrow, 2006.

Reasoner, Vic. *The Hope of the Gospel: An Introduction to Wesleyan Eschatology* Evansville, IL: Fundamental Wesleyan, 1999.

Rhemick, John R. *A New People of God: A Study in Salvationism.* Des Plaines, IL: The Salvation Army, 1993.

Rightmire, R. David. "Sacraments." In *Historical Dictionary of the Salvation Army*, edited by John G. Merritt. 487-90. Lanham, MD: Scarecrow, 2006.

———. *Sacraments and the Salvation Army: Pneumatological Foundations.* Studies in Evangelicalism. Metuchen, NJ: Scarecrow, 1990.

———. *Sanctified Sanity: The Life and Teaching of Samuel Logan Brengle.* Alexandria, VA.: Crest, 2003.

Rose, Jonathan. *The Intellectual Life of the British Working Classes.* 2nd ed. New Haven: Yale University Press, 2010.

Bibliography

Salter, Darius. *Spirit and Intellect: Thomas Upham's Holiness Theology*. Studies in Evangelicalism. Metuchen, NJ: Scarecrow, 1986.
Sandall, Robert, et al. *The History of the Salvation Army*. 7 vols. London: Nelson, 1947–86.
Satterlee, Allen. *Turning Points: How the Salvation Army Found a Different Path*. Alexandria, VA: Crest, 2004.
Sheldrake, Philip. *Images of Holiness: Explorations in Contemporary Spirituality*. Notre Dame, IN: Ave Maria, 1988.
Snyder, Howard A. *The Radical Wesley: And Patterns for Church Renewal*. Eugene, OR: Wipf and Stock, 1996.
Stackhouse, John G, editor. *Evangelical Ecclesiology: Reality or Illusion?*, Regent College Theology Conference, Vancouver. Grand Rapids: Baker Academic, 2003.
Stafford, Ann. *The Age of Consent*. London: Hodder and Stoughton, 1964.
Stanley, Susie Cunningham. *Holy Boldness: Women Preachers' Autobiographies and the Sanctified Self*. Knoxville, TN: University of Tennessee Press, 2002.
Staples, Rob L. *Outward Sign and Inward Grace: The Place of Sacraments in Wesleyan Spirituality*. Kansas City, MO: Beacon Hill, 1991.
Stevenson, Herbert Frederick, editor. *Keswick's Authentic Voice*. London: Marshall, 1959.
Street, Robert, and International Spiritual Life Commission. *Called to Be God's People: The International Spiritual Life Commission, Its Report, Implications and Challenges*. London: The Salvation Army International Headquarters, 1999.
Streett, R. Alan. *The Effective Invitation*. Grand Rapids: Kregel, 1995.
Streiff, Patrick Philipp. *Reluctant Saint?: A Theological Biography of Fletcher of Madeley*. Peterborough, UK: Epworth, 2001.
Taggart, Norman W. *William Arthur: First among Methodists*. London: Epworth, 1993.
Telford, John. *The Life of John Wesley*. London: Kelly, 1906.
Terrot, Charles. *The Maiden Tribute: A Study of the White Slave Traffic of the Nineteenth Century*. London: Mutter, 1959.
Unsworth, Madge. *Maiden Tribute: A Study in Voluntary Social Service*. London: Salvationist Publishing and Supplies, 1954.
Volf, Miroslav. *After Our Likeness: The Church as the Image of the Trinity*. Sacra Doctrina. Grand Rapids: Eerdmans, 1998.
Walker, Pamela J. "A Chaste and Fervid Eloquence: Catherine Booth and the Ministry of Women in the Salvation Army." In *Women Preachers and Prophets through Two Millenia of Christianity*, 288–302. Berkeley: University of California Press, 1998.
———. *Pulling the Devil's Kingdom Down: The Salvation Army in Victorian Britain*. Berkeley: University of California Press, 2001.
Watson, Bernard. *A Hundred Years' War: The Salvation Army 1865–1965*. London: Hodder and Stoughton, 1964.
———. *Soldier Saint: George Scott Railton, William Booth's First Lieutenant*. London: Hodder & Stoughton, 1970.
Weddle, David L. *The Law as Gospel: Revival and Reform in the Theology of Charles G. Finney*. Studies in Evangelicalism. Metuchen, NJ: Scarecrow, 1985.
White, Charles Edward. *The Beauty of Holiness: Phoebe Palmer as Theologian, Revivalist, Feminist, and Humanitarian*. Grand Rapids: Asbury, 1986.
White, Vernon. *Atonement and Incarnation: An Essay in Universalism and Particularity*. Cambridge: Cambridge University Press, 1991.
Whitehead, Alfred North. *Science and the Modern World*. Lowell Lectures. 1925. Reprint. London: Free, 1997.

Bibliography

Wilson, Bryan R., editor. *Patterns of Sectarianism: Organisation and Ideology in Social and Religious Movements.* Heinemann Books on Sociology. London: Heinemann, 1967.

Wilson, P. W. *General Evangeline Booth of the Salvation Army.* New York: Scribner's Sons, 1948.

Winston, Diane H. *Red-Hot and Righteous: The Urban Religion of the Salvation Army.* Cambridge: Harvard University Press, 1999.

Wood, Laurence W. *The Meaning of Pentecost in Early Methodism: Rediscovering John Fletcher as John Wesley's Vindicator and Designated Successor.* Pietist and Wesleyan Studies. Lanham, MD: Scarecrow, 2002.

Woodall, Ann M. *What Price the Poor?: William Booth, Karl Marx and the London Residuum.* Aldershot, UK: Ashgate, 2005.

Wright, Neil R. *Boston: A History and Celebration.* History of Boston Project. Salisbury, UK: Frith, 2005.

Yuill, Chick. "Restoring the Image." In *Catherine Booth: Her Continuing Relevance*, edited by Clifford W Kew, 52–85. London: The Salvation Army International Headquarters, 1990.

Smith, Timothy L. *Revivalism and Social Reform: American Protestantism on the Eve of the Civil War.* Baltimore, MD: John Hopkins University Press, 1980.

Salvation Army Journals and Magazines

Bond, Linda. "Our Life of Holiness: Can Our Holiness Teaching Survive?" *Word and Deed* 11.1 (2008) 17–28.

Cameron, Helen. "Women and Men in Ministry, Leadership and Governance." *Word and Deed* 9.2 (2007) 63–88.

Davisson, Philip W. "Catherine Booth and Female Ministry: Foundations and Growth." *Word and Deed* 6.1 (2003) 50–65.

Eason, Andrew Mark. "The Salvation Army in Late-Victorian Britain: The Convergence of Church and Sect." *Word and Deed* 5.2 (2003) 3–27.

Green, Roger J. "Facing History: Our Way Ahead for a Salvationist Theology." *Word and Deed* 1.2 (1999) 23–29.

Howe, Norman. "The International Commission on Officership: A Report." *The Officer*, August 1999, 18–20.

Jewett, Vern. "An Examination of Ecclesiastical Authority in the Salvation Army." *Word and Deed* 2.1 (1999) 54–64.

Larsson, John. "Salvationist Theology and Ethics for the New Millennium." *Word and Deed* 4.1 (2001) 9–23.

Miller, Andrew S "Eschatological Ethics: The Army's Hospitable Legacy." *Word and Deed* 10.1 (2007) 39–60.

Miller, Andrew S. "Suffering for and to Christ in William Booth's Eschatological Ecclesiology." *Word and Deed* 14.1 (2011) 19–36.

Mills, Douglas W. "The Doctrine of the Church in the Methodist Heritage." *Word and Deed* 8.2 (2006) 23–34.

Needham, Philip. "We Believe in the Holy Catholic Church." *Word and Deed* 10.1 (2007) 5–22.

Orsborn, Albert. "The World Council of Churches." *The Officer*, March/April 1954, 73–78.

Rightmire, R. David. "Holiness and the Ethical Dimensions of Brengle's Eschatology." *Word and Deed* 10.1 (2007) 23–38.

Bibliography

———. "Samuel Brengle and the Development of Salvation Army Pneumatology." *Word and Deed* 1.1 (1998) 29–48.
Robinson, Barbara. "Andrew Mark Eason. Women in God's Army: Gender and Equality in the Early Salvation Army." *Word and Deed* 6.1 (2003) 90–93.
———. "The Wesleyan Foundation of Salvation Army Social Work and Action." *Word and Deed* 7.1 (2004) 33–42.
Robinson, Earl. "The Salvation Army: Ecclesia?" *Word and Deed* 2.1 (1999) 5–15.
———. "Salvationist Ecclesiology: Past, Present, and the Way Forward." *Word and Deed* 9.1 (2006) 9–42.
Wiseman, Clarence. "Are We a Church?" *The Officer*, October 1976, 435–39.

Journals and Magazines

Abraham, William J. "The End of Wesleyan Theology." *Wesleyan Theological Journal* 40.1 (Spring 2005) 7–25.
Altholz, Josef L. "The Mind of Victorian Orthodoxy: Anglican Responses to "Essays and Reviews", 1860–1864." *Church History* 51.2 (1982) 186–97.
Anderson, Olive. "Women Preachers in Mid-Victorian Britain: Some Reflexions on Feminism, Popular Religion and Social Change." *The Historical Journal* 12.3 (1969) 467–84.
Barth, Markus. "BEM: Questions and Considerations." *Theology Today* 42.4 (1986) 490–98.
Brittain, John. "William Arthur's the Tongue of Fire: Pre-Pentecostal or Proto Social Gospel?" *Methodist History* 40.4 (2002) 246–54.
Bundy, David. "Thomas Cogswell Upham and the Establishment of a Tradition of Ethical Reflection." *Encounter* 59.1 (1998) 23–40.
Byrn, Robert T. "Butler's Analogy: Its Dangers." *The Irish Church Quarterly* 10.37 (1917) 40–48.
Carwardine, Richard. "The Second Great Awakening in the Urban Centre: An Examination of Methodism and the 'New Measures.'" *The Journal of American History* 59 (1972) 327–40.
Clapper, Gregory S. "Wesley's 'Main Doctrines' and Spiritual Formation and Teaching in the Wesleyan Tradition." *Wesleyan Theological Journal* 39.2 (2004) 97–121.
Collins, Kenneth J. "A Hermeneutical Model for the Wesleyan *Ordo Salutis*." *Wesleyan Theological Journal* 19.2 (Fall 1984) 23–37.
———. "The Soteriological Orientation of John Wesley's Ministry to the Poor." *Wesleyan Theological Journal* 36.2 (2001) 7–36.
Dayton, Donald W. "Asa Mahan and the Development of American Holiness Theology." *Wesleyan Theological Journal* 9.1 (1974) 60–69.
———. "The Doctrine of the Baptism of the Holy Spirit: Its Emergence and Significance." *Wesleyan Theological Journal* 13.1 (1978) 114–26.
Del Colle, Ralph. "John Wesley's Doctrine of Grace in Light of the Christian Tradition." *International Journal of Systematic Theology* 4.2 (2002) 172–89.
Dieter, Melvin E. "Laurence W. Wood. The Meaning of Pentecost in Early Methodism." *Wesleyan Theological Journal* 38.1 (2003) 242–46.
Dyck, Arthur J., and Carlos Padilla. "The Empathic Emotions and Self-Love in Bishop Joseph Butler and the Neurosciences." *Journal of Religious Ethics* 37.4 (2009) 577–612.

Bibliography

Erickson, Joyce Quiring. "'Perfect Love': Achieving Sanctification as a Pattern of Desire in the Life Writings of Early Methodist Women." *Prose Studies* 20.2 (1997) 72–89.

Gallagher, Sally K. "The Marginalization of Evangelical Feminism." *Sociology of Religion* 65.3 (2004) 215–37.

Grave, S. A. "The Able and Fair Reasoning of Butler's Analogy." *Church History* 47.3 (1978) 298–307.

Guelzo, Allen C. "An Heir or a Rebel? Charles Grandison Finney and the New England Theology." *Journal of the Early Republic* 17.1 (1997) 61–94.

Hovet, Theodore. "Phoebe Palmer's 'Altar Phraseology' and the Spiritual Dimension of Woman's Sphere." *The Journal of Religion* 63.3 (1983) 264–80.

Howe, Renate. "Five Conquering Years: The Leadership of Commandant and Mrs H. Booth of the Salvation Army in Victoria, 1896 to 1901." *Journal of Religious History* 6.2 (1970) 177–97.

James, Edward W. "Butler, Fanaticism and Conscience." *Philosophy* 56.218 (1981) 517–32.

Johnson, James E. "Charles G. Finney and a Theology of Revivalism." *Church History* 38.3 (1969) 338–58.

Long, Kathryn. "The Power of Interpretation: The Revival of 1857–58 and the Historiography of Revivalism in America." *Religion and American Culture* 4.1 (1994) 77–104.

Macquiban, Timothy S. A. "Soup and Salvation: Social Service as an Emerging Motif for the British Methodist Response to Poverty in the Late Nineteenth Century." *Methodist History* 39.1 (2000) 28–43.

Maddox, Randy L. "Responsible Grace: The Systematic Perspective of Wesleyan Theology." *Wesleyan Theological Journal* 19.2 (Fall 1984) 7–22.

———. "Wesley's Understanding of Christian Perfection: In What Sense Pentecostal?" *Wesleyan Theological Journal* 34.2 (Fall 1999) 78–110.

Mathers, Helen. "The Evangelical Spirituality of a Victorian Feminist: Josephine Butler, 1828–1906." *Journal of Ecclesiastical History* 52.2 (2001) 282–312.

McGonigle, Herbert. "Pneumatological Nomenclature in Early Methodism." *Wesleyan Theological Journal* 8.1 (1973) 61–72.

Murdoch, Norman H. "Evangelical Sources of Salvation Army Doctrine." *Evangelical Quarterly* 59.3 (1987) 235–44.

———. "Female Ministry in the Thought and Work of Catherine Booth." *Church History* 53.3 (1984) 348–62.

———. "William Booth's in Darkest England and the Way Out: A Reappraisal." *Wesleyan Theological Journal* 25.1 (1990) 106–16.

Noll, Mark A. "Common Sense Traditions and American Evangelical Thought." *American Quarterly* 37.2 (1985) 216–38.

O'Brien, Wendell. "Butler and the Authority of Conscience." *History of Philosophy Quarterly* 8.1 (1991) 43–57.

Outler, Albert. "John Wesley: Folk Theologian." *Theology Today* 34.2 (1977) 150–60.

———. "A Focus on the Holy Spirit: Spirit and Spirituality in John Wesley." *Quarterly Review* 8.2 (1988) 3–18.

Rainey, David. "The Established Church and Evangelical Theology: John Wesley's Ecclesiology." *International Journal of Systematic Theology* 12.4 (2010) 420–34.

Randall, Ian M. "Evangelical Spirituality and the Church Catholic." *The Way* 45.3 (2006) 95–112.

Bibliography

———. "Lay People in Revival: A Case Study of the '1859' Revival." *Transformation* 26.4 (2009) 217–31.

———. "The Pentecostal League of Prayer: A Transdenominational British Wesleyan-Holiness Movement." *Wesleyan Theological Journal* 33.1 (Spring 1998) 185–200.

———. "Spiritual Renewal and Social Reform: Attempts to Develop Social Awareness in the Early Keswick Movement." *Vox Evangelica* 23 (1993) 67–86.

Raphael, D. Daiches. "Bishop Butler's View of Conscience." *Philosophy* 24.90 (1949) 219–38.

Roberts, M. J. D. "Evangelicalism and Scandal in Victorian England: The Case of the Pearsall Smiths." *History* 95.320 (2010) 437–57.

Rose, Jonathan. "Rereading the English Common Reader: A Preface to a History of Audiences." *Journal of the History of Ideas* 53.1 (1992) 47–70.

Scotland, Nigel. "Evangelicals, Anglicans and Ritualism in Victorian England." *Churchman* 111.3 (1997) 249–65.

Shepherd, Victor. "From New Connexion Methodist to William Booth." *Papers of the Canadian Methodist Historical Society* 9 (1993) 91–107.

Smith, Timothy L. "The Doctrine of the Sanctifying Spirit: Charles G. Finney's Synthesis of Wesleyan and Covenant Theology." *Wesleyan Theological Journal* 13.1 (1978) 92–113.

———. "The Holiness People and the Doctrine of the Holy Spirit." *Quarterly Review* 8.2 (1988) 49–70.

———. "Righteousness and Hope: Christian Holiness and the Millennial Vision in America, 1800–1900." *American Quarterly* 31.1 (1979) 21–45.

Snyder, Howard A. "The Babylonian Captivity of Wesleyan Theology." *Wesleyan Theological Journal* 39.1 (2004) 17–24.

Sturgeon, Nicholas L. "Nature and Conscience in Butler's Ethics." *The Philosophical Review* 85.3 (1976) 316–56.

Sutton, William R. "Benevolent Calvinism and the Moral Government of God: The Influence of Nathaniel W. Taylor on Revivalism in the Second Great Awakening." *Religion and American Culture* 2.1 (1992) 23–47.

Swain, Shurlee. "In These Days of Female Evangelists and Hallelujah Lasses: Women Preachers and the Redefinition of Gender Roles in the Churches in Late Nineteenth-Century Australia." *The Journal of Religious History* 26.1 (2002) 66–77.

Taiz, Lillian. "Applying the Devil's Works in a Holy Cause: Working-Class Popular Culture and the Salvation Army in the United States, 1879–1900." *Religion and American Culture* 7.2 (1997) 195–223.

Truesdale, Al. "Reification of the Experience of Entire Sanctification in the American Holiness Movement." *Wesleyan Theological Journal* 31.2 (1996) 95–119.

Underwood, Grant. "Millenarianism and Popular Methodism in Early Nineteenth-Century England and Canada." *Wesleyan Theological Journal* 29 (1994) 81–91.

Walker, Pamela J. "Andrew Mark Eason. Women in God's Army: Gender and Equality in the Early Salvation Army." *The American Historical Review* 109.3 (2004) 976.

Walkowitz, Judith R. "The Politics of Prostitution." *Signs* 6.1 (1980) 123–35.

Whidden, Woodrow W. "Eschatology, Soteriology and Social Activism in Four Mid-Nineteenth Century Holiness Methodists." *Wesleyan Theological Journal* 29 (1994) 92–110.

White, Charles Edward. "Phoebe Palmer and the Development of Pentecostal Pneumatology." *Wesleyan Theological Journal* 23 (1988) 198–212.

Worthen, J. F. "Joseph Butler's Case for Virtue: Conscience as a Power of Sight in a Darkened World." *The Journal of Religious Ethics* 23.2 (1995) 239–61.

Wynkoop, Mildred Bangs. "Theological Roots of the Wesleyan Understanding of the Holy Spirit." *Wesleyan Theological Journal* 14.1 (1979) 77–98.

Theses and Dissertations

Buss, Paulo Wille. "Integrity and Integration in Ecclesiastical Historiography: The Perspective of Mosheim and Neander." DSTh diss., Concordia Seminary, 1994.

Darrie, Stephanie Mary. "The Editorial Work and Literary Enterprise of Louis Aimé-Martin." PhD diss., University of Exeter, 2009.

Macquiban, Timothy S. A. "British Methodism and the Poor: 1785–1840." PhD diss., University of Birmingham, 2000.

Murdoch, Norman H. "The Salvation Army: An Anglo-American Revivalist Social Mission." PhD diss., University of Cincinnati, 1994.

Petri, Laura. *Catherine Booth's Religious Development*. Translated by Elizabeth Balshaitis. PhD diss., Lund University, 1925.

Pugh, Benjamin Alan. "Power in the Blood: The Significance of the Blood of Jesus to the Spirituality of Early British Pentecostalism and Its Precursors." PhD diss., University of Bangor, 2009.

Valtanen, Krista Amy Gabriela. "Catherine Booth: Preacher and Theologian?: A Study of the Exhortations and the Message of Catherine Booth." PhD diss., University of Exeter, 2005.

Web Pages

de Souza, José Carlos. "Towards an Inclusive, Missionary and Peregrine Ecclesiology: Recovering Lost Links of the Wesleyan Tradition." Online: http://divinity.duke.edu/oxford/docs/2007papers/2007-4Souza.pdf.

Eason, Andrew Mark. "The Salvation Army and the Sacraments in Victorian Britain: Retracing the Steps to Non-Observance." Online: http://www.thefreelibrary.com/Fides+et+Historia/2009/June/22-p52138.

Green, Roger J. "Why Social Holiness?" The Salvation Army. Online: http://e-summit.org/conference/Why-Social-Holiness.html.

Grider, J. Kenneth. "The Governmental Theory: An Expansion." Online: http://www.libraryoftheology.com/writings/atonement/Governmental_Theory_Explained-KenGrider.pdf.

Grinsted, Stephen. "Hallelujah Bands." The Salvation Army. Online: http://www1.salvationarmy.org.uk/uki/www_uki_ihc.nsf/vw-sublinks/74F3065589B270418025709E0038DDA4?openDocument.

Hattersley, Roy. "A Biographer Forever." Online: http://textualities.net/author/roy-hattersley/.

Hill, Patricia R. "Uncle Tom's Cabin as a Religious Text." Online: http://utc.iath.virginia.edu/interpret/exhibits/hill/hill.html.

The Salvation Army. "A Strategic Framework for the United Kingdom Territory with the Republic of Ireland." Online: http://www2.salvationarmy.org.uk/uki/www_uki.nsf/0/B4692EF122DF933180256F97005545EC/$file/Library-StrategicFramework.pdf.

Index

Aikin, Samuel, 93
Aitken, Hay, 17
Anderson, Olive, 162
Arminius, Jacobus, 49
Arthur, William, 56, 63, 70–71, 77, 79, 113, 116, 145

Baggaly, William, 111n173
Baillie, Donald M., 200
Bangs, Nathan, 76
Barnes, Alfred, 15, 33, 35, 40
Barratt, T. H., 191
Baxendale, David, 3
Bebbington, David W., 5, 57n159, 61, 64, 66, 73, 110, 129n52
Beecher, Lyman, 93–94
Begbie, Harold, 5, 13, 164, 179
Bennett, David, 5, 11n79, 129n56, 157
Benson, Edward White, 134
Beza, Theodore, 34
Boardman, William, 61, 63–65, 68–70, 105–6, 115, 193
Booth (Charlesworth), Maude, 168
Booth (Schoch), Cornelie, 168
Booth (Soper), Forence, 175
Booth, (William) Bramwell, 13, 25, 98–99, 134–36, 168–70, 175, 178–79, 195–96
Booth, Abraham, 11
Booth, Ballington, 14, 168
Booth, Catherine (Daughter), 14, 168
Booth, Emma Moss, 15, 168
Booth, Evelyn Cory (Evangeline), 21, 24
Booth, Herbert Henry Howard, 18, 168
Booth, Lucy Milward, 21
Booth, Marion, 18
Booth, William, 2, 5, 10–18, 20–22, 24–26, 28, 40–4, 42n8, 47, 52–54, 57–58, 61, 63, 65–66, 71–74, 78–79, 81, 92–93, 106–12, 119–21, 124, 127–32, 134, 136–37, 143–44, 146, 148–49, 152, 156–57, 164–66, 169–72, 174, 176, 178–80, 193–97, 202, 208–12
Booth-Clibborn, Arthur, 168
Booth-Tucker, Frederick, 4, 22, 24, 68, 92–93, 98–99, 109, 129, 172–73, 186
Borgen, Ole, 189–90
Bowmer, John Coates, 192
Bradwell, Cyril, 171
Bramwell, William, 112
Bramwell-Booth, Catherine, 4, 7, 11n79, 53, 129n56, 164–65
Briggs, Elizabeth, 33
Bundy, David, 105
Bunting, Jabez, 71
Burrows, Eva, 120
Buss, Paulo Wille, 123n17–18, 123n21, 124n23, 124n25–26, 142
Butler, Joseph, 7, 39–41, 106, 210
Butler, Josephine, 2, 155

Index

Carlile, Wilson, 129
Carpenter, Minnie, 211
Carvosso, William, 62–63
Carwardine, Richard, 143n130
Caughey, James, 17, 18, 71
Chadwick, Owen, 5, 10n62, 185n40
Chiles, Robert, 36, 91
Chisholm William, 141
Clarke, Adam, 15, 67, 74, 77, 80, 101, 112, 159
Clifton, Shaw, 3
Clouse, Robert, 82
Cobbin, Ingram, 15
Collins, Kenneth J., 33, 38–39, 44, 48–50, 91, 125, 127
Cooke, William, 13, 133, 192
Cory, John, 18
Cory, Richard, 18
Coutts, John, 185n43

Davidson, Randall Thomas, 134
Dayton, Donald, 103, 115
Dean, Harry, 202n119
Dieter, Melvin, 70–71, 73, 76n85, 105–6
Doddridge, Philip, 15
Dodwell, Henry, 15
Dow, Lorenzo, 143
Dunning, H. Ray, 33, 44

Eason, Andrew, 5, 6, 120n5, 163–67
Edwards, Jonathan, 32, 35, 41n72, 93, 95
Erickson, Joyce Quiring, 64n21
Ervine, St John, 5, 134, 176

Finney, Charles, 7, 17, 33–35, 39, 46, 50, 79, 85, 92–102, 106, 112, 116, 118, 143, 193, 206, 210
Fishbourne, Edmund Gardiner, 104, 109
Fletcher, John, 7, 33, 49, 53, 56–57, 59, 60–62, 74, 77, 79–80, 85, 93, 107–8, 111–16, 118, 146, 149, 193–94, 200, 206, 210
Fletcher, Mary Bosanquet, 13, 62, 64, 112, 116, 161
Foster, Frank, 32, 38
Fry, Elizabeth, 161

Gough, John, 13
Grant, Brewin, 107,
Green, Roger, 5, 7, 42–43, 61, 66, 120, 134, 148, 154, 194–95, 209
Grider, J. Kenneth, 31
Grotius, Hugo, 31, 32, 34, 160
Grundell, John, 132
Guelzo, Allen C., 95n71
Gunton, Colin, 138–139, 201

Hamilton, James E., 101n103–4, 101n106, 103–4
Hardman, Keith, 34, 93–96
Harris, Richard Reader, 110
Hattersley, Roy, 5, 6, 61, 66, 211
Heath, Elaine, 67, 74
Hill, Harold, 5, 120n5, 137n100, 175
Horridge, Glen, 5, 23n161, 169, 173n155
Hulme, Samuel, 13n95
Hurrell, Elizabeth, 161

James, John Angell, 133
Johnson, Samuel, 161

Kent, John, 61, 66, 68–69, 72–74, 82, 84, 106, 185n41, 209
Kilham, Alexander, 132–33, 136
Knight, John, 91
Küng, Hans, 200–201

Larsen, Timothy, 13n95, 85n3
Larsson, John, 120–21, 169n128
LeClerc, Diane, 165
Leech, Kenneth, 3
Liddell, Henry George, 15

232

Index

Lightfoot, Joseph Barber, 24, 134, 140
Locke, John, 15
Lunn, Henry, 179

Macquiban, Timothy S. A., 156
Madden, Edward H., 101n103–4, 101n106, 103–4
Maddox, Randy, 113–14, 188
Mahan, Asa, 63, 85, 101–5, 112–13, 116
Mallett, Sarah, 33, 161
Marsden, Isaac, 143–44
Marsh, Catherine, 161
Martin, Aimé, 161
McGonigle, Herbert, 46n99
McGrath, Alister, 3
McKinley, Edward, 198–99
Miley, John, 32, 35, 36
Miller, Andrew, 57
Moltmann, Jürgen, 149–50
Moore, Henry, 64n21, 112n76
Morgan, Richard Cope, 85, 105
Morley, Samuel, 21
Mosheim, Johann Lorenz, 7, 123, 142, 186, 206
Mossner, Ernest, 40
Mumford, John (Brother), 6
Mumford, John (Father), 6, 7, 8
Mumford, Sarah, 6, 7, 8
Murdoch, Norman, 5, 22, 23, 58n165, 61, 107, 155, 164, 210

Neander, Augustus, 7, 123–24, 186–87, 206
Needham, Philip, 120
Nicol, Alex, 169

Orr, James Edwin, 17, 61, 72–73, 211
Orsborn, Albert, 121–22, 140, 150
Outler, Albert, 44, 49, 128, 190

Paget, James, 24

Palmer, Phoebe, 14, 16, 17, 18, 54, 56, 61, 63–69, 71–72, 74–84, 85, 90–91, 105–6, 112–13, 115, 161, 165, 193, 206, 209
Palmer, Walter, 14, 16, 17, 18
Parkhurst, John, 15
Payne, George, 11
Penelhum, Terence, 40
Pollard, George, 171
Pollock, J. C., 111
Porter, Ian, 155

Rabbits, Edward Harris, 10
Rack, Henry, 33
Radcliffe, Reginald, 17
Rader, Paul, 152, 202
Railton, George Scott, 136, 168, 174, 195
Rainey, David, 128n47, 128n49
Randall, Ian, 3, 110
Read, Harry, 3n14
Reasoner, Vic, 57n159
Redford, George, 96
Rees, Arthur, 14–15, 157–61
Reid, Thomas, 105
Rhemick, John, 4
Rightmire, David, 5, 61, 186, 193, 196–201, 209
Roberts, M. J. D., 108n154
Robertson, Roland, 120n5, 176
Robinson, Edward, 15
Robinson, Barbara, 167
Rogers, Hester Ann (Miss Roe), 112, 116, 161
Rose, Jonathan, 7
Rowe, Elisabeth, 62, 112n177

Salter, Darius, 105–6
Sandall, Robert, 169
Satterlee, Alan, 203
Schleusner, Johann Friedrich, 15
Scott, Robert, 15
Shadford, George, 143
Shaw, George Bernard, 23

Index

Sheldrake, Philip, 3
Shepherd, Victor, 133n74
Smith, Hannah Pearsall, 73, 106, 108–9
Smith, Robert Pearsall, 73, 104, 106–8, 116
Smith, Rodney (Gipsy), 169–72
Smith, Timothy L., 156
Snyder, Howard, 114–15, 122
Socinus, Faustus, 34
Stacey, James, 17
Stanley, Susie, 61n4, 166
Staples, Rob L., 190
Stead, William T., 1, 2, 58, 119, 155, 170–71, 191, 199–200
Stephen, Leslie, 129n54, 132n72
Stowe, Harriet Beecher, 106
Streiff, Patrick, 80, 146n150, 193
Sturgeon, Nicholas L., 40n69
Sutton, William R., 35n38

Taylor, Nathaniel, 35, 94
Thomas, David, 11, 13, 30, 128–30, 136, 156–57, 207, 210
Thomson, William, 185
Truesdale, Al, 76–77

Underwood, Grant, 147n162
Upham, Phebe, 106
Upham, Thomas Cogwell, 85, 105–6, 116

Valtanen, Krista, 5, 6, 26, 43, 58, 77, 198, 205
Varley, Henry, 107
Volf, Miroslav, 136n98, 149

Walker, Pamela, 5, 15n107, 15n110, 110–11, 143n29, 153, 157, 167, 195, 208
Watson, Richard, 15, 33, 35–38, 113
Weaver, Richard, 17
Webb-Peploe, Hanmer William, 109–10
Weddle, David, 34, 46n97
Wesley, John, 7, 28, 32–33, 38–39, 41–46, 48–50, 53–54, 57–59, 60–62, 79–80, 82, 85, 89–94, 97–101, 107–8, 113–16, 118, 123–28, 136, 146, 149, 156, 165, 181, 188–93, 200, 203, 206, 210
Westcott, Brooke Foss, 134
Wheatley, Richard, 68n42
Whidden, Woodrow, 82
Whitby, Daniel, 15
White, Charles, 56n152, 67, 74–77, 79–82
Whitehead, Alfred North, 76
Wiley, H. Orton, 118
Wilkinson, George Howard, 134
Winston, Diane, 5
Wiseman, Clarence, 122n13
Wood, Laurence, 56–57, 112–14, 146n151
Woodall, Ann M., 23n163, 155
Wright, Edward, 171
Wright, Neil R., 8n45
Wynkoop, Mildred Bangs, 83, 118

Young, Robert, 16
Yuill, Chick, 4, 61, 67–68, 70, 78

www.ingramcontent.com/pod-product-compliance
Lightning Source LLC
Chambersburg PA
CBHW051638230426
43669CB00013B/2348